BELIEVING IN LIGHT AFTER DARKNESS

BELIEVING IN LIGHT AFTER DARKNESS

Displacement and Refugee Resettlement

MOLLY FEE

UNIVERSITY OF CALIFORNIA PRESS

University of California Press
Oakland, California

Library of Congress Cataloging-in-Publication Data

Names: Fee, Molly, author
Title: Believing in light after darkness : displacement and refugee resettlement /
    Molly Fee.
Description: Oakland, California : University of California Press, [2026] | Includes
    bibliographical references and index.
Identifiers: LCCN 2025035033 (print) | LCCN 2025035034 (ebook) | ISBN 9780520416307
    cloth | ISBN 9780520416314 paperback | ISBN 9780520416321 ebook
Subjects: LCSH: Refugees—United States—Social conditions | Refugees—
    Government policy—United States | Refugees—Services for—United States |
    Refuge (Humanitarian assistance)—United States
Classification: LCC JV6601 .F44 2026 (print) | LCC JV6601 (ebook)
LC record available at https://lccn.loc.gov/2025035033
LC ebook record available at https://lccn.loc.gov/2025035034

Manufactured in the United States of America

GPSR Authorized Representative: Easy Access System Europe,
Mustamäe tee 50, 10621 Tallinn, Estonia, gpsr.requests@easproject.com

35 34 33 32 31 30 29 28 27 26
10 9 8 7 6 5 4 3 2 1

To Rick

Contents

Contents

Preface

AMONG THE BARRAGE of executive orders signed within hours of Donald Trump's second term as president was "Realigning the United States Refugee Admissions Program," which suspended refugee resettlement on January 27, 2025, exactly eight years after he signed the first of his travel bans. This executive order immediately halted the future resettlement of refugees to the United States, including those who had already made it through the long approval process and were simply awaiting their scheduled flights. The executive order stated that "entry into the United States of refugees under the USRAP [U.S. Refugee Admissions Program] would be detrimental to the interests of the United States."[1] If we learned anything from the first Trump administration's drastic cuts to refugee admissions, it was that ending resettlement is much more harmful.

The first Trump administration used a "death by a thousand papercuts" strategy to systematically dismantle the

USRAP, reducing arrivals and weakening the Resettlement Agencies that support refugees in communities across the country. The second time around, President Trump and his staff returned with a more definitive approach, forever changing the modern USRAP as we have known it since Congress passed the Refugee Act of 1980 with bipartisan support. The research for this book took place in 2018 and 2019 during the first Trump administration, under the shadow of its overtly antirefugee and anti-immigrant policies. As I reach the final stages of writing this book, US resettlement once again finds itself under threat.

The Trump administration's rationale for halting future resettlement relies on a series of facile falsehoods that mischaracterize the USRAP. The executive order suggests that resettlement poses a risk to national security. All refugees admitted through the USRAP pass through an extremely rigorous and lengthy protocol of interviews and screenings carried out by numerous government agencies, including the Department of State, U.S. Citizenship and Immigration Services (USCIS), the Department of Homeland Security, and the National Counterterrorism Center. This process typically takes eighteen to twenty-four months, making resettled refugees the most vetted group arriving in the US.

As I discuss throughout this book, the US model of resettlement undoubtedly has its challenges and shortcomings. Nonetheless, resettlement is a deeply important pathway for refugees who have ended up in camps and urban areas in countries of asylum due to a combination of politics, persecution, and climate change. Confined to places that are designed to feel temporary despite their increasing permanence, these refugees lack the rights that many of us take for granted. For such refugees, resettlement may be the only possible alternative to future generations being born into a life shaped by insufficient healthcare, food insecurity, and limited opportunities.

Resettlement has only ever been a reality for less than 1 percent of refugees globally, with the US historically welcoming more refugees through resettlement than all other countries of resettlement combined. UNHCR, the United Nations Refugee Agency, predicts that 2.9 million refugees will need resettlement in 2025. By abdicating its leadership and shutting its doors to future arrivals, the US government has made it even less likely that these refugees will get resettled. Families awaiting reunification with loved ones will endure even longer separations. While some aspects of the US model of resettlement fall short of offering newly arrived refugees the support they need to gain their footing, resettlement still offers refugees a different path forward, particularly for younger generations.

The admissions levels of up to 125,000 refugees per year set by the Biden administration did not, as President Trump claims, "compromise the availability of resources for Americans." As this book demonstrates, arriving refugees receive an extremely limited amount of public funds and are immediately put on a pathway to economic self-sufficiency. The USRAP provides significantly less financial support than other countries of resettlement do, and a 2017 study found that resettled refugees contribute more to the US economy in taxes than they receive in public assistance, not to mention the immediate and longer-term net benefits that refugees bring communities across the country. Refugees have helped to revitalize smaller cities throughout the US by opening businesses, renting vacant apartments, and sending children to schools in places experiencing population decline. Though President Trump sews doubt about refugees' ability to incorporate into the US, research has shown that within six years of their resettlement, refugees have higher employment rates than their US-born counterparts. As this book shows, the refugees who have arrived in communities across the country simply want to build a stable and secure life for their families, a reality that proved impossible in their country of asylum.

Not only are the Trump administration's actions built on misconceptions, but they also ignore the many reverberating harms that follow a suspension of the USRAP. As we saw eight years ago, halting resettlement will cost hundreds of jobs. The ten national Resettlement Agencies have already been forced to lay off hundreds of staff throughout the country as offices reduce operations or close their doors. Beyond Resettlement Agencies, the constellation of organizations and local businesses that provide services for arriving refugees will lose an important client and customer base, resulting in more job losses and a greater economic impact.

The damages that come with suspending resettlement stretch well beyond US borders. The significant cuts to resettlement during the first Trump administration carried far-reaching ripple effects that impaired the humanitarian infrastructure that supports refugees around the world. As in 2017, the UNHCR has begun to restructure and lay off staff responsible for processing resettlement cases overseas. Just as we know that resettlement does not take resources away from US citizens or carry national security risks, we know all too well the wide-ranging damages that will follow a suspension of this important program.

This book details many of the ways that the USRAP does not adequately set arriving refugees and service providers up for success. Given the massive scope of the policy changes that have taken place since I carried out my research, my hope is that this book will become a tool to help imagine a more hospitable model of US resettlement when it is time to rebuild.

Acknowledgments

NUMEROUS REFUGEE CRISES AND WARS have unfolded during the research and writing of this book. As I reflect on the words of the people who trusted me with their experiences of forced migration and resettlement, my thoughts have been with those displaced from Afghanistan, the Democratic Republic of the Congo, Gaza, South Sudan, Tigray, and Ukraine, where the search for safety and security is increasingly met with obstacles and unfavorable options.

This book was only possible because of the many people in San Diego and Boise who let me into their lives. I am forever grateful for their trust, candor, and thoughtfulness. Doing the work of resettlement alongside the caseworkers and many other Resettlement Agency staff in each city was truly meaningful, and I am incredibly lucky to have learned from the best. I am indebted to everyone who agreed to sit for an interview and share their expertise, intimate experiences, and recommendations. This book, as well as my own understanding of forced migration and resettlement, is better off for what they taught me.

Thank you to Graeme Rodgers for believing in this project in its earliest form and helping to make it a reality and to the leadership and staff of the International Rescue Committee's (IRC) San Diego and Boise offices. Though I will not list their names in the interest of maintaining anonymity, I benefitted tremendously from their warm welcome and openness. I am thankful to the generous funding that supported my fieldwork in San Diego and Boise, including the National Science Foundation's Graduate Research Fellowship Program and Doctoral Dissertation Research Improvement Grant, P.E.O. International, and UCLA's Department of Sociology.

I was fortunate to have learned how to think like a sociologist in the Department of Sociology at the University of California, Los Angeles. I received exceptional training as a migration scholar and ethnographer though coursework, working groups, and other opportunities for intellectual growth. I also benefitted from steadfast guidance and mentorship throughout my PhD studies. Thank you especially to my advisor, Roger Waldinger, for always showing interest in my research and for asking just the right questions to make my work stronger. And thank you to my other committee members: Gail Kligman for the generosity of her time through written feedback and in conversation, Edward Walker for helping me build connections between refugee resettlement and political sociology from my earliest days at UCLA, and David FitzGerald for his steady encouragement from the beginning and his thoughtfulness in connecting me to so many opportunities. I was lucky to learn from many other faculty members who provided important support that ultimately helped shape my trajectory and this book, especially Lauren Duquette-Rury, Aliza Luft, Rubén Hernandez-Leon, Cecilia Menjívar, and Ching Kwan Lee. Thank you also to Nicky Fox for her kindness and mentorship.

During my time at UCLA, I learned so much from the rich and interdisciplinary community of scholars at the Center for the Study of International Migration and the Migration Working Group. I benefitted from friends and colleagues who offered support and feedback on my work, including Chiara Galli, Andew Le, Peter Catron, Phi Hong Su, Tahseen Shams, Tianjian Lai, Nihal Kayali, Leydy Diossa, Nathan Hoffmann, and Deisy Del Real. Thank you to Rawan Arar whose friendship, guidance, and encouragement helped me through graduate school and beyond. I am also grateful to many other colleagues and collaborators who have enriched my understanding of refugee resettlement, including Jessica Darrow, Heba Gowayed, Blair Sackett, Jess Howsam-Scholl, Odessa Gonzalez Benson, and Ashley Cureton.

I was extremely fortunate to write this book while I was a Postdoctoral Prize Research Fellow in Sociology at Nuffield College, University of Oxford, which gave me the gift of time to focus on this project. I am grateful to Dave Kirk, Lucie Cluver, and Eleni Kechagia-Ovseiko for their support. Thank you also to Ridhi Kashyap, Des King, Mobarak Hossain, Juliana de Castro Galvão, Pablo Geraldo, David Kretschmer, Daniela Urbina, Anette Stimmer, and Mariana Borges Martins da Silva. While at Oxford, I had the great privilege of finding an intellectual home at the Refugee Studies Centre. Thank you especially to Matthew Gibney, Tom Scott-Smith, Catherine Briddick, and Naohiko Omata for welcoming me and providing me with a place to share my work and engage with such an exciting group of scholars.

This book has benefitted from the careful feedback and expertise of many trusted readers. Thank you to Jeff Crisp, Matthew Gibney, Loren Landau, and Tom Scott-Smith for your valued critiques and suggestions during my book manuscript workshop. I also deeply appreciated the comments provided by others who read part or all of this manuscript at various stages of the writing process, including David FitzGerald, Roger Waldinger, Gail Kligman, David Cook-Martín, Rawan Arar and her fall 2024 undergraduate class (Seeking Refuge: A Global Perspective on

Refugee Displacement), Jake Watson and his spring 2025 graduate class (Immigration, Assimilation, Identity), and Gretchen Caldwell, as well as the anonymous reviewers at the book proposal and full manuscript stages. Their questions and advice have undoubtedly improved this book; any shortcomings or errors are my own.

I received exceptional mentorship prior to my graduate studies which was integral in shaping my intellectual trajectory. Mary Laurita and Joachim Faust at Washington University in St. Louis taught me how moments of discomfort are those most worth examining further. At the American University of Paris, Christian Joppke introduced me to the questions central to the international migration literature and Geoffrey Gilbert encouraged me to move beyond disciplinary boundaries as I honed my research interests. While at the Center for Applied Linguistics, Sarah Moore, Terrence Wiley, and Beatriz Arias generously offered their mentorship and attention to my career growth, helping me to understand and investigate the tensions between policy and practice, which became formative to how I study refugee resettlement.

I am excited to continue my professional journey at the University of South Florida's Department of Sociology and Interdisciplinary Social Sciences. Thank you to Sara Green, Chris Ponticelli, David Jacobson, Elizabeth Aranda, Vrinda Marwah, Alejandro Marquez, Jamie Sommer, Beatriz Padilla, Will Tyson, Laurel Graham, Jim Cavendish, Frank Biafora, S Crawley, Melissa Sloan, and Fransheska Andaluz for your warm welcome.

I am grateful to the University of California Press for their interest in this book. Thank you especially to Naomi Schneider and Aline Dolinh for your enthusiasm for and care with my manuscript. It was a pleasure working with Boise-based batik artist Amiri Osman as he created *Le Paradoxe* for the book's cover. I deeply appreciate Amiri's willingness to share his talent and artwork for the cover. And thank you to Bruce Tarbet for photographing this artwork in such a timely manner.

Portions of the introduction and chapter 3 appeared in Molly Fee, 2025, "Displacing Refugees: Resettlement and the Reconstitution of Families," *Social Problems*, online first. Tables 2 and 3 appeared in Molly Fee, 2025, "Once a Refugee, Always a Refugee? The Social Construction of Refugee Status After Resettlement," *Ethnic and Racial Studies* 48(3):498–519.

Thank you also to the Fee family, the Frelich family, the Doerr family, and the Tyson family for being an added source of reassurance throughout this journey. Thank you especially to my parents, Joan Frelich and Jim Fee, who were always so encouraging of my passions, regardless of how different they may have been from their own. Though I wish they could have seen this book, the unwavering support they gave me continues to help me take such rewarding risks in my career.

Thank you finally to Rick who has been resolute in his encouragement and has stood alongside me at every step of this process, starting from when I applied to graduate school. I am grateful for his confidence in my ambitions, for knowing when I needed time to think and write, and for always betting on me, even when it made life more challenging in the short-term. And thank you to Roan who has made everything so much more rewarding.

INTRODUCTION

GEOFFROI WAS THREE YEARS OLD when his family fled war in the Democratic Republic of the Congo (DRC) and found safety in a refugee camp in Rwanda in the late 1990s. Describing the camp where he lived for fifteen years, Geoffroi told me, "It wasn't a good life. . . . We were living in bad condition[s]." During their first eight years there, his family lived in a tent that Geoffroi described as "not like, you know, a home." His family was then moved to a more durable two-room house, but it was cramped for eight people, and they had to use a shared bathroom facility in the community. For Geoffroi, life in the camp was characterized by food insecurity, inadequate healthcare, and limited opportunities.

Camp residents were provided with an allotment of beans and maize. Not only did they have to make it stretch throughout the month, they also used it as a form of currency to pay for other goods in the camp economy. Making this ration last was a constant struggle. Though education in the camp was free through the ninth grade, Geoffroi's two older brothers dropped out to earn some money to help the rest of the family. Geoffroi knew that his brothers had "sacrificed their lives" for the benefit of the family.

Geoffroi's mother first pursued resettlement in 2005. When other families around them began leaving for their resettlement destinations, she inquired about the progress of their case only to learn that it no longer existed. They got another chance to pursue resettlement in 2009. By this point, Geoffroi's family had grown to fourteen people, which included his older siblings' spouses and children who now had separate resettlement cases. His siblings' families were approved for resettlement to the US, while Geoffroi, along with his mother and younger siblings, were notified that their case was still pending. Geoffroi felt ambivalent about this mixed news. Though he was happy for his siblings, his future still felt so uncertain. He added, "Some[times], you celebrate, and sometimes you don't, because some of your [family] members are going to get a chance to go, but then you're like, 'Well, what about us?'"

As his family awaited news of their resettlement, Geoffroi was nearing the end of high school, which required tuition payments beyond the ninth grade. Though Geoffroi would soon be eligible to take a national exam to earn his high school diploma in Rwanda, he did not register because it seemed likely that their resettlement would get approved before he could sit for the exam. If he was not going to complete his degree in Rwanda, it felt pointless to continue paying to attend high school. But as his siblings' families left for the US, the approval process for Geoffroi, his mother, and younger siblings dragged on. The national high school exam came and went, and Geoffroi's classmates earned their diplomas while he looked on. He said, "You are waiting, you thought you were going to leave the country, and you're still there. People that were in the same year with you, they have the diploma. You don't have yours. Then you're like, 'What's going on?'" Amid the obstacles and hardships of growing up in a refugee camp, Geoffroi had worked hard for his education, but the resettlement process strung him along regardless of his life plans.

A year after the first members of his family had departed for the US, Geoffroi was enrolled in a computer class. One day he received a phone call from his mother telling him that their resettlement had finally been approved. They would be leaving the camp in one week. After Geoffroi returned home, his family sent him to the market to do some errands in preparation for their upcoming journey. While on the bus, he got another call telling him, "Hey, you need to get off the bus right now. We're leaving." Without warning, their departure had been moved up to that very day. Geoffroi recounted, "The car was right there, waiting for us to go in and then leave the country. . . . It was like, 'Wait, what?' . . . My bag was empty." He did not even have time to change his clothes before getting in the car that took his family from the refugee camp to Kigali for their flight. After years of uncertainty and waiting, Geoffroi was given a moment's notice of his resettlement, as if leaving behind the world he had inhabited for the past fifteen years was of no consequence.

He felt completely unprepared and only knew a little about what awaited him in Boise, Idaho. On what turned out to be the day of his departure, Geoffroi had been on his way to the market to buy some new clothes. Beyond wanting to feel prepared for his first weeks in a new country, Geoffroi also acknowledged a cultural dimension to having a new outfit for the journey. He noted how when people finally depart for their resettlement destination, "they just want to make sure they're dressed. They look good, right?" Resettlement is momentous, and dressing for the occasion was a way to mark its significance and assert dignity. He added that resettlement is "a big event. It's actually like a ceremony." As someone prepares to leave, friends and family visit, celebrate, and come to say their goodbyes. Geoffroi explained how for those left behind in the camp, these departures, though joyous, were somewhat akin to a death. He said, "It's like if someone was passing away. It's like, 'Well, goodbye. May God be with you.'" This sense of finality was fueled by the prevailing assumption that when people are resettled, they never come back. But given his family's hasty departure, Geoffroi was denied much of this ceremony.

Despite the unanticipated rush and hectic departure, Geoffroi was thrilled. His siblings who had already been resettled in Boise gave him some clues about what life would be like there. They told him that food was plentiful, that there would be people to help them, and that they would be able to make friends who spoke their language. But he was most excited about the opportunities he would have in the US. His brother told him, "You will get a chance to go back to school. You can graduate from high school. If you want, you can go to college. It will be up to you. . . . You get a lot of opportunities here." Geoffroi said, "That's why I was really excited." He remembered thinking, "I can't wait to get there. I just want to be able to go back to school." Given the complications of daily life in the camp in Rwanda, Geoffroi explained that resettlement to the US was imagined as a kind of heaven where food, money, and opportunity existed in abundance. He added, "That's the thing that you dream of. You always dream to go to school, to be able to have opportunities to do things that you want." This idealized image of life in the US was propped up by the transformative effects of even small sums of money sent back to loved ones in the camp. His family in Boise told him, "We're secure. You're not going to worry about who's going to knock on your door." Resettlement was a life-altering opportunity for Geoffroi to leave behind the difficulties of his childhood.

He arrived in Boise in the summer, when daylight lasts late into the evening. His older siblings were able to help Geoffroi, his mother, and his younger siblings navigate all the novelties of life in a new country. He was impressed by the speed with which food could be cooked in a microwave given the hours it used to take to prepare a meal over an open flame in the camp. His brother had a computer and introduced

Geoffroi to the wonders of Facebook. Geoffroi was eager to start high school in the fall but was taken aback by pressure from his Resettlement Agency to forgo his education for work. According to Geoffroi, one of the staff members told him, "Well, you're the only one that speaks a little bit of English. You need to go to work to help your family." His older siblings were taking care of their own families, so it was up to Geoffroi to help his mother and younger siblings. Geoffroi said, "But my dream was to go to school and be able to change [my] life." Though the Resettlement Agency pushed for full-time employment as the only way to cover his family's expenses, Geoffroi did not want to give up on his dream of finishing high school after finally making it to the US. He wondered, "Can I do both?" Geoffroi continued, "When you are in the place where you've had nothing . . . [and] you get the chance," he thought, "let me take my chances." Through the help of members of the Boise community, he enrolled in high school against the Resettlement Agency's advice.

He started school that fall in the eleventh grade, but his schedule quickly became grueling. When school let out, he would take the bus downtown where he would catch a van that drove him to his job forty minutes outside of Boise. By the time he finished work around 11 p.m. or midnight and got dropped back off downtown, the city buses were no longer running. He either had to wait for someone to pick him up, which could take another hour, or he would bike home. As temperatures dropped in the winter, this commute was punishing. Geoffroi said, "It was a real tough experience. It was really hard for me. . . . Sometimes you have to bike, freezing your butt. . . . You get home. Your hands are frozen. You have to take a shower, and you go to bed around 2 a.m. . . . So I wasn't getting enough sleep." On nights when he still had homework to finish, he would be up until 3 a.m. or 4 a.m. before catching the bus to school at 6:45 a.m. the next day. Thinking back on those early months in Boise, Geoffroi admitted, "Yeah, this is not a life that I expected. It was really, really hard."

During that first year in the US, Geoffroi's mother passed away, and he was left to support and care for his younger siblings. His older siblings' apartments were not big enough to take them in, so rent fell to Geoffroi. Despite his added responsibilities, Geoffroi graduated from high school in two years and went straight to a four-year university. He benefitted from the support of community members who helped him budget and save as much money as possible. Though he had not yet completed his degree at the time of our interview, he had gotten married and started his own family, working full-time as a caregiver for people with mental illness. After a difficult resettlement, Geoffroi had found stability and, most importantly, a home in Boise. He said, "I love Boise so much. . . . I call Boise home, because it's quiet. . . . I have two kids, so I have to make sure I live in a place where they are safe." He added, "It's a good place where you can raise your kids and be able to make a living." Though Geoffroi noted that Boise's low minimum wage made it difficult to save money, he did not consider moving elsewhere because it would mean losing everything he had worked so hard to build. After all that it took to make a good life in the seven years since his resettlement, he saw no appeal in uprooting again.

This book brings to light the tensions and contractions of refugee resettlement. Though much is gained with resettlement, it is complicated by what is lost along the way. Resettlement was something that Geoffroi's family wanted, yet it nonetheless came with new hardships and disruptions. Geoffroi dropped out of school in Rwanda in anticipation of his departure, but he had to wait more than a year to leave, a reminder of how little of this process was in his control. Because of the resettlement program's emphasis on nuclear families, parts of Geoffroi's family were processed as separate cases, and they did not know if or when they would be reunified.[1] As thrilled as Geoffoi was to learn that he was finally departing for Boise, he was not given the time to prepare for such a significant move or say goodbye to the community where he had grown up, resulting in a disorienting departure. Along with the relief and excitement of making it to Boise, Geoffroi encountered new challenges. He was free of struggles such as food scarcity and physical danger but faced economic hardships that made daily life insecure in new and unexpected ways. While resettlement had remedied many of the struggles that had shaped Geoffroi's youth, getting settled in Boise came with displacing effects that were both startling and distressing. Yet despite such a difficult start, Geoffroi had succeeded in making a home in Boise where his US-born children could grow up with the security and stability that were so meaningful to Geoffroi as a parent.

In the chapters that follow, this book details the long and difficult process of resettlement, shedding light on the benefits and hardships that accompany what the US and other countries characterize as a form of humanitarian protection.[2] Resettlement has traditionally been framed as a solution to displacement and a program of social, political, and economic integration for refugees. According to the UNHCR, the United Nations Refugee Agency, refugees' "predicament [is] definitively solved through resettlement."[3] But by examining the complexities and contradictions of refugees' lived experiences,[4] this book reveals that initial resettlement comes with displacing effects for newly arrived refugees. I reframe resettlement as a time of disruption and disorientation as refugees navigate the rules and expectations of a new country. Rather than a solution that marks the end of their displacement, resettlement has destabilizing consequences that extend through refugees' early months in the US. Resettlement itself becomes another relocation in a series of displacements that began when refugees were first forced to leave their homes. This book reveals that resettlement is not purely benevolent; it can create new conditions of uncertainty and vulnerability.

Drawing on over one thousand hours of ethnographic fieldwork at a Resettlement Agency in two US cities and over one hundred interviews with refugees and service providers, this book centers refugees' experiences to explore more deeply what makes resettlement so disorienting. Refugees arrive in the United States with ambitions and competencies as well as the lingering effects of loss and trauma. Once in their destination, people like Geoffroi begin receiving financial and social service support provided by a federally funded local Resettlement Agency. This assistance, however, comes with formal and informal terms that demand compliance and dictate their socioeconomic incorporation. As refugees try to establish themselves in a new country and adapt to the expectations of their assistance, they may find that the rules and realities of US resettlement do not always align with their aspirations and notions of dignity. Even though refugees may experience early resettlement as another displacement, many, like Geoffroi, do eventually achieve permanency and stability.

At the core of this book are the experiences of those like Geoffroi who arrived through the US Refugee Admissions Program (USRAP) and have worked so hard to build a brighter and more secure future for themselves and their families. I show that the challenges of forced migration in combination with policy decisions made by the US government affect refugees' well-being as they go through the resettlement process. This book progresses both chronologically and thematically to reveal how refugees navigate the displacing effects of resettlement as they reestablish their familial, professional, and social lives in a new country.

Geoffroi is among the more than three million refugees who have arrived in cities across the US through the USRAP since it was formally established by the US Congress in 1980. Resettlement is considered one of three durable solutions for refugees, offering an alternative to the temporariness, limited rights, and insecurity of protracted displacement in refugee camps and urban areas in countries where refugees seek asylum.[5] Typically a last resort for refugees who will likely never be able to safely return to their home country or integrate meaningfully in the country of asylum, resettlement can be life altering and even lifesaving. It provides legal status and social services, thus offering refugees the opportunity to build permanent and safe futures as full members of society. Despite being an important pathway for particularly vulnerable refugees, resettlement is exceedingly rare. In contrast to asylum seekers, who make increasingly dangerous journeys by land and sea in hopes of gaining protection, refugees who have already received this internationally recognized status may be considered for a finite number of resettlement spots while they wait in countries of asylum. This drawn-out process can take years or even decades, with no guarantee of approval. Considering that less than 1 percent of refugees are resettled, resettlement has been likened to "winning the lottery," as it is a seemingly arbitrary process for a highly coveted outcome.[6]

The US is among the two dozen countries that resettle refugees, historically accepting more refugees annually than all other countries of resettlement combined. Once refugees arrive in the US, they benefit from the support of a local Resettlement Agency tasked with carrying out a highly standardized federal program of assistance provided to every refugee who arrives through the USRAP, regardless of the resettlement destination. Each arriving family, or "case," is assigned a case manager, who becomes responsible for their initial well-being, including airport pickup, housing, disbursing financial assistance, and connecting them with other services and supports during their first weeks and months in the US.

In this way, the USRAP stands out as an anomaly in US immigration policy. While the US has extensive federal *immigration* policies that regulate entry into the country, it does not have a comparable *immigrant* policy to address what happens after migrants arrive.[7] At best, migrants entering the US encounter little formal welcome, and at worst, they are subjected to a hostile environment.[8] As a result, social scientists have traditionally studied US refugee resettlement through the lens of integration.[9] Yet alongside resettlement's comparatively exceptional forms of support, the refugee experiences discussed throughout this book show that it is far from straightforward. The USRAP has been described as the *"only* affirmative integration program at the federal level,"[10] but studies have also shown how it continually falls short of achieving this outcome. How can we categorize the experience of resettlement, which offers a tremendous opportunity yet is simultaneously filled with hardships and disappointments?

This book draws on extensive ethnographic fieldwork and interviews in San Diego, California, and Boise, Idaho, from 2018 to 2019 to contextualize resettlement within the broader scope of refugees' lives and to reveal all of the tensions that exist within this ostensible program of humanitarian protection. I show that the very programs of relief intended to support refugees as they settle constrain their choices, create economic insecurity, and expose them to new forms of trauma. I foreground the difficult nature of resettlement given all the ways that refugees must cope with the past while gaining their bearings in a new country. Social scientists typically rely on refugees' labor market participation, English language proficiency, and educational attainment as indicators of incorporation, yet these benchmarks obfuscate less measurable yet deeply meaningful aspects of refugees' lives.[11] By shifting away from framing refugees as a "problem to be solved"[12] or managed, I focus instead on the consequences of the policies and programs that shape their lives. In reality, resettlement is another uprooting and readjustment for refugees who have already rebuilt their lives numerous times.

By offering displacement as an alternative framework for understanding refugees' initial resettlement, this book foregrounds the small yet accumulating indignities, disappointments, and harms that accompany the benefits and forms of support available to arriving refugees. This book centers on everyday aspects of refugees' lives to show how and why resettlement is so disruptive and disorienting. With a comprehensive focus on the resettlement process, which begins in the country of asylum and extends through a refugee's first eight months in the US,

I examine key moments when refugees interact with the formal re-settlement program, a distinct period that shapes numerous aspects of their lives, including familial integrity, economic stability, and trust in the system that welcomed them.

Alongside its many challenges, resettlement nonetheless comes with tremendous opportunity. The early weeks in the US also bring long awaited moments of relief, such as dropping a child off for her first day of school following years of interrupted education or shopping in a supermarket after suffering from food insecurity. Resettlement offers newfound rights and safety in tandem with daily struggles and con-straints. These incongruities make early resettlement difficult to clas-sify. The lens of displacement reflects all of the contradictions wrapped up in the US model of resettlement.

For a year I volunteered as a Resettlement Agency casework assis-tant, with six months at the International Rescue Committee's (IRC) San Diego, California, office followed by six months at their Boise, Idaho, office. Given the nature of my research, which included both shadowing Resettlement Agency staff and supporting them as they as-sisted their refugee clients, this book also draws attention to the ser-vice providers who are tasked with providing resettlement assistance on a daily basis. As the implementers of this standardized and feder-ally funded program of support, Resettlement Agency caseworkers, employment specialist, and other staff work tirelessly and creatively to carry out this notoriously insufficient program and to meet the needs of their diverse refugee clients.[13] Resettlement Agencies are chroni-cally understaffed and underfunded. As this book demonstrates, many of the tensions that arise during early resettlement are rooted in the structural and material constraints that shape how Resettlement Agen-cies carry out their work. Because Resettlement Agency staff are the messengers of this highly regulated, monitored, and time-limited assis-tance, they often become the targets of blame and dissatisfaction when resettlement falls short of expectations.[14] With a deep attention to the structural limitations of Resettlement Agencies, I explain not only *how* resettlement unfolds but *why* it is carried out this way.

A PROGRAM OF INTEGRATION
OR ANOTHER DISPLACEMENT?

The prevailing discourse on durable solutions frames resettlement in opposition to displacement, implying that, upon resettlement, refugees' "problems" have been resolved. Due to the political construction of resettlement as a scarce resource, along with the symbolic value attached to resettlement countries in the Global North, scholars and policymakers have highlighted that resettlement offers an exceptional pathway for select refugees, which stands in stark contrast to the experiences of those who remain in difficult conditions in the Global South or take dangerous routes to seek asylum.[15] Yet even those categorized as privileged under immigration law can experience vulnerabilities through the very programs that set them apart.[16] Bureaucracies reify categories and implement policies that create and maintain inequalities.[17] Though resettled refugees benefit from essential humanitarian protection and services, the gains of resettlement may be accompanied by new and unexpected hardships.

Displacement is an undertheorized concept that has been used interchangeably with forced migration, creating an assumed overlap that may not accurately reflect refugees' lived experiences.[18] Disentangling the *event* of forced migration from the *process* of displacement is more representative of complex realities.[19] The destabilizing effects of displacement are not solely limited to a refugee's migration as it is more than just a "technical problem" that can be solved by humanitarian aid.[20] For example, geographer Ali Ali found that Iraqis suffered from displacement before they became refugees.[21] Anthropologist Stephen Lubkemann's study of the effects of war in Mozambique revealed that those who fled experienced less displacement than their counterparts who could not migrate, creating "displacement in place."[22] I build on this research to show how the social process of displacement also extends into the initial resettlement stage, even after refugees' forced migration has supposedly been resolved.

Central to Ali's conceptualization of displacement is the role of coercion. When people must make life-altering choices under severe constraints, they face "immoral proposals" in which the available options all carry significant consequences that disrupt accepted baselines of security and ways of being.[23] While people do exercise agency when faced with immoral proposals, they are nevertheless choosing among a set of outcomes that are determined by powerful people and institutions, and all carry negative costs. Refugees contend with immoral proposals at numerous junctures along the forced migration trajectory, as they make consequential choices within highly constrained contexts.

Throughout this book, I draw attention to the immoral proposals and coercive dynamics embedded within the USRAP that exacerbate refugees' feelings of displacement. When someone is approved for resettlement before the rest of her family, she must decide whether to leave alone without the guarantee of future reunification or delay departure and potentially give up any chance of ever getting resettled. Once in the US, refugees must accept the first job offer secured by their employment specialist or risk the termination of essential services and financial assistance, compelling work that may be a poor match for their physical or mental health. During their first several months in the US, despite lingering misgivings, refugees feel pressured to sign paperwork out of fear that if they do not, they will lose access to the critical funds needed to pay rent. The programmatic constraints and resource scarcity within which Resettlement Agency service providers work create situations that lead them to present their refugee clients with immoral proposals. Despite their awareness of the structural harms embedded within the USRAP, these service providers find themselves trapped as they perpetuate coercive and problematic dynamics.

Considering the circumstances of their forced migration and long stays in countries of asylum, many refugees are highly dependent on the USRAP when they first arrive in their resettlement destination, making it financially and logistically unfeasible to break away from the programmatic constraints imposed upon them. As I detail in the following chapters, early resettlement is filled with moments of forced compliance. While resettlement is disorienting under the best of circumstances, this book reveals how the US approach to resettlement exacerbates refugees' feelings of displacement, adding to the hardships and challenges that come with settling in a new country. Not only do humanitarian programs not immediately remedy refugees' displacement, they can create conditions that prolong it.[24]

Displacement is assumed to be "the process of relocation under dire circumstances."[25] Yet the experiences of refugees resettled to the US shows how displacement can also occur under *favorable* circumstances. Displacement encompasses a "disruption of key life projects,"[26] which causes a "multifaceted 'package of losses'"[27] that affect relationships, material security, rights, and well-being. This accumulation of losses highlights the processual nature of displacement; it affects people's lives in both catastrophic and mundane ways.[28] Displacement is destabilizing, permeating multiple domains of one's life. It is "hidden in plain sight" and negotiated on a daily basis.[29] In contrast to an event-centered approach, understanding displacement as a social process reveals that it is "so much more than simply people being forced to leave their place of residence."[30]

Refugees resettled through the USRAP arrive with social rights that grant financial and social service support, immediate inclusion in the welfare state, and a pathway to citizenship.[31] They receive initial services from a federally funded Resettlement Agency for up to eight months, after which they can transition to general public assistance programs. Simply framing the resettlement program as exceptional, however, is misleading. Research has simultaneously shown that refugees encounter a distressing reality upon resettlement.[32]

Numerous studies have identified the USRAP's insufficiencies—the ways it falls short of stated objectives and leaves newly arrived refugees to cope with difficult and disappointing circumstances.[33] Given that refugees are benefitting from these services and forms of assistance, why are they experiencing such adverse circumstances? Scholars have demonstrated that immigrants' interactions with public institutions shape their political and economic incorporation.[34] This book shows that the programs and forms of assistance that greet refugees upon arrival have meaningful consequences.

STRUCTURAL HARMS AND WELFARE IN THE US

Research has revealed how laws and policies shape the life chances of marginalized groups, particularly different categories of immigrants in the US.[35] Routinized practices that govern the distribution of resources can stratify life chances and well-being. Pervasive and embedded harms exist silently in ordinary institutions and are often only apparent to those directly affected or in proximity to those experiencing these harms, rendering them largely invisible.[36] Exploitation, inequality, and poverty, particularly when produced or perpetuated by the state, result in diminished educational and professional opportunities, housing and food insecurity, and poor health outcomes, producing slow and persistent damage that extends to multiple facets of life.[37]

The scholarship on structural violence has identified not only how people suffer but also the systems that cause their suffering, including the adverse outcomes of the taken-for-granted practices of everyday institutions.[38] For those affected, the harms endured are no less damaging in the absence of malicious intent. An important trait of structural violence is the lack of an easily identifiable perpetrator,[39] as suffering is produced by state and social institutions, not individual offenders.[40] In contrast to interpersonal violence, this type of "violence is built into the structure and shows up as unequal power and consequently as unequal life chances."[41]

The welfare state is one institution that plays an active role in stratifying society.[42] When social policies are tied to markers of class and labor market status, they further reinforce social disadvantage.[43] As the rise of neoliberalism and welfare state retrenchment took hold and spread internationally,[44] US welfare reform—and specifically the Personal Responsibility and Work Opportunity Reconciliation Act of 1996—replaced guaranteed cash aid with workfare requirements that made ongoing assistance contingent upon engagement in job seeking activities.[45] Means-tested benefits, which are allocated according to income level, and market solutions became the remedy to the "problem" of welfare dependence, employing punitive strategies to promote self-reliance and enforce work.[46] Ongoing retrenchment of the US welfare state has particularly disadvantaged vulnerable groups, such as immigrants, who over time have been pushed out of programs of relief.[47] Whether the result of neoliberalism or a combination of market solutions and nativism, welfare reform inhibited most immigrants' access to social services.[48]

As certain groups have been excluded over time from federal welfare, refugees resettled in the US have been deemed deserving of assistance in ways that other immigrants have not and have continued to enjoy social rights.[49] But research has shown that this deservingness has limitations. The programs that provide newly arrived refugees with access to services and benefits are informed by and at times delivered through the US welfare system.[50] Moreover, the USRAP has also undergone its own retrenchment both in duration and amount of support, favoring employment over financial assistance. What began as an ad hoc system of assistance for select refugee groups turned into a formalized and uniform program of refugee-specific welfare established by the Refugee Act of 1980.[51] Since the resettlement of Vietnamese and Cubans in the 1970s and 1980s, refugee-specific services have been reduced from thirty-six months of transitional assistance to eight months of support, and the level of financial assistance has not always kept pace with the rising cost of living.[52]

The structural harms embedded within the USRAP are obfuscated by refugees' relative privilege, particularly when compared to those who arrive undocumented, have temporary status, or are seeking asylum. Resettlement offers legal status, financial assistance, and social service benefits. Yet, as this book shows, structural harms exist within the very forms of assistance that set refugees apart as privileged. Policies designed to protect particular groups can be embedded within broader institutions that exacerbate existing vulnerabilities.[53]

The USRAP provides arriving refugees with resettlement-specific benefits and social service support (see table 1), both of which extend through refugees' first several months in the US. Resettlement also makes refugees eligible to enroll in federal and state-based public assistance programs, including the Supplemental Nutrition Assistance Program (SNAP, or food stamps), Temporary Assistance for Needy Families (TANF), the Woman, Infants, and Children (WIC) Program, Supplemental Security Income (SSI), and Medicaid.[54] Despite what may look like a generous approach to provisional membership, the USRAP is nonetheless informed by the same neoliberal propensities as other social policies in the US.[55] Contemporary resettlement is motivated by the dual goals of early employment and economic self-sufficiency, which are framed as the means through which refugees will achieve linguistic and cultural integration.[56]

Research has pointed to the neoliberalization of the USRAP.[57] The retrenchment of the US welfare state changed the political environment for programs of relief, including for refugees. Despite a reduction in benefits over time, it is important to recognize that refugees have nonetheless retained access to certain social rights that have been

TABLE I
Refugee-specific forms of assistance (at the time of fieldwork in 2018–2019)

Program	Description	Amount	Time frame
Reception & Placement (R&P) Assistance	One-time per capita grant provided to the Resettlement Agency for initial setup expenses	$1,125 per person	To be spent during the first ninety days
Refugee Cash Assistance (RCA)	Cash aid typically used for single refugees, refugee families who do not qualify for TANF, refugees not enrolled in Matching Grant, or non-minor children in families enrolled in TANF	Per month, varies by state and family size San Diego: Single case: $345 Case of two: $561 Boise: Single case: $382 Case of two: $514	Through the first eight months
Matching Grant Program	Monthly cash aid and employment services for particularly "employable" refugees; carries six months of ineligibility for RCA and TANF	$355 per person per month, including family members, plus funds for transportation	Financial assistance for four months, employment assistance for six months
Refugee Medical Assistance	Medical insurance administered by the state	N/A	Through the first eight months

stripped from most other immigrant groups. By focusing on what refugees no longer receive, scholarship on resettlement has paid less attention to the interactions between refugees and the institutions that continue to serve them—albeit on a reduced scale.

By looking closely at how refugees interact with services during initial resettlement, this book examines how the structural harms within the USRAP exacerbate the displacement that comes with resettling in a new country. Resettlement is disruptive to numerous aspects of refugees' lives, including career ambitions and a sense of home and belonging.[58] This book proposes displacement as an alternative framework for understanding how refugees' lived experiences interact with this standardized program of resettlement. Resettlement is important and at times lifesaving, yet it is nonetheless a displacing process that is unsettling to refugees' lives. Though resettlement may be a migration that is favorable and desired because it offers safety and benefits, it still engenders the "loss, disruption, and disorientation"[59] associated with displacement.

Rima, a young Iraqi woman, struggled when she first arrived in San Diego. Though she had pursued resettlement with her parents and sibling, her case was approved first. Taking the opportunity for resettlement meant leaving for San Diego without them. She had extended family in San Diego already, but she felt alone and insecure as she tried to navigate her new surrounds—all while worrying about her family's safety as they awaited news of their case. Despite her training as an engineer, Rima was soon told by her Resettlement Agency to forget about her prior career. Life in San Diego was expensive, and she needed to begin earning an income as soon as possible. She felt pressured to accept a job so as not to lose her remaining financial assistance. During her first year in the US, Rima continued to flounder. After marrying another Iraqi refugee who had been resettled several years earlier, she relocated to Boise, Idaho, to join him. With his support and the help of his network in Boise, Rima began to build the life she had envisioned for herself. The rest of her family's resettlement case was soon approved, and they joined Rima and her husband in Boise. Reflecting back on her early resettlement experience, Rima said, "Even if you have hard moments, you have to believe there is a light after this darkness." Six years after her arrival in the US, Rima said, "I dreamed of coming to the United States [to] have a normal life and be safe, raise my children here, and I'm kind of this person now."

Despite the disruptive and disempowering effects of resettlement, people like Geoffroi and Rima find ways to navigate their circumstances by developing means of survival,[60] believing that light will come after the unexpected darkness of early resettlement. Refugees draw upon and adapt strategies amid significant constraints, asserting their agency in the face of loss, disenfranchisement, and coercion.[61] Refugees arrive in the US with aspirations of safety and security that they work hard to realize despite numerous unanticipated obstacles. They are not simply victims of the inequalities embedded within US institutions. Upon resettlement, refugees navigate the unfamiliar landscape of a new country and system, striving for the most stable future for their families.

THE POLITICS OF RESETTLEMENT

Resettlement is framed by both the UNHCR and the US government as a life-saving tool of humanitarian protection for vulnerable refugees. According to the UNHCR, resettlement is "the careful selection by governments for purposes of lawful admission of *the most vulnerable refugees* who can neither return to their home country nor live in safety in neighboring countries."[62] Similarly, the USRAP "provid[es] critical protection for *the most vulnerable refugees.*"[63] As scholars have shown, however, humanitarian programs are inherently political and are not impartially benevolent.[64] While resettlement offers legal status, rights, and services to particularly vulnerable refugees, it also acts as a form of "humanitarian governance" characterized by both care and control.[65]

The Refugee Act of 1980 established that the objectives of resettlement are "to achieve economic self-sufficiency among refugees as quickly as possible" and "ensure that cash assistance is made available to refugees in such a manner as not to discourage their economic self-sufficiency."[66] The Refugee Act therefore frames successful resettlement through the dual goals of early employment and economic self-sufficiency, which shape the services provided upon arrival. It is in this sense that the politics of refugee protection are misaligned with the politics of resettlement. Refugees are not selected for resettlement based on their employability, yet their success depends on it once they arrive. Policies that differentiate refugees as vulnerable and deserving of resettlement stand in conflict with the constructed "needs narrative"[67] that refugees encounter in the US, which immediately categorizes them as low-income residents who must be discouraged from becoming dependent on programs of relief. Despite being the very same people, refugees undergo a discursive transformation when they land, creating a dissonance that is disorienting for new arrivals.[68]

The USRAP's quick shift from humanitarian protection to punitive workfare creates programmatic whiplash for refugees as soon as they depart for their resettlement destination. Prior to boarding their flight, refugees sign a travel loan promissory note agreeing to begin repaying the US government for the cost of their airfare six months after arrival through monthly installments over three years. To put the size of this debt into perspective, a Congolese family of six arrived in San Diego, California, with a travel loan of more than $6,000, while the loan for an Afghan family of seven exceeded $9,000. In exchange for safety, social services, and a pathway to citizenship, resettlement carries pecuniary conditions that shape a refugee's early months and years in a new country. This interest free travel loan is framed as an "opportunity" for refugees to establish a credit history.

Attention to the legal fictions that separate "refugees" from "migrants" reveals the incongruity between the politics of refugee protection and the politics of resettlement.[69] Characterizations of resettled refugees as either vulnerable recipients of aid or low-income residents who must be pushed into employment are both oversimplifications. Those deemed vulnerable and in need of resettlement have nonetheless been finding ways to survive under harsh circumstances, just as those who have finally been resettled are still managing the lingering effects of forced migration and trauma. The pathway to resettlement is complicated, carrying multiple and interacting needs and ambitions, and refugees' experiences do not neatly fit convenient political categories.

While pushing against these legal fictions, this book also takes seriously certain factors that make resettlement distinct from other forms of immigration to the US, as it remains important to recognize the critical differences that shape refugees' experiences. The people I met throughout my fieldwork detailed the grief of losing their home and homeland, the constraints that came with being recipients of humanitarian aid, the lack of agency when someone else decides when you leave and where you will go, the challenges of arriving in a resettlement destination where they knew no one, the absence of material resources upon arrival, and the necessary reliance on service providers. While it is critical not to overstate the exceptional nature of resettlement, as refugees interact with many of the same institutions as other immigrants and low-income populations, it is also imperative not to overlook the circumstances that meaningfully differentiate refugees' experiences in the US. The refugees who arrive through the USRAP would otherwise have had no way to get to the US. They also do not have the option to return to their country of origin. Policies matter for "shaping the freedoms and unfreedoms" that refugees encounter.[70] The decisions of the USRAP and the Resettlement Agencies that greet them upon arrival are exceedingly consequential for their initial experiences.

THE UNITED STATES REFUGEE ADMISSIONS PROGRAM

There is no international obligation to welcome refugees through resettlement, and it is up to each government to decide how to incorporate the refugees they accept. The USRAP takes a one-size-fits-all approach to resettlement, providing all arriving refugees with the same scope of services and level of financial support over a fixed time-line regardless of their country of origin or their destination in the US.[71] This standardization of assistance is a feature of the bureaucratization of humanitarian practice.[72] Refugees' first ninety days in the US fall under the Reception and Placement (R&P) period, during which their assigned Resettlement Agency caseworker secures housing, enrolls them in various resettlement-specific and general public assistance programs, and attends to other needs such as accessing medical care and enrolling children in school. In order to cover the expenses associated with this initial period, Resettlement Agencies receive a one-time per capita R&P grant with each new arrival, which at the time of fieldwork was $2,125 per person, with $1,125 to be used for the arriving refugee's expenses and $1,000 to cover the Resettlement Agency's administrative costs and staff time.

Soon after landing in their resettlement destination, refugees are enrolled in refugee-specific and general assistance programs that, depending on their personal circumstances and family composition, provide some level of support for four months or longer. While the R&P period covers initial arrangements, these ongoing programs focus on transitioning refugees to economic self-sufficiency through time-limited assistance in the interest of early employment, which stands in stark contrast to resettlement models in other countries that offer refugees a longer runway for adjustment.[73] Additionally, refugees may have access to an array of other programs—such as in-house English classes, job readiness training, vocational training, and youth services—offered by their local Resettlement Agency that are funded by the federal Office of Refugee Resettlement, local government, or private entities. These ongoing services are typically intended for "extended" refugee clients beyond the initial resettlement period and within their first five years in the US. Figure 1 illustrates the different pathways of assistance available to refugees after arrival.

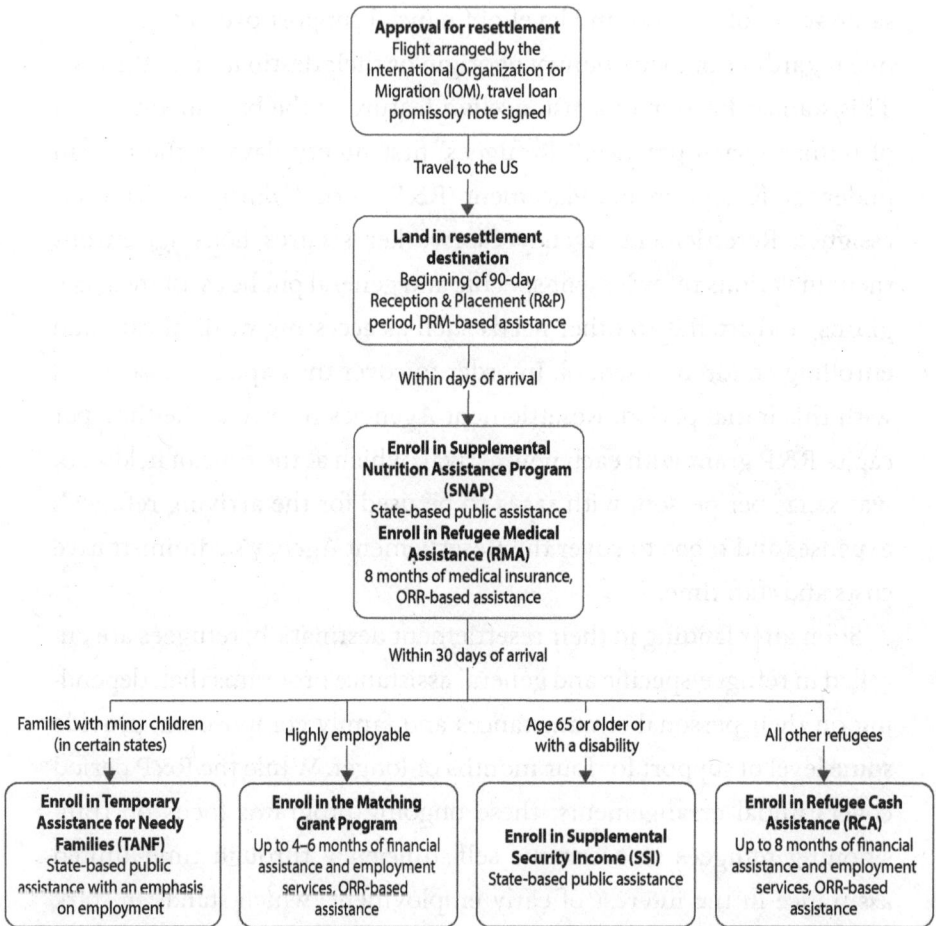

Approval for resettlement
Flight arranged by the
International Organization for
Migration (IOM), travel loan
promissory note signed

Travel to the US

**Land in resettlement
destination**
Beginning of 90-day
Reception & Placement (R&P)
period, PRM-based assistance

Within days of arrival

**Enroll in Supplemental
Nutrition Assistance Program
(SNAP)**
State-based public assistance
**Enroll in Refugee Medical
Assistance (RMA)**
8 months of medical insurance,
ORR-based assistance

Within 30 days of arrival

Families with minor children (in certain states)	Highly employable	Age 65 or older or with a disability	All other refugees
Enroll in Temporary Assistance for Needy Families (TANF) State-based public assistance with an emphasis on employment	**Enroll in the Matching Grant Program** Up to 4–6 months of financial assistance and employment services, ORR-based assistance	**Enroll in Supplemental Security Income (SSI)** State-based public assistance	**Enroll in Refugee Cash Assistance (RCA)** Up to 8 months of financial assistance and employment services, ORR-based assistance

Figure 1. Resettlement process and assistance programs.

THE GEOGRAPHY OF RESETTLEMENT: SAN DIEGO, CALIFORNIA, AND BOISE, IDAHO

The resettlement destination for refugees arriving as "free cases"—that is, without an established close contact already in the US—is decided during a weekly meeting of government officials and representatives of the ten national Resettlement Agencies. Approved cases are assigned to Resettlement Agencies in a round-robin-style process that allocates refugees to resettlement destinations across the country based on considerations such as family size, medical needs, and the capacity of local Resettlement Agencies. These resettlement destination decisions have changed the landscape of the foreign-born population across the US.[74] For approved cases with a "US tie," typically a family remember or close friend already in the US, they will be resettled within the same community as their tie and must reside within one hundred miles of their local Resettlement Agency, as opposed to fifty miles for free cases. While refugees can move within the US as soon as they arrive, relocating as a secondary migrant comes with financial and logistical costs that can complicate the initial resettlement process. Secondary migration is poorly tracked and often happens when new arrivals seek out extended family or an established co-ethnic community elsewhere in the country, as the support of social ties may outweigh the associated costs of relocation.

This book looks at how the resettlement process unfolds in two dissimilar resettlement destinations. Local factors are meaningful for arriving refugees as cities and states vary in their ethnic and racial diversity, cost of living, levels of public assistance, and labor markets.[75] With the exception of sociologist Jeremey Hein's research on Cambodian and Hmong refugees in four US cities, most studies of US refugee resettlement have examined either a single geographic site or similar destination types.[76] This book examines how refugees interact with the federally standardized USRAP in two types of resettlement contexts, offering important insights into how local characteristics do and do not matter in shaping refugees' initial experiences.

The top fifty cities of resettlement over the past twenty years include both traditional immigrant gateway cities and new immigrant destinations, typically smaller cities where refugees make up a larger proportion of the foreign-born and total population.[77] This divergence creates different contexts of reception for refugees.[78] In large cities that have long welcomed immigrants, refugees join diverse communities with a substantial foreign-born population. In contrast, when refugees are resettled in new destinations, their visibility is heightened.[79] Where a refugee is resettled matters, as place-based policies and racialized discourses affect how those resettled learn to frame their belonging.[80]

The USRAP is nationally standardized, yet resettlement is implemented locally and experienced by refugees within the context of their resettlement destinations. The various characteristics of a resettlement destination comprise a constellation of features that make them hospitable and challenging in unique ways. While large urban areas tend to have more diversity, co-ethnic organizations, public transportation, and employment opportunities, they also typically have higher costs of living, and affordable housing tends to be of poor quality. Moreover, not everyone considers large cities to be desirable. Smaller cities and towns may offer a lower cost of living, affordable apartments, industries with stable employment opportunities, and the ability to mobilize community volunteerism. Yet local institutions may be poorly equipped to manage linguistic diversity, co-ethnic communities may be nonexistent, and public transportation may be insufficient. New destinations are critical to the implementation of the USRAP, and while they have long-term potential as resettlement destinations, they often involve growing pains. Though the size and pace of these smaller locales may be appealing to some refugees, the lack of anonymity in a racially homogenous community is undesirable to others.[81]

While most migrants exercise some choice about where they settle, following familial and community ties, job offers, or educational opportunities in the US, this geographic allocation process of the USRAP, especially for free cases, is a distinctive feature of resettlement. The differences between traditional cities of immigration and new immigrant destinations informed my research design and case selection. San Diego and Boise have resettled similar refugee groups over the past two decades (see table 2), yet these cities contrast in a number of ways (see table 3). To study if and how city- and state-based characteristics shape

TABLE 2

Top four countries of origin for refugee resettlement
in San Diego and Boise, FY2002–2020

| | San Diego, CA | | Boise, ID | |
Country	Number of refugees	% of all refugees resettled in San Diego	Number of refugees	% of all refugees resettled in Boise
Iraq	5,449	30.7	1,216	12.8
Somalia	2,871	16.2	1,124	11.8
Burma	2,106	11.9	1,189	12.5
DRC	1,492	8.4	2,056	21.6

SOURCE: WRAPS (2020)

TABLE 3

San Diego and Boise demographics

	San Diego	Boise
Population (2020 Census)	1,386,932	235,684
Refugees resettled FY2002–2020	17,767	9,519
Resettled refugees as % of total population	1.3	4.0
Resettled refugees as % of all refugees resettled in the US between FY 2002–2020 (987,564 refugees)	1.8	1.0
% Non-Hispanic white residents	41.5	81.2
% foreign-born population (2018–2022 estimates)	24.9	6.7
Resettled refugees as % of the city's foreign-born population	5.1	60.3

SOURCE: American Community Survey and WRAPS (2020)

resettlement experiences, I gained research access through the International Rescue Committee's (IRC) Resettlement, Asylum, and Integration office as well as their local affiliate Resettlement Agencies in San Diego and Boise. At the time of my fieldwork, the IRC was one of four local Resettlement Agencies in San Diego and one of two in Boise.

I carried out six months of ethnographic fieldwork at the IRC's San Diego office, immediately followed by six months at their Boise office, working several days per week as a volunteer casework assistant, setting up apartments for impending arrivals, helping with airport pickups, accompanying clients to appointments, providing transportation, and serving as an ad hoc interpreter for francophone clients. In this capacity, I saw families experience the many highs and lows that come with the initial stages of their resettlement. I also conducted over one hundred interviews with refugees, service providers, and community partners whom I met during my fieldwork. Sixty of these interviews were with people who had been resettled for at least one year, offering important perspectives on longer-term trajectories.

As opposed to focusing in depth on some of the people I met during my fieldwork, I instead draw on a breadth of examples throughout this book in an effort to show how the displacing effects of resettlement were shared among refugees from different countries of origin, contexts of asylum, and resettlement destinations. I have also chosen not to provide detailed descriptions of Resettlement Agency service providers, referring to them instead by their job titles. Resettlement Agencies are small organizations, and this lack of detail was necessary in order to maintain workers' anonymity.

While the characteristics of resettlement destinations do matter in shaping refugees' experiences, this book also shows that many of the circumstances that refugees encounter upon arrival are shared regardless of local context. My research took place in very different cities, yet similar issues of disappointment, disrupted family structures, financial insecurity, and loss of trust reveal the institutionalized and overpowering nature of federal policy during initial resettlement, which creates comparable conditions regardless of destination. As the following chapters demonstrate, microlevel dynamics may differ between San Diego and Boise, but macrolevel experiences of displacement were shared across sites. In both cities, newly arrived refugees work long shifts in manual labor jobs, endure drawn out commutes, and rely on inconsistent charity while their caseworkers tirelessly patch together different forms of assistance in order to keep their clients housed. Each city may have its own set of variables, but arriving refugees and Resettlement

Agency staff face a similar set of obstacles that result in struggle and disillusionment. Though resettlement experiences are place dependent in many ways, this book reveals how much is also shared.

The IRC is one of ten national Resettlement Agencies with twenty-nine affiliate offices in communities across the US. I selected two affiliate offices of the same national Resettlement Agency as field sites to minimize variation in organizational culture. While several national Resettlement Agencies are faith-based organizations that oversee a wide range of programs for vulnerable populations, the IRC specializes in assistance during humanitarian disasters and for forced migrants.

The IRC is an international organization that has provided support and services to refugees, displaced populations, and victims of war around the world since the 1930s. What began as a response to Albert Einstein's plea to help those targeted by Naziism when Hitler assumed power in Germany has turned into a global organization with offices in more than forty countries. Throughout the twenty-first century, the IRC expanded its international presence as wars and political crises unfolded throughout the world. While the IRC responds directly to crisis-affected areas and in countries of asylum, it has also worked consistently in US resettlement since the Cold War.[82] The IRC staff located throughout the world all work under a unified code of conduct called the "IRC Way" that foregrounds integrity, accountability, and service.

San Diego, California

San Diego is a large and sprawling city located at the US-Mexico border. It is home to the San Ysidro Port of Entry, the busiest land border in the US, and has welcomed refugees since the earliest days of the USRAP, even before resettlement was formalized through the Refugee Act of 1980. A Resettlement Agency casework staff member in San Diego characterized it as a "since 1975 site" for resettlement as opposed to other cities, which he characterized as "late to the party." California, and San

Diego in particular, have long been among the top resettlement destinations in the US.[83] San Diego is also a diverse city in which less than half of the population is non-Hispanic white. One quarter of the city's population is foreign born, and despite having such a large resettlement program, refugees who arrived through the USRAP between 2002 and 2020 make up only 5 percent of the city's foreign-born population.

With its desirable climate and coastal location, San Diego is among the most expensive cities to live in the US. Though California offers low-income residents a comparatively generous safety net relative to other states and San Diego's minimum wage reached $16.30 per hour in 2023, these advantages do not offset consistently high rental prices. Resettlement in San Diego was long centered in the diverse and more affordable neighborhood of City Heights, which over time has become home to Somali, Congolese, and Burmese communities. However, as the rising cost of housing in City Heights outpaced periodic and minimal increases to resettlement assistance, Resettlement Agencies expanded their operations to neighboring El Cajon in the 2010s, a smaller city about twelve miles east of San Diego that had previously been a resettlement destination for Iraqi refugees, particularly the Chaldean minority group. At the time of my fieldwork, resettlement activities had shifted to housing almost all new arrivals in this smaller city. In 2018, the San Diego IRC office relocated their resettlement casework staff from City Heights to their expanded El Cajon satellite office. San Diego's geographic size, insufficient public transportation, and high housing costs made this type of auxiliary office a necessity. Over time, the IRC's City Heights and El Cajon offices have together grown into a robust hub that provides comprehensive services to refugees and other immigrant communities, including extensive vocational training programs, career development support, legal services, English classes, financial services, and youth programming. Though the initial R&P program is the backbone of every Resettlement Agency, it has since become only a small part of what the City Heights and El Cajon offices do as an organization.

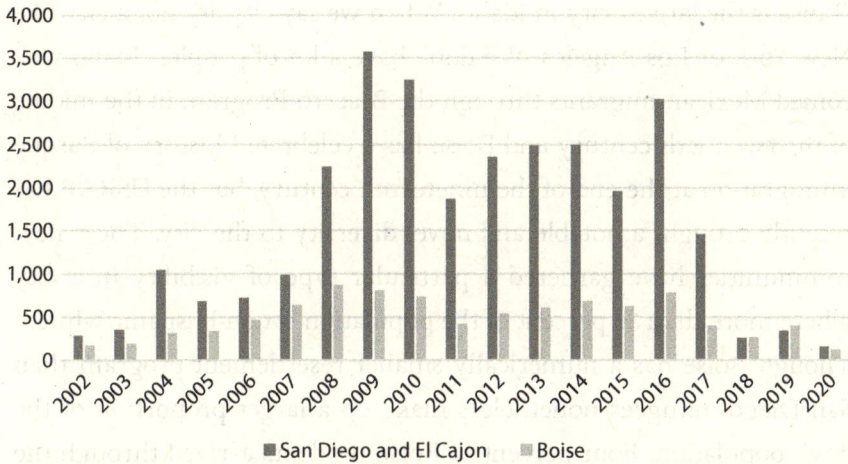

Figure 2. Number of refugees resettled in San Diego/El Cajon and Boise, FY2002–2020. SOURCE: WRAPS (2020).

San Diego offers extensive co-ethnic support through a proliferation of well-established and newer community-based organizations as well as the comforts of numerous markets that offer a range of familiar goods and foods. Yet certain factors, including the cost of living, geographic size, and an inefficient public transportation system, create daily challenges for recently arrived refugees. As I discuss in subsequent chapters, long commutes to jobs across San Diego County add hours onto the workday and rental prices encourage overcrowding in small apartments as refugees try to make ends meet each month. Nevertheless, local institutions, such as public schools, community colleges, and social service agencies, are well equipped to support residents from diverse backgrounds and languages.

Boise, Idaho

Boise, in contrast, is not typically considered a destination for immigrants in the US. At a Cultural Orientation class in Boise, the instructor described their surroundings to a group of newly arrived refugees:

"Boise is the largest city in Idaho. When we say city, it's not a city like New York or Los Angeles. We don't have a lot of people." Idaho welcomed Mexican migrants through the Bracero Program in the middle of the twentieth century and Boise has a celebrated history of Basque immigration at the end of the nineteenth century, but the USRAP has recently brought a notable and novel diversity to the city. These new communities have garnered a particular type of visibility in a city where more than 80 percent of the population is non-Hispanic white.[84] Though Boise has a numerically smaller resettlement program than San Diego, refugees nonetheless make up a larger proportion of the city's population. Four percent of Boise residents arrived through the USRAP over the past two decades, and resettled refugees comprise more than half of Boise's foreign-born population.

With its smaller size and population, Boise prides itself in being a welcoming and neighborly community within a state that at times has been vocally hostile to resettlement. Boise became a certified Welcoming City in 2019 and has proactively established numerous public programs to better support residents who arrived through the USRAP, including the Neighbors United initiative and the Refugee Liaison Officer position within the Boise Police Department.[85] The resettlement program benefits from a culture of active local engagement and volunteerism, particularly from faith-based groups, but the organizational climate makes it challenging for co-ethnic communities to build a formal presence with a seat at the table, relying instead on less formalized networks of support. It has taken time for local institutions such as schools to respond to changing demographics in the city.

The IRC's Boise office was a smaller operation than their San Diego counterpart and centered more directly on initial resettlement services. By virtue of being in a state that offers little to no public safety net, the Resettlement Agency also spent much of its time responding to the needs of extended clients who in San Diego would have sought support from numerous other public and private organizations. The

Resettlement Agency also did not have access to a reliable network of large local donors, who often fund supplemental programming in Resettlement Agencies in other parts of the country. To keep the program viable in the often adverse political context of Idaho, the Resettlement Agency had staff dedicated to community engagement efforts and state-level advocacy in hopes of moving the needle in favor of resettlement and making Idaho a more welcoming state.

Though the cost of housing has increased rapidly in recent years, Boise still offers an affordability that is out of reach in San Diego. Some residents who arrived through the resettlement program have even achieved homeownership either in Boise or neighboring cities, a near impossibility in San Diego. Yet Boise's minimum wage is set by the state, which has remained at $7.25 per hour since 2010. While employment opportunities are closer to refugees' homes, the local bus system does not operate overnight or on Sundays, times that are common for employees in the service industry. Nonetheless, I met numerous people in Boise who were thankful to have been sent there. As for Geoffroi, Boise was a peaceful community that offered his young family the safety and security they desired. A caseworker from the Idaho Department of Health and Welfare echoed this sentiment, telling a newly arrived family of three at the end of their welfare enrollment appointment, "I wish you and your family lots of success and happiness in Idaho and especially Boise. It's one of the best places to raise a family in America."

STUDYING RESETTLEMENT AT A TIME OF RESTRICTION

Given the timing of my fieldwork in 2018 and 2019, my research was deeply shaped by the xenophobic and restrictionist politics of the first Trump administration. Within his first week in office, President Trump dealt the first of many debilitating blows to the resettlement program by signing the January 2017 travel bans. During the subsequent four years, US resettlement reached historic lows. The number of actual arrivals plummeted along with the annual ceiling that sets the cap for the total number of refugees who can be resettled in a given year; the annual ceiling went from a high of 110,000 at the end of the Obama administration in fiscal year 2017 to a low of 18,000 in fiscal year 2020. Once viewed as a goal to strive for, the annual ceiling became a limit not to exceed. Beyond just reducing the number of refugees resettled, the Trump administration also systematically undermined the infrastructure that keeps the resettlement program operational by creating new roadblocks to refugee processing and weakening the institutions that support refugees once they arrive.[86] This strategy, which a Resettlement Agency staff member in San Diego referred to as "death by a thousand papercuts," strained Resettlement Agencies to the point that they had to lay off employees and shutter offices. National security concerns and the growing asylum backlog were used as scapegoats to increase obstacles and reduce resources.[87] During my fieldwork, Resettlement Agency staff were let go, leaving their colleagues to wonder if they would be next.

Over the course of my research, it felt like a small miracle every time a refugee crossed the threshold of the airport arrivals terminal, making it to the US despite the increasingly unfavorable odds. The travel bans caused a near complete halt in the arrival of certain refugee groups that had been resettled in both cities, including Somalis and Syrians. As a result, the majority of new arrivals I met throughout my fieldwork were Congolese refugees, a group that was already being resettled in growing numbers and not affected by the travel bans.

These national policies had ripple effects at the local level, affecting tangential industries that had developed a symbiotic relationship with Resettlement Agencies. A local furniture company in San Diego that used to supply low-cost essentials when Resettlement Agency caseworkers set up apartments for new arrivals had a sudden drop in business. The public school districts in San Diego and Boise both lost their newcomer programs when there were no longer enough incoming students to justify the budget. An administrator in the Boise School District explained, "Trump happened, and the kids stopped coming. If kids stop coming, we don't get money." My research was shaped by the deep uncertainty caused by these policies. At the same time, each long-awaited reunion and act of local support seemed that much more meaningful.

STRUCTURE OF THE BOOK

This book progresses both chronologically and thematically through the stages of a refugee's resettlement. When taken together, the chapters show that displacement permeates numerous domains of a refugee's life, disrupting their expectations, familial integrity, sense of home, financial stability, and educational trajectories, all of which ultimately shape their trust in the system that welcomed them. Along with the opportunities and benefits afforded by resettlement, these chapters examine the ongoing challenges that follow forced migration and protracted displacement. This book demonstrates how the inevitable difficulties of resettling in a new country are compounded by the everyday and accumulating struggles, indignities, and coercive dynamics embedded within the USRAP.

Chapter 1 contextualizes resettlement within the broader scope of refugees' lives by examining the period leading up to a refugee's departure for the US. This chapter reveals that resettlement is another unplanned step in refugees' forced migration trajectories. Resettlement has complex meanings in countries of asylum. While it represents hope for a different future, it also involves leaving loved ones, communities, and familiar places behind. I detail how refugees manage the complicated and drawn-out referral and approval process for resettlement and face the uncertainty that comes with long periods of waiting as their fates rest in the hands of far-removed bureaucrats. At several junctures, refugees encounter reminders of how little of this process is within their control, as flight dates can be changed and destinations can be switched at the last minute. Once refugees do depart for the US, they embark on a long and exhausting trip. All of the stages that precede refugees' arrival in the resettlement destination create a context of disorientation from which they begin the arduous process of settling in a new country.

Chapter 2 picks up right after refugees land in their resettlement destination and are first welcomed by their Resettlement Agency caseworker. Refugees are immediately put on a fast moving and highly standardized "conveyor belt of services" within days of arrival. Despite feeling unprepared and unsettled, refugees are expected to quicky make consequential decisions that affect their ongoing assistance. As newly arrived refugees are still gaining their bearings, this rigorous pace is punctuated by days of solitude, and for some, initial resettlement is marked by loneliness. During this time, refugees grapple with the terms and conditions of life in the US, which may not align with the expectations they formed in their countries of asylum, resulting in confusion, disappointment, and even regret. As refugees become more familiar with their new communities and the rules of US resettlement, they must reconcile this reality with their aspirations for the future. This chapter details how the early weeks of resettlement are shaped by refugees' initial interactions with their Resettlement Agencies.

Chapter 3 looks at how resettlement is experienced within families and explores the various ways that the resettlement process reshapes kinship structures. The priorities of the USRAP are at times incompatible with the realities of familial life, particularly when it has been transformed by forced migration. Some refugees face the impossible choice between separating from loved ones or forgoing the opportunity for resettlement. Along with separating and reconstituting family units, resettlement can disrupt dynamics between parents and children. Parents may feel a loss of authority at home, particularly when they are warned that certain types of discipline are against the law. Family separations and conflicts make resettlement all the more destabilizing. These changes take place as refugees are trying to make a new home, which may be forestalled as they find themselves, by necessity, in temporary accommodations or crowded apartments rented at occupancy limits. This chapter centers on the numerous ways that resettlement becomes disruptive to key dimensions of refugees' familial lives.

Chapter 4 focuses on how the USRAP's dual goals of early employment and economic self-sufficiency ultimately resettle refugees into poverty. This approach to resettlement promotes rapid incorporation into low-wage work and uses poverty-level income as its benchmark of success, regardless of refugees' prior professional backgrounds. While Resettlement Agencies encourage entry-level manual labor jobs in order to get their clients employed as quickly as possible, this type of work is a poor match for older refugees or those in poor health. For refugees looking to rebuild their careers in the US, such positions can feel belittling. As an extension of the US welfare state, resettlement employment services and financial support follow a punitive approach that seeks to prevent dependence and requires refugees to accept their first job offer or risk losing assistance. As a result, refugees feel distraught and stuck, barely making ends meet each month. By exposing refugees to economic insecurity, the USRAP makes them vulnerable to new forms of trauma.

Chapter 5 explores the ongoing relationship between refugees and the Resettlement Agency service providers tasked with supporting them. Over time, as refugees' expectations go unmet and as they confront repeated disappointments, their trust begins to erode, making refugees wary of their caseworkers and the Resettlement Agency that welcomed them. This chapter shows that mistrust between refugees and service providers inheres in the structure of the resettlement program, as refugees lack choice, agency, and control over early financial decisions. Resettlement Agency staff are the custodians of refugees' meager resettlement assistance, using it in ways that may run counter to refugees' expectations and preferences. When refugees lose trust in service providers, they develop a reluctant dependence on their Resettlement Agency out of financial necessity. As a result, refugees may end the formal resettlement period with suspicions and doubts about the support they received, undermining their confidence in the people who helped them.

The book concludes with reflections on refugees' longer-term incorporation, as the losses and disappointments faced by adults may be outweighed by the gains and opportunities enjoyed by their children and future generations. I offer policy recommendations about how the USRAP could better account for and attenuate the displacement that comes with resettlement by addressing the programmatic conditions that lead to unmet expectations and distress. These recommendations seek to center the expertise of people who have gone through the resettlement process themselves. As the USRAP currently stands at a crossroads, having fallen victim to the partisan politics of the second Trump administration, this book concludes by reasserting the importance of resettlement as well as potential ways to rebuild in the future.[88]

Believing in Light After Darkness shifts away from understanding initial resettlement as a solution and time of integration. Resettlement is simultaneously shaped by excitement and relief as well as disorientation and disappointment. While resettlement does succeed in addressing many of the core challenges that afflict refugees in countries of asylum, such as food insecurity, inadequate medical care, limited opportunities, and immobility, resettlement is far from a simple resolution to the difficulties of forced migration, particularly when it comes with new and unexpected hardships.

Resettlement may ultimately be a "good" displacement, but it is nonetheless disruptive. The lens of durable solutions gives a false sense of closure to refugees' challenges. By untangling the displacing effects of resettlement that are inherent in the complexities of forced migration from those that are the product of policy priorities and models of service delivery, this book shows that durable solutions do not immediately resolve displacement, as refugees continue to experience instabilities that affect their families, economic security, and psychosocial well-being. Resettlement will always be a difficult undertaking, but structures of assistance can exacerbate or mitigate the extent of this displacement.

Drawing attention to the displacing effects of resettlement does not imply that resettled refugees remain in a permanent state of displacement. Integration and belonging are multidimensional. Despite having been resettled, it takes time before refugees find "secure belonging."[89] This book builds upon previous scholarship that centers refugees' perspectives of their own resettlement[90] to underscore the complex lived realities of forced migration. Situating resettlement within the broader scope of refugees' lives reveals how the resettlement process becomes one more uprooting in a succession of displacements that began when refugees were first forced to leave their homes.

1

DEPARTURE

EVER SINCE HER FAMILY'S home burned down in Syria, Yara
has felt like she has been on the move, even after coming to
the US. Initially resettled to a city in the southwestern US
where they knew no one, Yara's family of six relocated to San
Diego eight months later to join the growing Syrian community. Though Yara and her siblings were doing well in school,
the compounding difficulties of inadequate housing, limited
employment opportunities, and the high cost of living in San
Diego made the family consider moving yet again. A year
after arriving in the US, Yara still felt far from settled.

After losing their home in Syria, Yara's parents did their
best to avoid becoming refugees, but the safety they found
with each internal relocation was short lived, prompting
them to move again. When Yara's father could no longer
work and the accommodations at a relative's home grew too
crowded, they were finally pushed to cross the border into
Jordan. During the nearly five years they spent in Amman,

Jordan, Yara's family lived in eight different houses. Yara explained that, with each move, "we had to clean up, and we had to take on everything, start all over again. That was really hard, to do all that again and again." Though the family was ultimately resettled after a stressful year of official interviews and appointments, arriving in the US did not remedy the feelings of displacement that had come to shape Yara's adolescence. To fully understand Yara's resettlement experience, it is imperative to first understand the persistent instability she endured in Syria and Jordan, an instability that continued to plague her family in the US.

Despite feelings of ongoing precarity, Yara admitted how little another move appealed to her. She said, "We don't really want to move, because it's been like moving since in Syria, when our house burned down. We have been moving so much. . . . We just wanted to settle down." For Yara, the prospect of moving again in the US was inextricably linked to all of the displacements that had come before. Though resettlement brought security to some aspects of their lives, Yara's family continued to experience a transience that began when they first lost their home in Syria. Yara was tired of moving, but a sense of rootedness remained elusive.

Refugee resettlement offers safety, yet it creates disruptions that can be overwhelming, disappointing, and confusing as refugees take on the arduous task of reestablishing their familial, social, and professional lives in a new country and language, all while navigating an institutional system that is not always intuitive or supportive. Upon resettlement, refugees must deal with everything that comes with leaving one home and building another in a new country. Though resettlement may offer legal status, rights, and services, it can nonetheless come with displacing effects that require significant acclimation and adjustment, all of which may clash with refugees' expectations of life in the US.

This chapter takes a step backwards to situate resettlement within the broader scope of refugees' lives. By examining the period and process leading up to refugees' arrival in the US, I demonstrate that the displacing effects of resettlement begin long before refugees land in the US. Resettlement is an institution whose scope and reach extends beyond its role as a migratory pathway or a program of humanitarian protection.[1] Prior to their arrival in the US, refugees in camps and urban areas have often been navigating the resettlement process for years.

The USRAP holds complex and contradictory meaning in situations of protracted displacement. For many refugees, resettlement is a highly coveted outcome, yet it requires a drawn out and unpredictable process filled with uncertainty.[2] The joy and relief of receiving an approval is followed by a long and exhausting trip to an unfamiliar destination, creating a disorienting context from which refugees must begin to make sense of their lives in a new country. Throughout this chapter, I discuss the overlapping highs and lows that accompany the process of gaining approval, all of which begin to shape refugees' resettlement.

Studies of resettlement typically focus on the experience of refugees once they have landed in the resettlement destination and explore what comes after their arrival. In an effort to move away from siloed approaches to understanding forced migration,[3] this chapter contextualizes resettlement within refugees' forced migration trajectories and lives. When refugees arrive in the US, they bring with them the hope of a secure future along with the grief of leaving behind communities and homelands. By situating resettlement within the life course, not only can we better understand the contradictory emotions that accompany resettlement, but we can also untangle the complex roles that resettlement has played in refugees' lives prior to their departure.

RESETTLEMENT CASES AND APPROVAL

For many in situations of protracted displacement, the resettlement process is measured in years, during which refugees have little certainty about whether, when, or where they will be resettled. Raphael, a Congolese father, and his family gained approval three years after they had begun the process and seventeen years after he had arrived in a refugee camp in Uganda. Gerard, a Burundian father, had already been living in a refugee camp in Malawi for fourteen years before he began the resettlement process, and he waited another five years before receiving a letter informing him of his family's approval. After such a long wait for such an exceptional opportunity, he could barely believe the news when the letter arrived. He said, "I didn't believe it 100 percent. . . . I'll believe it when I'll be in the airplane. . . . Then even at the airport, I said, 'No, no,' and then in the airplane, we could look at each other and [say], 'Yes, really, we are going.'" For Gerard, like so many others, the underlying disbelief that this life-changing opportunity would ever become a reality was only quieted when his flight finally took off.

When refugees are living under particularly dire circumstances in the country of asylum, they may benefit from an expedited process. Tresor, a young Congolese man, and his family had their case expedited due to the injuries his father and one of his siblings had sustained during a violent attack on their refugee camp in Burundi, which killed his mother and many others. Even so, it took four years before they finally departed for the US. When compared to others he knew, their processing and approval had indeed been speedy. He noted how others who had been in the same camp and had cases at the same time were either only just arriving in the US ten years later or were still awaiting approval. Andre, a young Congolese man, had the opposite experience. After he was arrested and tortured, it became increasingly unsafe for him to remain as a refugee in Zimbabwe. In light of ongoing threats, his case was quickly pushed through by the UNHCR and approved by the US government. Within a short period and with little time to digest the news, Andre told me, "I found myself on the plane, and I was coming to Boise."

During the resettlement process in countries of asylum, refugees may experience several starts and stops. Back-to-back appointments and interviews can be followed by months of silence. After refugees' cases are referred to national governments by the UNHCR, they may be considered by a variety of countries of resettlement, and refugees can feel as though their fates are being passed around from one country office to another—with little certainty about the future. Two years before Rosine's family departed for the US, they had been progressing through the Dutch resettlement process but were rejected the following year because of complications with their extended family structure. A year later, this Congolese family of six began the interview process for Canadian resettlement, only to be notified soon after that they could also begin the process for the US. Ultimately the US was the first to accept Rosine's family, and they departed several months later. Each change in the country of resettlement created a new potential fork in the road. These changes were "so confusing" for Rosine, as they came with unsolicited advice from fellow camp residents about where life would be better. But in reality, they had little control over the outcome.

The uncertainty that accompanies these periods of waiting can feel agonizing and fuel gnawing doubt and fear.[4] Pascaline's family had to wait more than a year between certain stages of the process. Though it seemed like the case for this Congolese family of five was moving ahead, it took a year and a half to schedule their predeparture medical screening. During this time, Pascaline explained, "you really lost hope." They heard no news for another year once they had completed the required medical screening, and Pascaline, a teenager at the time, tried to push the prospect of resettlement out of her mind. Then, without warning, the family was notified that they would be leaving for the US in just two months. After years of false starts and drawn-out waiting, they had only two months to prepare for such a monumental move. Like Gerard, it was not until Pascaline arrived at the airport that she allowed herself to think, "Well, I guess I'm really leaving."

As refugees wait for such a consequential decision with little control over the outcome, it may feel as though time is being manipulated by those wielding power, resulting in significant uncertainty.[5] After Yara's family underwent the predeparture medical screening and cultural orientation required before refugees depart for the US, Yara assumed that their travel date would be imminent, as these were the final steps in the process. Yet six months passed with no news. During this time, Yara said, "we just had to wait. . . . We were afraid, because sometimes they will not accept your file, and they will just close it, and they don't tell you that they didn't really accept it. . . . So we would call them every day." Finally, they received notification of their approval along with a departure scheduled for seventy-two hours later. Then their flight date was moved up by a day. Yara explained the panic that followed, "We didn't know what we were packing. Like it's just everything in bags." Not only did Yara's family have to frantically prepare for resettlement in less than forty-eight hours, but their abrupt departure left no time to say their goodbyes to family and friends beyond the few who lived close by.

Seeming manipulations of time along with a lack of control or predictability all contribute to the disorienting nature of resettlement. In describing his family's departure for the US, Bernard, a Burundian father, likened it to his experience of fleeing home. Under the threat of immanent violence, a refugee's primary objective is leaving. After spending many years in a refugee camp, Bernard was once again just focused on getting out. When the opportunity for resettlement comes, Bernard explained, "You say, 'Let's go.'" Once approved, departure may be hasty, leaving refugees with little time to process such a big change. Such hurried exits deny refugees like Yara proper goodbyes to family and friends with whom future reunions are uncertain. Though this departure may ultimately be favorable and desired, it nonetheless contains parallels reminiscent of the earlier displacements that forever uprooted their lives.

Given all of the work and anxiety that go into the resettlement process,[6] the moment of approval is typically filled with unadulterated joy and relief. Tresor told me that he would never forget the day his family learned that their case had been successful. They had simultaneously hoped for this day while also assuming that it would never actually happen. Tresor and his siblings knew that their father received a phone call each time their family's case progressed to the next stage of the resettlement process, and they had come to associate his cell phone's ringtone with updates from the UNHCR. Whenever they heard an incoming call, they would pepper their father with questions, "Is that the UN? Is that the UN? Who's calling you?" Tresor admitted, "We were always excited" when the phone rang, eagerly anticipating updates about their case. One day after their father answered his phone and began to cry, Tresor said, "We just knew it was, then, the time."

When Pascal, a young Congolese man, and his family learned of their approval, he could hardly believe it. He said, "Oh man, I was so, so, so happy about it. . . . It's like you were dreaming, but it's actually true." For Ashina's family, after five difficult years living in Kampala, Uganda, getting approved for resettlement to the US "was the best moment." Ashina, a young Congolese woman, was a teenager at the time of their approval. She was most excited about being able to go to school without worrying about the interruptions that had interfered with her education in Kampala. Remi, a Congolese father, felt like all the work he had put into his family's resettlement process over a nine-year period had finally paid off. He said, "I felt very, very glad. I was excited, super excited, because it was a fight, going and coming back disappointed, going and coming back disappointed. Then finally they say yes, you've succeeded. Now you can go get ready. I was very, very excited." After fifteen years in a refugee camp in Tanzania, the last nine of which were spent pursuing resettlement, Remi's family was finally leaving.

But this joy can also be tempered by concerns about what might await them in the US. Though Aadam, an Afghan father, was very happy to be coming to the US, his mind was full of questions about how he and his wife would navigate moving to a place where they knew no one and did not speak the language.

THE IMPORTANCE OF RESETTLEMENT

Though resettlement is an exceedingly rare pathway for refugees in situations of protracted displacement, it nonetheless serves as an important means of humanitarian protection. Countries of asylum that host the majority of the world's refugees often rely on political tactics to make refugees' lives feel temporary by design even if they reside there for years. Limited political rights, restricted movement, nonpermanent shelter, and exclusion from the formal economy were all reasons why Serge, a Congolese father, likened the camp in Tanzania where he lived for fifteen years to a prison. Similarly, when Yonas described his life in the refugee camp in Ethiopia where he spent eight years of his youth, he said, "Life in refugee camps, it's hard; it's tough; it's [a] struggle. When I first ended up in [the] refugee camp, we used to eat once a day. There wasn't enough food, there weren't jobs, there wasn't money." He remembered having to strategize when to eat his daily meal. In light of these circumstances, resettlement is of great significance, offering an alternative to a life shaped by the food and housing insecurity, poor healthcare, and limited professional and educational opportunities characteristic of protracted displacement.

These daily struggles come to shape how refugees view resettlement and imagine what might be gained by coming to the US. For Bastien, a young Congolese man who experienced constant food scarcity during the thirteen years he lived in a camp in Tanzania, resettlement, and in particular the US, was synonymous with unhindered access to food. For others, resettlement was imbued with a general sense of hope for a better future. In the Kenyan camp where Rosine lived for five years, important updates to the status of residents' resettlement cases were posted to a centralized board. Given the hardships she, her siblings, and single mother endured, that board held great symbolic value. "The board," she explained, "that was our hope."

Amid the imposed temporariness of protracted displacement and limited opportunities, resettlement allows refugees to plan for an imagined future in a way that seems impossible within the context of their current circumstances. Hanad was born in Ethiopia to Somali parents who had fled the civil war. After his mother passed away, he dropped out of school in the fourth grade to work. While his family remained in the refugee camp, he went to live with his uncle in a nearby village where he began working as a cart pusher. During this time, Hanad's life took on a bleak monotony. He explained, "It's like there's no hope for [the] future. I just go and wake up and go to work and come back. That's it." Within such contexts, resettlement offers a different path forward. When Patrick's family learned that they had been approved for resettlement to the US, it finally seemed like they could mend their lives in a way that felt impossible in the camp in Tanzania where they had lived for fifteen years. He said, "We lost everything, and we never know how we are going to put it back together." Patrick was a young child when his family fled the DRC. He experienced all of the limitations that come with growing up in a refugee camp. For Patrick, coming to the US meant "I started thinking about my future."

Likewise, resettlement became a turning point for Raphael and his young children. In stark contrast to their life in the refugee camp in Uganda where, he explained, "you can't do anything because you are temporary. . . . [or] plan for your future because you are temporary," resettlement meant that Raphael could work, his children could pursue their education, and they "would be comfortable." Ten years after her family's arrival in the US, Paw Eh, a young Karen woman originally from Myanmar, reflected on how much the trajectory of her life had diverged from that of her friends who had remained in the refugee camp in Thailand where she had grown up. Paw Eh had graduated from high school in San Diego and was attending a four-year university. Her friends who never left had married young and become mothers, raising a new generation in the camp. She said, "It's just sad for me because I know that's how I was going to end up. . . . And me being here and hearing that I was just like, wow, that could have been me."

Not only does resettlement make another future possible, but it may be the only viable path forward for refugees experiencing particular vulnerabilities, such as critical health conditions or disabilities. In these cases, resettlement means access to lifesaving care. Cawil, a young Somali man, was acutely aware of the importance of proper medical treatment. During the seventeen years that his family lived in a refugee camp in Kenya, his father died after untreated wounds from a broken leg grew infected. At a young age, his sister began suffering from frequent seizures, which she simply had to endure in the absence of appropriate health care. Resettlement became the only way for Cawil's single mother to get her daughter the medication she needed to manage her condition. When they arrived in San Diego, Cawil's sister had her first doctor's appointment at the age of fourteen.

Beyond difficult circumstances, refugees may be unsafe in the country of asylum whether due to conflicts that permeate borders or to new forms of discrimination. Less than a year after Tresor's family fled the DRC for a camp just over the border in Burundi, an armed attack killed more than 150 people in the camp, including his mother, and wounded others. Similarly, Thierry and his family continued to experience violence during the six years they spent in Kampala, Uganda, after fleeing war in the DRC. In addition to being arrested in Kampala on a few occasions, Thierry's home was set on fire, killing his mother and severely burning his brothers, after which, he said, "life became really super dark." Had they not been able to pursue resettlement, Thierry told me that his family thought, "maybe we should just go back [to the DRC] and die [at] home."

Even when war and conflict in the home country are resolved in official terms, the scars of violence, persecution, and forced migration may make return feel like an impossibility. Political scientist Wendy Pearlman has shown that living under an oppressive and authoritarian government may mean that the country of origin never actually felt like "home" in the first place.[7] In such cases, resettlement becomes the only way forward, particularly if countries of asylum and international organizations stop providing aid. When the Second Liberian Civil War ended in 2003, David's mother refused to bring her children back to the country they had fled under such dire circumstances. But as peace was declared in Liberia, the aid they had been receiving as refugees in Sierra Leone ceased. Life became even more challenging as David, along with his brother and cousins, had to work manual labor jobs in order to afford their school fees. His family's eventual resettlement provided an alternative to the limbo they experienced in Sierra Leone. For David and others enduring difficult and precarious conditions in countries of asylum, resettlement, however unlikely, became the chance for another life.

AN UNANTICIPATED MIGRATION

Though resettlement may be an exceptionally meaningful and even lifesaving alternative to protracted displacement, it is not something that refugees plan for when they first leave their home countries and is rarely assumed to be a possibility until it happens. After Pascal's family fled the DRC and ended up in a refugee camp in Tanzania, he assumed that his life would forever be spent in this camp should the situation not improve back home. He explained, "Once we were in a refugee camp, you don't think that you'll go anywhere else. . . . The only thing you're thinking is, 'This is my life, and this is [the] place I found.'" Likewise, Thierry had never intended on moving to the US. While growing up in the DRC and even after fleeing to Kampala, Thierry said, "I never dreamed of coming to America." It was only after his family had endured forced migration and displacement, his mother had died, and his brothers were injured that resettlement became a potential outcome. Resettlement was an onward migration that had never been a part of Pascal's or Thierry's initial life plans, existing only in relation to their forced migration.

Places of first asylum, including refugee camps, may therefore feel permanent rather than like a "stepping stone" to the US.[8] Because resettlement is unreliable and rare and often only becomes possible long after initial displacement, refugees continue their lives and do their best in camps and urban areas despite challenging circumstances. By fully acknowledging refugees' lives in countries of asylum, however difficult they may be, we can better understand how resettlement is displacing. With resettlement, refugees must "imagine a future they never expected."[9]

A refugees' trajectory is rarely linear or premeditated and may be comprised of several discrete migrations over the life course, some of which could never have been anticipated at the outset. Andre was eight years old when war started in the DRC. As the situation worsened, his family moved from their home city to a village to put distance between themselves and the violence. When conditions improved a couple of years later, they returned and found their house still standing. His family rebuilt their life only to have it shattered two years later. War returned, and in the chaos, at the age of twelve, Andre was separated from the rest of his family. "School [and] family scattered all over," he explained. "I couldn't find them, and they kept pushing me out from another city to another city and finally all the way out of the country." Unsure of the fate of his family and in an effort to find safety, Andre continued to move south, down the eastern part of the DRC before eventually crossing the border into Zimbabwe where he was informed that he was now a refugee. In the nine years that followed, Andre lived in four more countries, moving each time after conditions became untenable. When Andre was resettled to the US, it became one more migration in a long series of displacements throughout his youth and adolescence, all of which had been more reactive than planful.

Like Andre, refugees may have already undergone multiple distinct displacements prior to their resettlement. Several people I met from Afghanistan were first displaced during war in the 1990s and returned in the early 2000s hopeful for a safe future following the US-led invasion of Afghanistan. But ongoing threats and deteriorating security years later drove them across borders once again. Aadam's life had been shaped by recurrent displacements: "I [had] grown up in a refugee life my entire life." When he was a child, his family moved to northern Afghanistan after their hometown became too dangerous. Then the Taliban took over, and his family fled to Pakistan a year later. After the new regime was established in Afghanistan in 2001, Aadam's family returned. He shared with me the joy of being back in his home country after living as a refugee in Pakistan. He said, "It was a new beginning for that country. . . . I finished my school and started working, and life was beautiful. Everything was awesome. Not from [a] luxury perspective, but I was home. I lived in my home. I was in my country. I was with my family, friends." As Aadam was establishing his career in Kabul, security in the city worsened. After an attack at his office killed several of his colleagues, he fled to Pakistan. Once again, Aadam became a refugee despite his efforts to build a life in Afghanistan. His resettlement to the US was another unplanned and unanticipated move after being forced to seek refuge in Pakistan for a second time.

The ever-changing politics of refugee selection[10] can quickly turn the impossibility of resettlement into a reality. Yonas had been living in a refugee camp in Ethiopia for five years before the US government designated residents of that camp as a priority for resettlement. Though these refugees still had to successfully undergo an interview and screening process, which took another three years for Yonas, anyone in the camp interested in pursuing resettlement to the US could now do so. Yonas explained that refugees lacked control over whether they got resettled and when. He said, "In the refugee camp, resettlement is not a right. You don't claim resettlement. You just wait there, and if any country requested or would like to resettle refugees, that's [when] you get a chance." For Yonas, what had seemed unlikely during the nine years he had spent as a refugee, fleeing first to Eritrea and then back to Ethiopia, all of a sudden became possible because of this new priority designation for the camp. Even after beginning the process, Yonas was cautious about making any assumptions, "When the process started it takes a long period of time. And you don't really know if you are really going to be qualified or not, [and] you go through multiple interviews, and multiple medical checkups. And you don't know what the qualifications and disqualifications are. It's a time of excitement and fear, until you get the approval paper at the end." It was only upon approval that an alternate life and future became possible for Yonas.

Heaven Crawley and Katharine Jones caution scholars against assuming that countries of first asylum and refugee camps are places of transit in which refugees simply wait for an opportunity to move on to the Global North. They instead view migration as a social process in which life continues in countries of asylum even amid hardships and subsequent migrations. They argue that refugees live "multi-layered lives in the 'in-between' places."[11] It is only when refugees move on or when the improbable outcome of resettlement occurs that countries of asylum undergo a rhetorical shift from a destination to an "in-between" transit country.[12] As Yonas's journey illustrates, the possibility of resettlement did not enter his life until nine years after fleeing his home. Until he received approval, the camp in Ethiopia was a place of immobility rather than a place of transit and mobility. Even within the harsh context of a refugee camp or impoverished urban area, refugees are creating and living lives prior to resettlement. In this sense, we can better understand how and why resettlement is displacing. While it may ultimately be a welcome and wanted migration, moving to the US is another uprooting that is disruptive and disorienting as refugees leave behind routines, communities, and means of survival. Refugees like Yonas and Andre must again figure out how to rebuild a meaningful life in a new country.

Not only is resettlement rare and never guaranteed, but it requires significant effort on behalf of refugees.[13] Resettlement does not just happen passively to refugees; they must actively seek it out. Warsame, a Somali father recounted how he engaged in a letter writing campaign in hopes of opening a pathway to resettlement for residents of the camp where he lived. When pursuing resettlement, refugees must undergo multiple appointments and rounds of interviews that can span years and may also require travel from remote refugee camps to centralized processing centers in neighboring cities. Eventual resettlement may even be the result of repeated cases after earlier failed attempts. Firas, a young Iraqi man, recounted his mother's stoic and tireless management of their family's resettlement process over a thirteen-year period. His mother concealed the persistence and work that went into this process. Each time their case was rejected, she would start again, simply telling her family that their case was still pending to shield them from disappointment, all while absorbing the emotional labor that went into their family's resettlement. Firas only learned of his mother's extreme efforts after they had finally been approved. Henri, a young Congolese man, shared how his mother silently managed their resettlement process over a ten-year period while their family lived in Zambia. Henri reflected on his mother's tenacity, overseeing the many components of their family's case while also raising young children in difficult conditions. Henri said, "It took my mom ten years or so. . . . My mom kind of kept it a secret from us. . . . I think back and I'm just like, Dang! How is she able to do that? . . . At that time, she had six kids, too."

Despite obstacles in the country of asylum, not all refugees necessarily view resettlement favorably. Bastien explained how the idea of resettlement was not equally enticing to all residents of the refugee camp in Tanzania where he grew up. Older residents in particular held onto dreams of an eventual return to the homeland. For them, there was little appeal to moving even further away when their home country still embodied everything they desired, so long as it was at peace. A service provider in Boise recognized how, all things being equal, resettlement was rarely a refugee's true preference. She said, "The majority of our families regardless of where they were displaced from, would say they would much prefer to go home rather than to have come here to the United States. Who wants to leave their home?"

As Joanne van Selm notes, "Many refugees do not want to resettle: fleeing for safety from a homeland where a person previously had a 'normal' life does not make that person suddenly want to move half-way around the world. Some resettle happily, seeing the opportunities a new life can bring for them or their children. Others are reluctant, but see it as the only way to move forward."[14] Western Europe and North America are not universally desired destinations,[15] and even when refugees do seek resettlement, they are operating under extremely limited options. Some refugees may be thrilled by the prospect of moving to the US, while for others resettlement is simply the best outcome of the worst-case scenario of forced migration, insecurity, and limited futures. In a perfect world, these refugees would never have to be resettled because they would never have had to leave their homes in the first place. Karam, an Iraqi father explained, "We are not here for leisure, not for fun. We're here because we were forced to flee. I mean, you wouldn't leave your family, you wouldn't leave your country, you wouldn't leave where you were born and raised for no sufficient reason. . . . War, discrimination, sectarian violence, a lot of components that push us to flee and come and try to start a new life. So we are not here because we choose to. We are here because we were forced to."

Maxime, a young Congolese man, reiterated this point, asserting that refugees would rather have never had to leave their home countries in the first place; they would have preferred instead to have lived a peaceful life uninterrupted by the wars and persecution that ultimately drove them to flee. He explained, "Nobody wants to leave Congo. . . . Everyone wants to stay in Congo. Nobody *wants* to leave." An Iraqi woman explained the emotional wounds that persisted long after she had left her country. In spite of the house, career, and family she enjoyed in Iraq, the threat of religiously motivated violence became unendurable. She put it quite simply, "You don't *want* to leave, but you *have* to leave," as the need to flee surpassed the desire to stay. This woman noted the particular pain she felt knowing that leaving Iraq meant forever losing her family's house, the place that embodied her sense of home.[16] A casework staff member in Boise acknowledged that if refugees did actually have a choice, they would probably never have become migrants in the first place. She said, "Where's the choice in any of this? No one's really choosing this. They'd like to stay home."

Consequently, resettlement may evoke complex and at times contradictory emotions, as feelings about what is gained are further complicated by what has been lost and what can never be. Though Aadam longed for his homeland and the life and community he left behind in Afghanistan, he was simultaneously ecstatic when he learned that his family had been approved for resettlement to the US: "It was kind of a dream, and I was not believing, like, I'm coming to US, and I will live my life in United States with my wife and my kids. It was amazing. At the same time, you have some nostalgia feeling about your home country. Still, I cry for Afghanistan. When something bad happens in that country, I cry from sadness. If something great happens, I cry for I'm away from that country and I'm not seeing and I'm not feeling." Refugees in protracted displacement must reckon with dreams that are at odds with reality. Manir, another Afghan father, explained, "Everybody likes their country, but the most important thing is our lives." The hope and relief of resettlement become complicated by grief and loss. Resettlement means reconciling the unlikeliness of an eventual return to the life they were forced to leave. Additionally, though refugees are living under difficult circumstances in refugee camps and urban areas, resettlement also means leaving behind the communities they built in the country of asylum.

For children born in the country of asylum, resettlement marks their first migration and is an uprooting from all they have ever known. Idil was nine years old when her family was resettled from a refugee camp in Yemen. Her parents fled civil war in Somalia in the 1990s and started a family after seeking refuge in Yemen. When Idil's family of six was approved for resettlement after multiple attempts and failed cases, Idil remembered thinking to herself, "What waits for us over there? How different is it going to be? I was really sad because we're going to leave, and we're going to leave everyone behind." She added, "I've only known that camp that I lived in. It was basically my home. I never met anyone else. I've never lived anywhere else. . . . In my mind, I was like, maybe we should stay. It was really sad. I wasn't ready for that huge change." Their impending move was fraught for Idil's mother as well, now a single mother of five. Despite the hardships she faced and the security that resettlement would offer her young children, moving to the US meant leaving behind the community she had built in Yemen. Idil continued, "I remember my mom was really sad, too, because she was like, 'I've known people for over twenty years and [I'm] just leaving them. I don't know if I'm ever going to see them again.' Yeah, my mom was really sad." For Idil's family, the benefits of resettlement were complicated by the loss of another home and the rupture of another displacement.

From Paw Eh's perspective as a child, the refugee camp in Thailand where she grew up was a place of joy because it was where she played with her friends: "It was really fun for kids because we don't really know the struggle behind the doors that our parents go through. . . . For us kids, it's fun, but for us to see the future, there's no future." Her family was approved for resettlement when she was ten years old. Paw Eh's eagerness to move to the US was tempered by the realization that she was leaving everyone and everything familiar behind. She said, "I was excited and really sad because I didn't want to leave my friends. And this is the place where I grew up, and this is the place where I want to be. But then I still want to come to America to have a better life. Even if I was a kid, I still know what a better life is."

Because of her family's multiple migrations, Pascaline struggled with what it meant to consider the refugee camp where she had spent her formative year as her home. After her parents fled the DRC, Pascaline was born in Tanzania. Then they moved to Botswana when she was four years old. She spent the next eleven years living in a refugee camp where her life was shaped by restricted rights, immobility, food insecurity, and poor medical care. She told me, "I'm just grateful to be out of there and healthy." She added, "I call it home because I don't really know what place to call home. . . . Botswana is what I know most of, and then we moved here. . . . It's really [the only] home that I know." Pascaline's family had not been looking to uproot again. Rather it was Botswana's poor treatment of refugees that ultimately pushed them to pursue resettlement. She explained, "I feel like people think we come here because we want to. . . . It wasn't our choice to leave Botswana and come here. They didn't want refugees there, so we had to leave, and then you don't choose where you're going. They just send you. . . . We uproot our lives somewhere else to come and start here, and it's a whole different world compared to where we come from, and everything, everything's so different." Even though she had been living under conditions of extreme hardship in Botswana, Pascaline's resettlement to the US still felt like another uprooting.

When families embark on the long and life-changing journey of resettlement, children rely on the signals around them to make sense of what lies ahead. Because of the drawn out and unreliable nature of the resettlement process, parents may spend years attending to paperwork and meetings, only to inform their children when departure is imminent. Even after a family's resettlement is approved, parents may still be wary of telling their children too much. Geoffroi, a young Congolese man, explained how cautious people had to be about the spread of information. Given the hardships of daily life in the refugee camp in Rwanda where he spent fifteen years, Geoffroi noted that jealousy drove some people to try to sabotage the resettlement of others. Upon gaining approval, he said, "You have to be careful. . . . The people, they have jealousy if you're actually saying that you're leaving the country. . . . They're living their life, right? But yours is going to change, but it's not going to affect them, their lives, right? Some people got killed because of that, the jealousy." In the days leading up to departure, the stakes are incredibly high. Geoffroi added, "Any time you get the news, you celebrate, but you have to be careful." Keeping children in the dark may be the best way for parents to ensure that no one ruins this opportunity for a different life.

At ten years old, Henri was too preoccupied by playing with his siblings to realize that the meetings he accompanied his parents to were actually the interviews that led to their resettlement. During the decade that Henri's mother spent managing the family's resettlement case, her six children were none the wiser. When they were finally approved and preparing to leave, Henri's parents did not let on about the finality of the trip. Henri assumed that they were just traveling somewhere temporarily. He explained,

> We all just thought we were just kind of going somewhere for a little bit. . . . The two days before we left my mom had all our family, probably fifty to one hundred people staying at our house, cooking food, celebrating. And I'm telling our friends, "I think I'm going somewhere. I'm not sure. My mom just has us packing." So I tell all my friends, "I'm going to come back this week, you know. I'm not going far." . . . Then in the morning while we're driving, I saw my teachers, and my mom was saying bye to them and I don't know why but she was just kind of like crying and stuff like that. Thanking them.

It was not until they arrived in Boise that Henri understood the permanency of their trip. He said, "My mom kind of just kept that as a secret until the moment that we started flying out and came to the States. . . .

And I was asleep, so I didn't know that we arrived in Boise. . . . And then in the morning [the next day] my mom was just like sitting us around. She's telling us, 'Yeah, now we're in the States. This is where we're going to be living now . . . You're never going to see home again.'" Now in Boise, Henri had to process his family's resettlement when it was already a fait accompli.

Similarly, Amara's parents did not reveal much to their children before their resettlement from Djibouti to Boise. Amara, a young Eritrean woman, was eleven years old when her family was resettled, and since she had had very little formal education, she did not yet have the context to understand that moving to the US meant moving very far away. She said,

> I think the first day it really hit me was the day that we were leaving. I remember we went to the UNHCR interview, and they asked us kids a couple of questions, like, "What do you want to be when you grow up?" . . . I remember that, but still, I made no connection to what was going on. Like my parents were trying to live abroad? No, I had no comprehension of that. But the day that we were leaving, I thought we were going to come back, but everyone was crying, and then I started to cry, because I was like, "Oh my gosh, we're leaving. And I think it means that we may not come back." Otherwise, why would they be crying, you know? So I would say the day that we were leaving was when it registered. Beyond that, there was nothing special in my mind about coming to America or anywhere, because I didn't go to school to know what that implied . . . but I was very conscious of the adults around me crying, and then I thought, "Maybe we're going far away."

In the absence of information, children like Amara piece together whatever clues they can from the adults around them.

Alongside dueling feelings of excitement and sorrow when a case is approved, refugees know that their resettlement is never guaranteed until they are sitting on the airplane bound for the US. Their hope for a different future can quickly be taken away should something unexpected happen prior to their departure. Unforeseen events or changes in federal policy can strand refugees with little warning. Dozens of approved cases became the collateral damage of President Trump's travel bans in 2017 when refugees from certain Muslim-majority countries became prohibited from entering the US and had their travel plans canceled, robbing them of their departure and leaving them in a precarious limbo.[17] This devastation repeated itself in 2025 when President Trump halted all refugee arrivals shortly after taking office. Predeparture medical screenings may also reveal certain excludable conditions and suddenly make someone inadmissible.

When Cyrille, a Burundian father, and his family were going through the routine checks leading up to their departure for the US, the health screening revealed that Cyrille's wife was newly pregnant with their second child. Due to the updates that had to be made to their case, the family's departure from Malawi was put on hold. This uncertainty gravely affected Cyrille's wife. He explained, "My wife was traumatized with the situation. She got to the point that nothing was interesting to her. She thought this is our end . . . no education, no money, and no future [in Malawi]. She was broken." When they finally left for the US three years later, Cyrille said, "Honestly speaking, I didn't believe them until I was in [the] airplane. When the airplane started moving, then I said, 'Yes, this is true.'" Such situations remind refugees of their powerlessness, with their future at the whim of bureaucrats and policymakers. Grace, a mother resettled from Kenya, shared how dehumanizing it was to be a refugee awaiting resettlement, as choice and control are taken away. Periods of uncertain waiting can take a toll on refugees, depleting them of their financial resources, emotional wellbeing, and physical health before they arrive in their resettlement destination.[18]

By situating resettlement within the full scope of refugees' migration trajectories and lives, I adopt what sociologists Rawan Arar and David FitzGerald call a "systems approach" to understanding forced migration.[19] When refugees are resettled to the Global North, they do not start a "new" life. Rather they continue lives that have been punctuated by uprootings and displacements. Like other migrants, refugees are transnational,[20] and it is important to recognize that they remain connected to places and people left behind. Resettling to the US is a complicated process that can simultaneously evoke hope, regret, excitement, and grief. Resettlement does not erase or undo all that came before, as refugees' pasts continue to inform their present and future through "entangled timelines."[21] Feelings of uncertainty may persist even as refugees gain newfound security and stable legal status.[22] The "solution" of resettlement does not resolve all that has been lost, as it is far from a panacea for the wounds of forced migration and multiple displacements.[23]

JOURNEYS AND DESTINATIONS

Though refugees may have received notification of their successful approval for resettlement to the US, they typically do not yet know their precise resettlement destination and may only learn of it shortly before their departure. Unless refugees are joining family members already in the US, so called "US-tie cases," resettlement destination decisions for "free cases" are made through a centralized allocation process. Approved cases are first assigned to one of ten national Resettlement Agencies, who then match them with one of their local affiliate offices based on a variety of considerations, including the Resettlement Agency's current caseload, capacity to house large families, and proximity to specialized care for complex medical cases. Notably absent from this allocation process is the preference of the arriving refugee. Yara explained how, without a US-tie, her family's resettlement destination was decided for them. She said, "They choose that. They don't give us a chance to choose. . . . We didn't have anyone here to tell them about, so they chose. . . . for us."

Patrick learned that his family was going to San Diego after they had left the camp in Tanzania and arrived at the Resettlement Support Center in Kenya where they underwent the final predeparture stages in preparation for resettlement. Kidane, an Eritrean father, found out that his family was going to San Diego three days before their travel date. Rosine's family had initially been informed that they would be going to Boston only to find out at the time of their departure that they were going to San Diego instead. She noted, "They will send you wherever they want to send you." Given how varied the more than 350 resettlement destinations are across the US, refugees' lack of involvement in the allocation process can feel disempowering and alienating.

Once refugees are informed of their destination, they only have a short time to make sense of this information before they board the airplane. They rely on their prior knowledge of US geography or do some cursory internet searches to have some grasp of where they will be continuing their lives. Shortly before his family's flight, Raphael was given some documents to sign. He explained, "I learned that in United States there are fifty states, and the best state where to live is California." When he saw that his family's travel itinerary ended in San Diego, he felt reassured and thought to himself, "I am going to a good place." Thierry had the opposite experience when he found out that his family was being resettled to Kentucky. He said, "We had no clue what freaking Kentucky is. They tell us, 'You're going to America.' 'Where?' 'Kentucky.' Like, 'What?'" He noticed on a map that it was near Chicago, a familiar point of reference from which he began to make sense of his resettlement destination.

While many people had some degree of familiarity with large cities and states in the US, no one I interviewed in Boise who arrived there as a free case had heard of it or of Idaho prior to learning that they would soon be moving there. After Nour, a young Iraqi woman, and her family were informed that they were going to Boise, she looked it up online. She told me, "I got shocked. . . . It's not like something I was thinking about, like the picture of USA." On the night before Pascal's family's departure, all of the families from the camp in Tanzania who were scheduled for resettlement the following day were brought together to have their baggage weighed and get information about their precise departure time. It was only then that they learned that they were going to Idaho. Pascal remembered, "I didn't even have an idea of where Idaho was on the map." In fact, he assumed that the man calling out each family's destination was telling his family that they were going to a city in Tanzania that sounded a lot like "Idaho." If being unfamiliar with Boise was not nerve-racking enough, offhand comments made by people in connecting cities en route did not provide any reassurance. As Pascal's family's itinerary routed them through Chicago, they spoke with a woman who seemed just as confounded as they were about Boise. After they told her where they were going, she replied, "What? I never heard of this town." Pascal remembered that his family looked at each other and wondered, "Wow, no one even know[s] where this place [is] even."

Despite his unfamiliarity with Boise, Tresor was somewhat ambivalent about his family's destination. He was just happy to be going to the US. They found out that they were going to Boise right before their flight. But, he said, "We didn't really care. It was the US. We were like, 'Okay, we're going to Boise, I guess.'" For refugees who have been unable to gain stability in countries of asylum, their resettlement destination, wherever it is, may come to symbolize the permanency they have longed for, a place they can come to see as their home. Toussaint, whose forced migration had taken him from his home in the DRC to Tanzania, Mozambique, and then South Africa, came to understand his resettlement destination as a type of destiny, something that was meant to be. In speaking of Boise, he said, "They choose me to be here. This is my destination. Let me create my life here. We spend more time all over because of the war. They just meant [for] me [to be] here. Let me be here." After becoming a migrant out of compulsion and living through years of difficult displacements as a result of war, Toussaint spoke of a prevailing desire to find meaning and rootedness in his family's resettlement.

Despite whatever sense of understanding or attachment refugees might begin to feel towards their assigned resettlement destination, sudden and unexpected changes remind them that they are not in control, which only adds to the disempowering and disorienting nature of this migration. As they prepared to leave for the US, Amara's family was informed that they would be resettled in the state of Georgia. During their layover in New York, they were told that their destination had been switched to Boise. This last-minute change was confusing and felt belittling. Thinking back on this moment, Amara said, "I remember they were just so matter of fact about it, the agents, but I guess there wasn't much they could have done." At that moment, her parents had no form of recourse and did not know whether to believe this new information. They felt robbed of any sense of control or ownership over their future in a new country. Though Amara was only eleven years old at the time, this moment left a lasting impression. She continued, "It's an unspoken kind of psychological impact, especially for the kids like me. It's something that follows you, because it gives you this impression that you weren't. . . . important enough." Last minute changes can make arriving refugees feel like pawns whose ultimate destination is of no consequences to far-removed decision makers. When refugees feel like their lives and futures are pins easily moved around on a map, resettlement feels even more displacing. Moreover, Amara's aunt, who had been resettled years earlier to the Midwest, had already made arrangements to greet the family in Georgia. Not only was this change in destination confusing, but it also disrupted their plans for a long awaited reunion.

Yonas was well aware of how quickly and unpredictably an itinerary could change. He had initially been scheduled to depart for Forth Worth, Texas, but was informed on his travel date that his flight had been cancelled. With little explanation, he was returned to the refugee camp in Ethiopia where he had lived. More than a year later, he finally received a new departure date. During a layover at the Miami Airport, an official provided the group of arriving refugees with information about their onward journeys. She told Yonas that his destination had been changed. He was now going to Boise, a place he had never heard of. When he asked her where it was, her reply did not offer much reassurance. She told him, "I don't know where it is, but I'm sure it's inside the United States." Yonas had good friends who had previously been resettled in Texas and were excited to welcome him. For reasons still unknown, he was sent to Boise instead.

The journey to the US is long and exhausting and may be comprised of several stages during which the excitement and uncertainty of what awaits is mixed with sadness for what is being left behind. When Rosine's family finally boarded the plane that transported them away from the refugee camp in Kenya where she had spent the previous five years, she remembered all of the conflicting and competing emotions as she said her goodbyes. She said, "It was feeling unreal, like is this really me going? But at the same time, I was so sad because I was leaving all my friends, everyone I have known. Like my friends, they were crying. I was so sad, but at the same time, I was like, 'Oh thanks God.' Because once you get in the plane you have to turn back and say bye to everyone. You see people crying out there. But I was so young, I was happy I was going to America." Likewise, when David's family left the refugee camp in Sierra Leone, he remembered, "We were so happy; but on the other hand, we were sad because, coming to a new place, we don't know anybody here. You're about to start your life over again. So, that was our feeling. It was happy. . . . But on the other side, it was not that happy." Paw Eh described how her infant brother's emotions became a mirror for what everyone else was trying to hold in as her family boarded the bus that took them away from the camp in Thailand where they had lived for ten years. She remembered, "My brother started crying. He was only a little baby, and he knows that we were leaving. . . . our home. He started crying, and everyone started crying." As the weight of the moment hung heavy in the bus, she added, "Fifty minutes into the drive, it was so quiet."

Refugees who are coming from camps located in remote areas in particular may have an interim stay at a Resettlement Support Center that ranges from one night to a couple of weeks before ultimately boarding their flight to the US. Refugees may still need to undergo final medical checks or cultural orientation. Though the bus ride from the camp was sorrowful, Paw Eh's mood lifted when they arrived at a hotel where they would spend the night before their very early flight the next day. As a ten-year-old, she delighted in the novelties of their hotel room: "It was so nice. It was my first time seeing water coming from the shower. The first time seeing a hairdryer and sleeping on a really soft bed. It was so cool. And then we woke up at three in the morning to go to the airplane."

Paw Eh and several others recounted how their predawn departures were harbingers of the exhausting journey ahead. Refugees' flights are arranged by the International Organization for Migration (IOM), and given the distances that refugees are usually traveling, itineraries route them through airports around the world. Refugees may travel for several days before they finally land in their resettlement destination. It might be the first time on an airplane for some, and for most, it is the furthest they have ever traveled. David's family flew from Sierra Leone to Senegal to Belgium to New York to Chicago, and finally, to San Diego. Firas recounted a particularly dreadful trip that took five days. Each leg of their journey included long layovers in airports where his family simply had to wait for their next flight without the basic amenities of a shower or a bed. He said, "It was a total of five days in the same clothes without taking your shoe off and stinking. . . . So we had to stay in the airport. The airport gets empty; it gets closed; it gets opened again—and we are still inside. . . . Five days just sitting on chairs [in] different airports." In addition to exhaustion, the food offered during flights may be unfamiliar and unappealing. Several people remembered how little and how poorly they ate during the trip.

For those who are navigating large airports for the first time, the journey can be very confusing, particularly when the spoken and written languages are unfamiliar. Haymar, a young Karenni woman, shared that once her family was without the assistance of the Burmese interpreter who had accompanied them on the first leg of their trip, they felt completely lost. "It was hard. . . . I didn't even know where I was, because I couldn't read the words." At one point, her family waited somewhere for several hours because they did not know where they were supposed to go next: "We didn't know what to do." Tresor explained how once his family could no longer use Swahili to communicate in airports, they just had to trust that they would make it to their resettlement destination. He said, "It was a little bit stressful because . . . we didn't know where we were going. We didn't speak any English. . . . We went from Burundi to Nairobi. And in Nairobi, we were still okay 'cause we were speaking Swahili. . . . And then, from Nairobi to New York. Even when we got to New York, everything went kinda dark. We knew we were somewhere safe. We were okay. But we didn't know what's gonna happen after that. . . . or where to go." Luckily their trip went as planned, and they were given directions at each juncture. Tresor said, "Whoever planned our trip did a very good job of having somebody meet us at the airport and show us where to go. Although we didn't know what they were saying, we just kind of follow blind. So, we ended up getting to Boise."

The unexpected, however, can always alter travel mid-route. One Congolese family's flight itinerary to San Diego had to be rerouted due to disruptions caused by a hurricane on the East Coast. Ashina's little sister got sick early in their trip and was having difficulty breathing. Once the family landed in New York, her sister was taken to the hospital for treatment. Four days later, after Ashina's sister had regained her strength, the family was informed that, unbeknownst to them, they had not in fact arrived in their resettlement destination. They were told, "Actually you guys are going to Boise." Describing the initial part of their trip from Uganda to New York, Ashina said, "I was so tired. Oh my God, this was so crazy. I would never do this again." When they learned that they had to board another flight to Boise, a place they had never heard of before, Ashina though to herself, "Another flight. . . . Oh my God, this is hell." Most refugees resettled in San Diego land at the Los Angeles International Airport, after which they are greeted by a van that drives them to San Diego. This drive, which takes a minimum of two hours, becomes another tiring and disorienting leg of their journey.

Ma Htet, a young Chin woman, and Hanad, a young Somali man, each told me how even after they had arrived in San Diego and were brought to their accommodations, they assumed that their journey was not yet over. They both kept expecting someone to come get their families to take them to yet another airport; it seemed impossible to imagine that they had finally arrived. After being taken to her family's new home in San Diego, Ma Htet said, "I thought we have to, again, keep moving forward. I didn't [think] we are in San Diego." It seemed more probable to Ma Htet that her family would be leaving again the next morning. For Hanad, it took time before the reality sunk in that he was in San Diego. He said, "I was still waiting for them to take me to the actual place. . . . I didn't know it was America." As time went on and no one came to pick up his family, Hanad figured, "Okay, this is America." Both Ma Htet and Hanad were youths when their families were resettled in the US. Amid the exhaustion, no one told them that they had arrived. After such a long trip, which took them through so many new places, their arrival in San Diego was so unceremonious they did not realize that they were in their new homes.

Depending on where a family is resettled, seasonal weather may be an extra shock and source of strangeness and discomfort. When

Warsame's family exited the Boise airport, it was dark and cold. They arrived on a winter evening, and as they took in their new surroundings, they were confronted with snow and below-freezing temperatures unlike anything they had experienced in their home country of Somalia or in the camp in Ethiopia where they had lived for eight years. Warsame recounted how much the weather shaped his wife's outlook on their life in this new place. She told him, "This is the place we are going to die." While acclimating to cold weather was a nonissue for refugees arriving to San Diego, it was an added layer of adjustment for those resettled to Boise, particularly during the winter months. The timing of Warsame's arrival gave them a hostile and inhospitable impression of the city.

As refugees prepare for and begin their journeys to the US, a series of preparations are already underway at their local Resettlement Agency. New arrivals are greeted at the airport by their Resettlement Agency caseworker and immediately transported to accommodations that have been secured for them. In many cases, an apartment has been rented and furnished ahead of time. Otherwise, they may be taken to a hotel or temporary accommodations while their caseworker continues to search for permanent housing. The caseworker will have already picked up a hot meal for the new arrivals to enjoy along with some other basics to hold them over until someone takes them grocery shopping. For families with young children, the caseworker may also bring over some toys or stuffed animals.

These modest preparations offer much relief to new arrivals who may have very little with them in a country they do not yet know. After such long journeys, arriving to a furnished home with freshly made beds, warm food, and other small comforts can provide long-overdue peace of mind. Food insecurity was a constant part of Paw Eh's childhood in the refugee camp in Thailand. She had always thought of the US as a place of wealth and prosperity where food was available in abundance and where "you don't have to be hungry all the time." When her family learned that they were going to the US, Paw Eh thought to herself, "[W]hen I go there, I'm going to get to eat apples and ice cream without having to eat just a tiny portion of everything." Paw Eh remembered her unabashed delight when their caseworker brought her family to their new home. She said, "It was so cool. When they opened the door, I started screaming because there was toys everywhere, and there was food on the table. There was grapes, there was chicken, there was so many food, there was ice cream, there was apples. . . . Yeah, it was really cool. . . . It was really fun. We always played. We always eat. We didn't have to worry about our food." For Paw Eh, resettlement had resolved many of the stresses that were routine throughout her childhood. Tresor also remembered how excited he was by all of the food that greeted his family after the long trip, "It was awesome . . . There was milk. There were fruits. There was all this food that we knew but we had never had before. So, we were like, 'Holy crap, this is awesome.' We were really happy to be in Boise and having all that stuff." For Raphael, this arrival marked the transition to his new life in the US with his two young children. He said, "The trip was too long. I was feeling tired, and then I just relaxed, and life just started from there."

Yet initial relief can be complicated by feelings of disorientation. After such a long trip, refugees experience jet lag as they adjust to new time zones, as well as a range of other unfamiliarities. Rosine explained that no one in her family could sleep that first night in their new apartment. They had not eaten well during the journey, but the new foods that their caseworker had supplied in their home held little appeal. She said, "The food was there, but it wasn't really familiar to us. The only thing we knew was the mayonnaise. And the milk used to taste so different. Just everything—it was different. Because even in the plane we didn't even eat for those two days. We were just like picking, picking." A well-intentioned caseworker in Boise made his typical preparations for an evening airport pickup, including ordering chicken kabob from a local restaurant as the hot meal. The following morning, the family informed their caseworker that they were vegetarian; they had been left with very little to eat the night before.

All of the change that comes with initial resettlement can be jarring, and it takes time for the mind and body to adjust. As chapter 2 explains, refugees are quickly confronted with a rigorous pace of resettlement services while also coping with the effects of their long journeys, including jet lag and exhaustion—not to mention the accumulation of the material, emotional, and physical costs of waiting for resettlement.[24] Two days after a young Congolese family was resettled from Tanzania to Boise, the father, Jose, shared with me that despite the abundance of food, he had had little appetite since his arrival. His body still ached from their long trip to the US, which had begun with a two-week stay in a transit center as his family underwent the final preparations for resettlement. They then embarked on a multi-leg flight itinerary from Tanzania to Boise, including layovers in the Middle East and Los Angeles, all with an infant in tow. Likewise, when Hanad thought back to those first few days his family spent in their new home, he said, "We didn't leave our home. Just sleeping. Because it's a long way to travel to here. I was confused. I was just sleeping. That's it. A headache." Though someone from the Resettlement Agency provided his family with a home orientation and made sure they were comfortable using the various appliances in their kitchen, Hanad remembered how fearful he was of venturing beyond the immediacy of their apartment, as the surrounding area felt so unknown. He added, "I didn't leave the house. I just—I stay home. . . . I was scared if I leave home, I cannot come back. Yeah, I was scared." Once Nour's family arrived in Boise, she did not know what to make of it and, like Hanad, found temporary refuge within her apartment. She said, "It's like a dream, and I'm not sure. . . . is [it] a good one or a bad one?" Though she was glad to have finally arrived, she still felt so uncertain about the life that awaited her in this unfamiliar place. She continued, "[I] just worry. . . . I feel safe here, but still I don't know what my life will be."

Cyrille explained just how discombobulating the journey can be. What begins as excited anticipation gives way to exhausted stress, as long flights become draining. "Imagine this. Most of the people [had] never got on a plane. It's their first time. The first airplane is so exciting for everybody. The second is not. But it's long, twelve hours, sitting." He added how much harder this trip is for families with young children, as adults must attend to their children's needs and help them through so much travel. Shortly after arrival, Resettlement Agencies commence the suite of standardized services delivered to each refugee. Refugees need to fill out forms and pay attention to orientations as early as a few hours after landing. Exhausted and overwhelmed, refugees try to take in and make sense of their surroundings while being pressed with questions and decisions related to their resettlement services. Under these conditions, refugees feel compelled to be amenable to everything their caseworker says, regardless of their own expectations or preferences. According to Cyrille, during these first days, refugees feel like they have no choice but to say yes to everything. Early in their resettlement, they may have no one else they can rely on for essentials such as food and shelter. Given the material circumstances of their migration and arrival in the resettlement destination, refugees are put in a position of immediate dependency that will shape how they initially interact with their caseworker.

CONTEXTUALIZING RESETTLEMENT

This chapter situates resettlement within the broader scope of refugees' lives. I examine both the meaning of resettlement in contexts of protracted displacement as well as how the long and uncertain process of gaining approval unfolds. Resettlement becomes another step of refugees' forced migration trajectories, a migration that was likely never planned for when they were first forced to leave their homes. Nonetheless, amid the everyday hardships of life in a refugee camp or urban area, the prospect of resettlement comes to embody hope for a different future.

Refugees arrive in the US with complicated histories, and the path ahead once in their resettlement destination is not straightforward. Long and exhausting journeys to unfamiliar destinations shape refugees' mental and emotional states during the early days in a new city and country. Understanding how resettlement fits within the bigger picture of refugees' lives foregrounds the difficulties of resettlement given how refugees must reconcile the past as they seek to build a future in a new country.

2

ARRIVAL

ON A FALL EVENING, Bonheur stepped out of the IOM van
that had just driven his family 125 miles from the Los Angeles
Airport to a parking lot at the San Diego Airport. His wife,
Esperance, and their two young children were still inside the
van, groggy and bleary eyed from their long trip, which had
begun in Kampala, Uganda. Once a law student in the DRC,
Bonheur had managed to escape the war years earlier after
facing political imprisonment. He and Esperance met as refugees in Kampala and did their best to raise a family under
very difficult circumstances. They had successfully made
it through the process for refugee resettlement and were
invited by the US government to rebuild their lives in California. Finally in San Diego, Bonheur and Esperance were
ready for their caseworker to take them to their new home.

A couple of weeks earlier, the San Diego Resettlement
Agency was informed by their national headquarters that
they would be receiving a Congolese family of four. This

notification set into motion a series of preparations that take place ahead of each new arrival. This family, or "case," was assigned to one of the Resettlement Agency's staff caseworkers who, from that point forward, took charge of nearly every aspect of the family's initial resettlement. Provided with only very basic biographical information about the family, the caseworker was on a tight timeline to secure, furnish, and stock a suitable home in the most economical way possible while still meeting strict housing guidelines outlined by the federal government. Regulations addressed everything from which siblings could share a bed to the required number of place settings for dishes and cutlery. Caseworkers make these arrangements all while attending to the needs of their other active cases.

Two days prior to the family's arrival, their caseworker and I prepared their one-bedroom apartment, which had just been vacated by another one of the Resettlement Agency's cases, who had left San Diego to join relatives in the Midwest a few weeks after their arrival. In the absence of professional cleaners, it fell to us to make sure that the unit was in suitable condition. We also made a trip to Walmart where we purchased everything that this family would need for a functioning home, including cookware, linens, and cleaning supplies. We made up their beds, hung towels in the bathroom, and set the table.

Under the streetlights of the airport parking lot, Bonheur helped his wife, who was several months pregnant, and their children get situated in the Resettlement Agency's minivan. As the caseworker drove them to their apartment in El Cajon, just east of San Diego, one of the children snored in the back of the van. Once at their apartment, the caseworker gave them a tour of their new home. They would all share the apartment's one bedroom, which had been outfitted with two adjacent double beds. The caseworker showed them the food that he had put away in their kitchen and went through a brief home-safety orientation, including demonstrations of kitchen appliances and bathroom fixtures as well as how to lock their front door. Late in the evening, we left the family to settle in, enjoy the hot meal that their caseworker had picked up from a local kabob shop, and get some rest.

The next day, their caseworker and I returned around noon for the family's required twenty-four-hour home visit. When we arrived, the apartment was filled with the smell of fried potatoes, which Bonheur had just cooked for his children. Jetlagged, they had all woken up early that morning and had already received a noise complaint from the unit below them. As we sat around the kitchen table, their caseworker explained that they would soon need to enroll in one of two employment assistance programs for newly arrived refugee families and that each program differed in its duration and amount of cash assistance. The caseworker stressed that Bonheur and Esperance had to make their choice quickly so that their family could begin receiving critical financial support to pay their $1,200 per month rent and other necessities while Bonheur looked for a job. This quick transition to employment did not surprise Bonheur. He remembered learning in the predeparture Cultural Orientation that when refugees arrive in the US, they "need to start working in the first week." Their caseworker asked Bonheur if he was ready. Bonheur replied enthusiastically, "More than ready!"

After their caseworker discussed several other pressing tasks to complete—school enrollment for their children, vaccinations, medical appointments, a welfare meeting—he paused to offer reassurance. He told them, "We'll go step by step. The next three months are going to be a lot. You'll go through lots of stress. Make sure to take care of yourself." But he warned them, "There will be a lot of enrollments, a lot of signatures." The caseworker added, "Once you get a job, everything will be solved." Though this caseworker was bombarding the family with details less than a day after their arrival, he told me later that the only way to ensure that clients remember something was to address it at the twenty-four-hour home visit, as that was when information stuck. Within a few days, the family made the decision to enroll in the

Matching Grant Program, a fast-track program for particularly "employable" refugees. Bonheur was a good fit given his strong English proficiency and prior work experience related to food service. Though this option offered Bonheur's family a larger sum of money per month than the county's TANF program (CalWorks), it only came with four months of cash aid and prohibited enrollment in CalWorks for six months, making it crucial that Bonheur gain employment quickly.

Nearly a month later, Bonheur and I chatted in the waiting room as Esperance finished up a prenatal appointment. Now that his family had settled in and felt more familiar with the intricacies of US resettlement, Bonheur lamented how pressured he felt to make such consequential decisions about his family's resettlement so soon after arrival. He recalled how little he understood about the differences between the two assistance programs he was presented with during their twenty-four-hour home visit. He felt so tired and new on that first day, and there had been too much information for his family to digest. He felt like he was poorly informed while making decisions that now carried significant financial implications for his family. He wished someone had taken more time to go over everything with him again. But they did not have that luxury. Their caseworker was required to tick off the mandatory services for each of his cases according to a tight timeline and, most importantly, to secure their timely enrollment in a cash aid program. Not only was this a requirement of the caseworker's job, given the resettlement program's notoriously barebones assistance, it was also imperative for safeguarding his clients' well-being in such an expensive city.[1] Despite his frustrations, Bonheur was nonetheless sympathetic of his caseworker, remarking how he seemed spread so thin, managing a workload that appeared to be too much for one person.

Once refugees have arrived in their resettlement destination, they begin the long and complicated task of settling in a new country. Their new community may feel very different from the ones they left behind, and the types of services and support they receive may not align with the expectations they formed in the country of asylum. Alongside their aspirations for the future, refugees arrive with expectations about what life will be like in the US based on information that they pick up from friends and family as well as during different stages of the resettlement process.[2] It is dispiriting when the reality with which one is faced differs drastically from these expectations. Karam, an Iraqi father, explained how surprised he was by just how difficult he found so many aspects of his adjustment in San Diego. He had worked with the US military in Iraq for several years prior to his family's resettlement, but "coming to the United States, it's kind of challenging for me because almost everything's new." He was not prepared for how much cultural adjustment awaited him and continues to be required of him seven years later. He added, "I'm still learning from my coworkers here, from the community, from my kids."

While resettlement to the US resolves many of the central problems that afflict refugees in their countries of asylum—including limited rights, restricted movement, and temporary legal status—this chapter reveals that arrival in the resettlement destination marks a new phase of the journey. Arrival involves its own challenges and hardships, as refugees once again undertake the arduous task of starting over in a new country. Though a formal system of assistance awaits, the provision of resettlement services begins rapidly and is time limited, creating a sense of disorientation as new arrivals try to gain their bearings. Refugees like Bonheur and Esperance must make consequential decisions quickly, yet the USRAP is far from intuitive and offers little room for customization or preference. This chapter explores how unmet expectations complicate the process of settling in a new country and community, as the relief of arrival is complicated by feelings of disappointment and even regret. As a former employment specialist in Boise noted, rather than being the solution to refugees' challenges, resettlement is more often "the beginning of new problems."

A "CONVEYOR BELT OF SERVICES"

With an exhausting pace of meetings and office visits shortly after landing in the resettlement destination, not to mention the challenges of language learning and cultural adjustment, the resettlement process can quickly feel alienating and impersonal. From the moment refugees arrive, they become the recipients of a highly standardized protocol of assistance, which a Resettlement Agency administrator in Boise described as a "conveyor belt of services." Strict federal guidelines combined with limited time and resources make it difficult for Resettlement Agency caseworkers to tailor service provision.[3] Meeting refugees' immediate material needs, such as housing, food, and public assistance enrollment, are prioritized at the expense of the human dimensions of adjustment. In the rush of initial service delivery, refugees are seldom offered the opportunity to connect more meaningfully with their caseworker or other Resettlement Agency staff. The early days and weeks of a refugee's resettlement are filled with appointments, paperwork, enrollments, and orientations. New arrivals are shuttled from one social service office to another, all while acclimating into a new home and community.

Farah thought that the years she spent studying English in Iraq would allow her to navigate the resettlement process with ease once she arrived in San Diego. Her assumptions were quickly proven wrong once she encountered this complex and byzantine program. She said, "With all the bureaucracy, with all the layers of forms . . . it doesn't matter. You have to live here long enough to understand the process, because it's confusing." As outlined in table 4, numerous core services must be delivered during the Reception and Placement (R&P) period, which spans a refugee's first ninety days in the US. Shortly after arrival, refugees find themselves on this fast moving "conveyor belt" which only intensifies the displacing effects of resettlement. After the end of the ninety-day R&P period, cases are administratively closed, though

TABLE 4
Reception and Placement (R&P) services

Time frame	Activity or service
Day 1 (arrival)	Airport pickup
	Brought to furnished housing (temporary or permanent)
	Initial home-safety orientation
	Hot meal and basic groceries provided
Day 2	24-hour home visit
	Intake paperwork
	Explanation of Reception and Placement (R&P) benefits
	Provision of check for pocket money
	Trip to the bank to cash check for pocket money
	First visit to the Resettlement Agency
	Receive donations of hygiene items, weather appropriate clothing, etc.
Within week 1	Welfare enrollment
	Social Security card application
	Medical appointment (blood draw and immunizations)
	First grocery shopping trip
	Service plan meeting
	Public transportation training
Within month 1	Enrollment in English classes; begin English classes
	Enrollment of children in school; begin school
	Enrollment in employment program; begin job readiness classes
	30-day home visit
	Sign lease agreement
	First rental payment
By month 3	Cultural Orientation
	Cultural Orientation assessment
	Family budget
	Begin employment

clients may continue to receive employment services from the Resettlement Agency or ongoing informal support from their caseworker.

Conspicuously absent from this process is the time for refugees to convey to service providers how they feel about their resettlement, what is most important to them, or their aspirations for the future. A Resettlement Agency administrator in Boise recognized this shortcoming. She admitted that during this time, "there's never an opportunity to be listened to." Initial service provision during the ninety-day R&P period can feel unidirectional, as Resettlement Agency staff must complete a regimented series of services in a short period of time without the flexibility to pause or adapt. This administrator acknowledged that for practical reasons attention to personal connections was not prioritized, as there was little time for caseworker to ask questions such as "What are your goals?" "What are your experiences?" "What are your drivers?" "What [is] important for you?"—which was the difference between being put on a conveyor belt and being treated like a person. Finding oneself on this fast-moving conveyor belt may be particularly challenging for new arrivals who are still struggling to cope with the circumstances of their forced migration and resettlement.

When Kazem arrived in Boise, he was still suffering from the traumas he had experienced in his home country of Iran and then in Turkey where he had fled alone. The absence of inquiries into his well-being combined with pressure to move him through the typical progression of R&P services repeatedly put Kazem in situations that further damaged his mental health. He said, "Especially in the beginning when I came, I was so sensitive. I could cry because I had a crazy life." As with all new arrivals, Kazem was expected to begin various programs and classes, but those settings only exacerbated his distress. He experienced flashbacks as he sat in classrooms with other newly arrived refugees. Kazem felt like his caseworker was ignorant of just how much he was still coping with so many dimensions of his displacement.

Casework staff must complete core R&P services within the time frame outlined in table 4 in order to comply with the requirements of the federal resettlement program. Caseworkers typically manage multiple cases simultaneously, sometimes with several arriving in the same week or even day. This workload contributes to a frantic and erratic pace of service delivery for new arrivals. Some days new arrivals are shuttled from one office to another as their caseworker checks off core services, which are followed by several days during which it feels like no one is checking on them. A casework staff member in Boise was sensitive to the fact that this model of service delivery was disorienting for newly arrived refugees. Either Resettlement Agency casework staff "are just grabbing clients left and right, trying to fulfill their own core service" or the clients "sit at home all day—they're super bored and isolated." She acknowledged "how scary that feels. To be like, 'I feel like I'm just drifting. Will anybody come to my help today?'" Refugees are provided no itinerary or roadmap for how each day or week will unfold. As she explained, "We give the clients no safety when they come here. It's like they feel abandoned. It's like [we] plop them in a house and are like, 'Look, we'll call you.'" She feared that this approach gave newly arrived clients the impression that "we're running around. Maybe we'll help you; maybe we won't." She wished the R&P period was in practice more supportive, which she believed would go a long way in creating a stable foundation that would allow clients to gain confidence and control. She noted, "I think the amount of trust would just skyrocket. Because we would be actually able to fulfill more promises or more expectations." Beyond just the content of services, the model and structure of service delivery matters.

When Bernard thought back to his first few days in Boise, he recalled how much time his family spent in their apartment, waiting for someone from the Resettlement Agency to stop by. Though caseworkers do make numerous house calls in the period immediately following arrival, visits tend to be short and for a specific purpose, such as completing paperwork or providing transportation to and from appointments. Though Resettlement Agency staff did come to Bernard's apartment, they would always depart after the task had been completed, once again leaving his family alone. He explained that, after they leave, "you stay inside. You don't have nobody to call, no friends, no anyone."

A casework staff member in Boise was concerned that this irregular pattern of assistance ran counter to their very goals of supporting newly arrived refugees. She said, "It's just our job to ease that transition. [We] should be blocking them from as much erratic interactions as we can." But casework staff do their best with a workload that may appear predictable on paper but frequently involves responding to unexpected client needs and crises that make it futile to set a schedule for the workday.[4] After a Congolese single mother of five in Boise remarked that she never knew when her caseworker would next visit, the caseworker hung a calendar on their kitchen wall where he began noting the date of his next visit before leaving their apartment. Providing more information offers new arrivals a greater sense of certainty and assurance.

The pace of R&P services and meetings can feel particularly overwhelming for refugees attending to caregiving responsibilities as well as their own physical and mental health. After nearly two months in San Diego, Nina, a Congolese mother of four, shared how much the resettlement process continued to exhaust her. She told me, "Life is too complicated here. It's giving me a headache. Everyone is so busy." Now that her husband Joseph had begun working six days a week, Nina managed the family's various appointments at social service agencies and attended English classes with her toddler in tow while her other three children were in school. The following day, while I sat with Nina and her toddler in the large waiting room of the Department of Motor Vehicles to apply for her State ID card, she wanted to know if life in the US would always require this many appointments and office visits.

Resettlement services and financial assistance programs are numerous and complicated, and the speed with which services are delivered during a refugee's first ninety days can be overwhelming. Because the initial R&P period is time bound, refugees are bombarded with programmatic requirements and bureaucratic processes, which often begin within hours of arrival. Whereas caseworkers have the perspective and experience to understand the long-term trajectory of resettlement, arriving refugees are at a knowledge deficit, lacking familiarity with how the winding journey of resettlement typically unfolds. The delivery of R&P services takes place in a vacuum of information, as refugees are without a clear roadmap. While Resettlement Agency staff are deeply familiar with what the R&P period entails and operate with an internalized schedule of service provision, refugees are ignorant of what exactly will be provided and when, as well as the important milestones of a "successful" resettlement. Though highly formulaic, R&P services are not intuitive from the vantage point of the client, leaving them unsure of what support remains and how their lives will progress, including how basic needs such as food and housing will be met. Without the perspective that comes with experience, refugees can only see as far as their current situation, which can be shocking, concerning, and disappointing.

Amara, whose family had arrived in Boise eighteen years earlier, felt like the most challenging aspect of their resettlement had been her parents' inability to gauge their progress during those early months. She explained, "We weren't sure about our case. Like are we good? Are we doing good? We didn't have checkpoints." Initial resettlement involves so many moving pieces, including housing, employment, language learning, cultural adjustment, and financial stability. For Amara's parents, the road ahead felt like a black box. She recalled the stress that her parents felt. She wished someone could have "[let] them know that it's okay to relax." She continued, "Because I think for my parents, they just felt like they were never doing enough." They would have benefitted from some reassurance and guidance on where to focus their energy at any given moment. Amara added, "just giving you an outline of the steps, I think that would be very good." While caseworkers can tell if a family is on track with federal resettlement objectives, refugees themselves do not have the luxury of this perspective, which heightens feelings of displacement and reliance on their Resettlement Agency caseworker.

When I visited Jose two days after he arrived in Boise with his wife and baby, he was anxious to talk to his caseworker. It was a Friday afternoon, and he would not see his caseworker again until Monday. Though the family had been to the Resettlement Agency the previous day for some of their initial intake meetings, Jose seemed restless. He was brimming with questions and eager to have a better sense of what lay ahead for himself and his family. They were in temporary housing and everything still seemed in flux. While his caseworker knew that over the coming days and weeks Jose's family would be taken grocery shopping, receive more money, move into permanent housing, enroll in English classes, and begin employment services, Jose was not privy to the routines of resettlement or the steps that would, in due course, be taken. Instead, he was focused on the fact that he would not see his caseworker for the next two days. When his caseworker stopped by a little later, Jose voiced his concern that he had only been to the Resettlement Agency once. He wanted to know when his family would see a doctor and when he would start working and earning money. He was ready to begin building a life for his family in a way that had not been possible in the refugee camp, yet he still felt in the dark about when or how that would happen. He told his caseworker, "We left [the camp] and came here for money, not to joke around." Without a clear sense of the progression of his family's resettlement, Jose was growing impatient.

While most studies of US resettlement critique the speed with which refugees are pushed into the labor market,[5] it is also important to note that many new arrivals, like Jose, are keen to begin employment. As I discuss in chapter 4, challenges stem less from the expectation that they work than from the type of jobs in which they are placed and the ramifications of these jobs for their economic security. Not long after this exchange with Jose, I interviewed his caseworker who brought up the exchange. He noted that clients "expect a lot in the first few days." He continued, "I was like, 'Dude, why are you complaining right now? This is the prime resettlement time. You can just do nothing and eat food and see your family that you haven't seen.'" This caseworker knew that Jose was about to jump onto the "conveyor belt of services" and understood that Jose had a rare moment to catch his breath and enjoy his reunion with relatives who had resettled in Boise previously. But a lack of information fueled Jose's anxieties about his family's future, particularly as the weekend loomed.

The ninety-day time frame that governs the provision of R&P services is arbitrary and does not necessarily align with the progression a refugee's integration. Amid all the newness that accompanies arrival in the resettlement destination, it can feel daunting to learn early on that case management services will formally end in three short months. Refugees' expectations of ongoing assistance and desire for support confront the reality of an underfunded and overstretched social service system. At Nina and Joseph's thirty-day home visit, their caseworker explained that their eventual transition away from the Resettlement Agency would take place now that so many of their core R&P services had been completed. He told them, "I'm not going to disappear. But new families are coming every month, and they need more help." Nina asked if they could still come to him after five or six months. Knowing that resettlement was never fully wrapped up by day ninety, their caseworker assured them, "Yes, we say three months, but it's always longer. It's for the rest of your life."

At the thirty-day home visit for Moise, a young Congolese man in Boise, the caseworker walked through a number of questions to gauge his resettlement progress. He still did not know how to get to a grocery store on his own, how to schedule a doctor's appointment, how to pay upcoming bills, or how to check his mail. While the official workflow of a caseworker assumes that clients' services end after three months, there is nothing magical about this official cutoff point. In reality, the need for ongoing support and someone to call during a crisis extends long past this time frame. This continuing assistance regularly takes caseworkers above and beyond their official duties, turning them into the shock absorbers of this abbreviated program by performing labor that largely goes unrecognized.[6]

Despite his reassurance, Nina and Joseph's caseworker could no longer maintain the intensity of support he had initially provided. He sought to encourage their independence, both for his own and his clients' benefit. He told them, "Try first, and then come to me if you need [help]. If I show you [how to do something] once, then I won't show you again." But his encouragement did not relieve Nina's anxieties, and the ticking clock of initial R&P services continued to trouble her. Almost two weeks later, she asked him, "After six months are you just going to leave us? We're still new." Though Nina had already been in the US for six weeks, her feelings of displacement lingered. She did not yet feel comfortable with the intricacies of life in San Diego, and she feared that her resettlement services would end before her family had found the stability and security that continued to elude them. The prospect of being without the regular support of their caseworker left Nina feeling uneasy.

Bastien recognized how this imposed timeline can make newly arrived refugees feel vulnerable and abandoned. Though, he said, "I never hear [about] people dying because of agents leaving them after three months," nonetheless "a lot of people are getting challenged because the agency are leaving them [at] the time they are not ready yet to be [by] themselves." A caseworker in San Diego echoed this sentiment. In his experience, the R&P period frequently extended beyond ninety days in practice, and he found the program's time frame to be "way unrealistic." He added that he had recently helped a family who had been resettled two years ago resolve an issue with their landlord. While Resettlement Agency staff do often provide ongoing assistance to "extended clients," the artificial cutoff date for R&P services adds unnecessary stress as refugees adjust after getting used to the intensity of initial R&P services. It also makes caseworkers feel overextended as they respond to the ongoing needs of clients for whom their responsibilities have technically ended. Maxime noticed that the expectations about transitioning off formal case management services was particularly difficult for those in San

Diego who had experienced protracted displacement in refugee camps. Refugees arrive in the US from a variety of backgrounds and histories of displacement, making them more or less ready to jump off of the conveyor belt of services when it comes to an abrupt end.

Alongside the challenges and stresses of those early days are welcome moments of levity. The first grocery shopping trip always serves as a reprieve from the meetings and difficult conversations that fill so much of a refugee's first week in the US. Immediately following Bonheur's twenty-four-hour home visit, his caseworker and I took him to a large discount supermarket where he succeeded in finding several familiar ingredients, including maize flour, a particular type of dried bean, and plantains. As we approached the checkout line, Bonheur was elated and exclaimed that this was "the best market in all of [the] USA!" I took Jose for his first grocery shopping trip six days after he arrived in Boise. He navigated the large store with enthusiasm, stopping frequently to ask questions about unfamiliar items like Gatorade, salsa, and caramel sauce. He was thrilled to find a particular variety of mushroom and filled a produce bag for his family. We also engaged in an exercise in cultural translation as Jose enlisted my assistance to locate various ingredients. On several occasions I used my phone to look up foods that were unfamiliar to me, such as linga linga, a leafy green from the amaranth plant, helping him find the best approximation of what he was looking for. As we left the grocery store, Jose posed for a picture with his full shopping cart. A decade after her arrival in San Diego, Farah still remembered the enjoyment of those early grocery shopping excursions, as she delighted in the range of dry cereal options compared to what she had been used to in Iraq.

THE SIGNIFICANCE OF A CASEWORKER

A newly arrived refugees' Resettlement Agency caseworker is not a neutral actor and plays an important role in shaping initial perceptions and impressions about the USRAP and life in the US. This relationship can feel exceptionally consequential to refugees during the initial stages of resettlement. In some instances, the Resettlement Agency caseworker may be the only person a new arrival knows in the country. During the early weeks, the caseworker is their access to shelter, food, funds, and information as well as their mode of transportation. While a good experience can offer a sense of relief and support, anything else can trigger disappointment and even fear. Remi appreciated everything his caseworker did for his family once they arrived in Boise after having spent fifteen years in a refugee camp in Tanzania. He explained that, upon arrival in the US, "you don't know where to start. And someone just comes, picks you up there, takes you to [a] home and start[s] feeding you, clothing you. I don't think you can forget those people because you have nowhere to go." He was grateful for the "material support" that his family received, including food, shelter, and clothing, because otherwise, "we didn't know where to start, where to knock." Particularly for free cases who arrive in a destination where they have no pre-existing social ties, the caseworker becomes their sole source of local information.

Tresor had such positive memories of the help that his family's caseworker provided after their arrival in Boise eleven years prior that he decided to pursue a career in social work, working with refugees and other vulnerable populations. He said, "It's because of the first impression that we got starting from the airport. When we got there, there were all these strangers happy to see us, helping us, and welcome signs. We didn't know any words they were saying, but they seem[ed] really happy, and they seem[ed] really excited to see us. So, it was really good to see and that's exactly what I wanna do because I want a stranger to feel the same way that I felt when I first got here." Tresor knew just how difficult resettlement had been for his father as a single parent. Tresor credits the support of their Resettlement Agency for allowing him to focus on his future. He continued, "They helped us with everything. . . . I was young. I was ambitious. I really wanted to get started. I think dad was probably really worried, but we were too young to be worried. I was just excited to start a new life."

On the contrary, the minimal reception from Kidane's caseworker made his family feel discarded with nowhere else to turn when they landed in San Diego. Refugees may be temporarily housed in hotels when an apartment has not been secured ahead of their arrival. Kidane was taken aback when his family was brought from the airport to a hotel, as he had been informed during predeparture Cultural Orientation that a home would be ready for them. They spent the following two days without sufficient food or guidance and without any contact from their Resettlement Agency. Kidane remembered, "Two days, nobody cared about us. Two days, just we are hungry . . . Nobody to ask for us, just they forget us." Kidane was shocked and dismayed. He said, "We broke our hair for that time." He continued, "At that time, we're hopeless. This is America. Where's the treatment? Where's the hospitality? . . . You know, I told my friend that I'm going back to Africa." During this initial resettlement period, refugees are put in a state of dependence, forced to rely on their caseworker whose responsiveness carries an outsized impact on their well-being.

The apparent support of one's caseworker can result from a variety of factors, including their caseload at any given moment. At the time of Pascal's family's arrival in Boise, their Resettlement Agency had one caseworker, who was managing services for all new arrivals. Though it was clear to him how overworked she was, it nonetheless affected the assistance they received. A caseworker in Boise admitted just how energy-intensive new arrivals were from his perspective. Apartment preparations, late-night airport pickups, home visits, enrollment forms, and appointments are draining, not to mention keeping up with services for other active cases. He described back-to-back arrivals as being "awful," noting how much "it sucks [the energy] out of you." Worn out from the previous day's arrival and services, a caseworker may need to head right back to the airport the following evening after a full day of work to greet another arriving case. This caseworker in Boise confessed that by the time the next family arrived, "you're doing it halfway. The second time, you're just going through the motions a little bit." The first forty-eight hours after a case arrives are physically, mentally, and emotionally depleting for the caseworker, not to mention the client.

Resettlement Agencies hold standard business hours, Monday through Friday from about 8 a.m. to 5 p.m. But the experience of resettlement—with all of the questions and uncertainties that arise during the early weeks—is not confined to conventional weekday business hours. Caseworkers often exceed these hours with uncompensated time attending to their clients. Yet despite their additional efforts, refugees' calls may go unanswered and their needs go unaddressed outside of formal opening times. This incongruity between the experience of being resettled and the work of resettlement is particularly salient for refugees who arrive in the US on Thursdays or Fridays. In such cases, refugees like Kidane may feel abandoned only twenty-four to forty-eight hours after landing. After Yara's family arrived on a Friday, they were left to themselves for the weekend, "We didn't see anyone for these two days, and it was scary." Likewise, Patrick's family struggled that first weekend when they ran out of the initial food that their caseworker had provided for them upon arrival. Come Sunday, the family of nine had nothing left to eat. They spent the day hungry, waiting for Monday to arrive.

Thierry noted how the resettlement program creates an overreliance on caseworkers who, because of professional limitations, will never be able to fully support the needs of new arrivals. He said, "If you are asked to work eight hours, it can't go beyond that. Because after five [o'clock], you're out. Yes, the refugee needs are beyond 5 p.m. I just came here from Africa, a refugee camp. I have no clue, and you make it so you're the only person that I rely on, and you leave me. I can't call you at night. I can't do anything. It's crazy." He added how he knew of families who went without food until their caseworker visited or who had been given food to hold them over that they could not eat. He noted that there had been some improvements more recently as Resettlement Agencies hired more caseworkers who came from the same national and ethnic backgrounds as their clients and could better connect new arrivals to community resources beyond the Resettlement Agency. Yet the hiring of co-ethnics may require these staff to perform significant additional labor beyond standard work hours—labor that goes underrecognized and uncompensated.[7]

Even during operating hours, Resettlement Agency caseworkers are typically busy managing services for multiple cases, several of which may be new arrivals, creating an asymmetry that leaves refugees feeling under supported. While each refugee has one caseworker to rely on, each caseworker must manage the urgencies of multiple cases, dividing their time and attention. Grace was taken aback when she was told to make an appointment with her caseworker for what felt like urgent needs. She explained, "You'll call your caseworker, and you're thinking they'll say, 'Hey, come in tomorrow at nine.' Or, 'I'll stop by.' And it's like, no: 'Why don't we meet on Thursday?' I'm thinking, 'You mean Thursday next week, and I have a need right now?'" Pascal recounted the same challenge when his family arrived in Boise. He remembered how they were left to struggle for days waiting for their appointments. He felt like his family's caseworker was very supportive, but their questions and concerns exceeded the hours of her workday. Though she had told them, "Call me any time you have a problem," she was not always able to answer the phone or respond in a timely fashion. While Patrick understood that it was just her job and that she also had a family and personal life, it still caused distress.

RECONSIDERING EXPECTATIONS

The displacing effects of resettlement are all the more disquieting for refugees because of the dissonance between their expectations about life in the US and the reality they encounter upon arrival. Even when resettlement evokes mixed emotions, it nonetheless represents hope for a different life. For Henri resettlement offered a paradigm shift for thinking about his future. Growing up in Zambia, Henri had envisioned his life unfolding in predictable ways, yet resettlement gave "us a sense of hope and create[d] a different future than we would have expected." Henri understood the US to be a place of opportunity, but he remained uncertain about how to achieve that after his family arrived in Boise. He said, "We were told about the American dream. How do you get the American dream?" Henri knew how much the significance of this shift weighed on his parents. He said, "I think the first couple of days were hard, especially on my parents. It was understanding now that they're able to bring six of their kids here and have a different future, have these dreams and goals and aspirations for their kids." Upon landing in the resettlement destination, expectations that formed prior to arrival are often tempered by an uncertainty about how to achieve them.

The "promise of resettlement" holds significant power in situations of protracted displacement and is even exploited by countries of asylum to manage large refugee populations.[8] Because the refugee groups prioritized for resettlement typically live in conditions of extreme vulnerability and precarity,[9] lofty expectations are often attached to resettlement. These expectations are fueled by information that circulates within countries of asylum and are further bolstered by the enduring power of the American dream. As Patrick contemplated his future in the US from a camp in Tanzania, he remembered thinking, "Oh man, we are going to live in paradise." Didier explained how his frame of references made it difficult to arrive with anything but high expectations. He said, "This is just a different environment compared to back home [in Uganda]. . . . You're told when you're back home how it was like a heaven on Earth. That's what you're told. You come here; you have a high expectation. You're like, 'Oh man, I'm going to chase my dreams here.'"

Given the reputation of the US as a country of wealth, power, and immigration it is difficult for refugees to fathom how little will be offered once they arrived. Hafiz, an Afghan father, was familiar with resettlement programs in Western Europe that offered housing and comprehensive financial support. He assumed that these policies extended to the welcome that his family of seven would receive once they arrived in San Diego. "We thought, yeah, the United States is a rich country, so even they will take care of our houses, right? But when we arrived here—no, it's 100 percent changed." While some refugees do eventually achieve the life that they aspired to in the US, it is not without struggle, sacrifice, and moments of disillusionment. Other refugees may confront obstacles that derail their aspirations for the stable, secure, and prosperous future they imagined.

Abdi, a young Somali man in San Diego, explained that these expectations are propped up by misconceptions about life in the US. He said, "It's really, really cool when you think you're going to United States. . . . Other people think that guy has really become rich." But after four years in San Diego, he knew just how far these images strayed from reality. He continued, "They're expecting [in] the United States . . . you're living easy lives. But actually we live real hard lives. And you have to work if you want to live here." Remi attributed this discontinuity to the vacuum within which refugees create their expectations before having gained accurate frames of reference: "When you are there, back there, you are determining your expectations by yourself, without having any reality in front of you. . . . And when you arrive here, there are some realities that you didn't think of when you were there, which means that you put your expectations higher than real. That's it. That's why people are disappointed." Consequently, when confronted with the realities of early resettlement, newly arrived refugees find themselves let down. Remi concluded, "They start from there with very big disappointment." He noted that expectations of prosperity can put some people in difficult financial situations before even leaving for the

US. Based on presumptions of future wealth, some refugees left the camp with unpaid debts that they assumed could easily be resolved once resettled.

At a community event in Boise, a Congolese man shared how the limitation imposed on refugees in Kenya heightened the contrast between the lived reality in the country of asylum and assumptions about future prosperity in the US. "In Kenya," he explained, "a refugee was like a useless person, worthless, so painful." Those he left behind in the camp held on to presumptions that did not reflect his new life in Boise. "In Africa, if they know you are in the US, they think you have too much money, a money tree." He added, "I sacrificed myself" by living as leanly as possible in order to send financial support to family members still in Kenya. Research has shown that, despite their own financial instability, refugees in the Global North often prioritize remittances ahead of their own well-being, at times even sending portions of their welfare assistance, which exacerbates their own economic insecurity and upholds misconceptions of their newfound wealth.[10]

Along with financial remittances sent to those left behind, migration scholars have also documented that migrants send social remittances back to loved ones, which may come in the form of information, goods, or images that reflect particular ideals about what life is like in the new country.[11] This research has found that in an effort to project stability and prosperity, social remittances do not always convey the complete picture of life in the new country.[12] Those who migrate are inclined to portray themselves as successful, omitting details of struggles or hardships in an effort to save face. Cyrille explained how this same pattern unfolded with resettlement. He said, "Once they got here, they don't want to tell the truth to people who stay in refugee camps. Instead, they are telling them lies. Try to show them that here, life is better. Hey man, I have car. They go take picture in Walmart, different places." These images of supposed wealth, comfort, and success further fuel expectations for those left behind.[13] On more than one occasion, newly arrived refugees asked me to take pictures of them posing in front of their shopping cart at the grocery store or in front of a Walmart, reinforcing the association of resettlement with prosperity. Cyrille noted that by a refugee's second week in the US, the novelty of resettlement begins to wear off as the reality of their situation sinks in. "People come here [with] over expectation. That's why first week is okay. . . . Second week, you see people becoming tough, losing trust." Unmet expectations dampen morale as the long road of resettlement begins.

In addition to the rumors that may circulate within countries of asylum, predeparture Cultural Orientation ahead of one's resettlement becomes a moment when expectations are established and concretized. Though the curriculum is intended to be general and apply to any resettlement destination in the US, it may nonetheless communicate information that poorly reflects the realities in a particular locale or is outdated. Given the diversity of cities and states across the US, predeparture Cultural Orientation may cultivate false expectations. Grace, who underwent Cultural Orientation in Kenya, referred to it as a "poor reference point," since there was no way to guarantee that it would match reality. She elaborated, "I'm not sure the orientation really prepares you for the reality on the ground." After Cultural Orientation in Malaysia, Ma Htet was left with the impression that life in the US would be easy, but, she explained, "when I got here, everything they told me was not true."

Some people referenced the fact that the course was taught by instructors who had not been to the US and used long-outdated materials, increasing the likelihood that the information taught was not a reflection of the reality that awaited. Moreover, the sheer excitement of an impending departure makes it easy to overlook information that runs counter to expectations and narratives of an easy life ahead. A service provider in Boise reported that some of her clients told her that, in all the anticipation, they did not "remember a single word that was spoken." She noted that the relief of getting approved for resettlement leads to thoughts like, "I'm finally going to be in peace; I'm finally going to be happy; I'm finally going to be taken care of"—and warnings of the challenges ahead do not stick. She explained, "When you're so excited, you may not hear all the hard things, and you might not want to hear all the hard things. . . . You're thinking America, land of opportunity. . . . You're not thinking you're being dropped into a place where you're going to make $7.50 an hour."

In the best-case scenario, predeparture Cultural Orientation conveys an adaptable framework through which newly arrived refugees can make sense of all of the complexities that come with resettlement in the US. One of the curriculum's modules is about how the stages of culture shock and adjustment follow emotional peaks and valleys. The high of landing in the US may be followed by the low of unfamiliarity. Over time, these highs and lows continue as refugees adjust to their new surroundings. This lesson stuck with Gerard when he arrived in Boise with his family, and he recognized this pattern as early excitement quickly gave way to challenges. He knew that overtime, his life would stabilize "slowly, slowly, slowly." Referring to the module on culture shock, he said, "We learned that from the workshops. When I reached here, it was more like, 'Ah, I was told this. I was told this. I was told this.'" But he also spoke of families that continued to struggle with their disillusionment.

Misguided and unmet expectations can leave new arrivals feeling as though they are worse off than before. Toussaint shared that disappointment tends to follow the initial relief of resettlement. He told me that refugees in Boise "feel frustrated," and think, "Ugh, I thought this is the better solution, but [it's] not." He added, "Everyone is happy when they just get resettled. But after some time, some of us, we feel, no, if I should know this, I should not come." Though resettlement offers newfound safety and rights, unforeseen disappointments accumulate during the first several weeks, resulting in disillusionment and distress. Toussaint noted that "resettlement [in the] US is a good solution for refugees," but the extent of the adjustment "makes refugees to feel uncomfortable." Considering the hardships that greet refugees upon arrival, the known challenges in the country of asylum may come to seem less daunting than the unknown challenges that lie ahead. Especially at the beginning, the displacing effects of resettlement can be overwhelming, and some refugees express regret. The enormity of this transition in the early months is not lost on resettlement agency staff. A casework staff member in Boise struggled with how best to convey to new clients that their lives were going to get a lot worse before they got better.

The experience of early resettlement is complicated by the fact that gratitude and disappointment can exist simultaneously. While refugees may know that resettlement is the best outcome for their families, it can be difficult to reconcile this knowledge with feelings of dissatisfaction. The realities of financial insecurity, minimum wage jobs, and poor housing complicate prior notions of what resettlement will be. Though Abdi and his family had not anticipated the struggles that greeted them in San Diego, they had nonetheless gained a newfound sense of freedom that had been lacking in their home country of Somalia and in the Ethiopian camp where they spent seven years. He said, "The only thing is we actually have and we really loved to have is freedom. . . . And actually the most important is to have freedom and to have something to eat." Despite unforeseen hardships, resettlement had afforded them relief from food insecurity along with rights, both of which were unobtainable within the context of a camp in Ethiopia.

Hafiz echoed this discord. Resettlement to San Diego meant that his family no longer had to live amid constant threats to their safety due to Hafiz's work with the US military in Afghanistan. Yet for Hafiz, gaining safety came at the expense of so many other aspects of his family's life. "Especially the first time, like two months, me and my wife crying all day and night. Why did we come here? Like everybody says we got a lot of things here, but . . . no, we lose a lot of things here. Only the one thing we can find is security . . . Only we find one thing here, and we lose a lot. We lose our mom, dad, families, love, our country, and, you know, country, everybody loves their country."

Prior to resettlement, refugees spend years functioning in survival mode, trying to fulfill their family's basic needs while keeping loved ones safe despite ongoing hardships, danger, and limited rights. Within the context of these challenges, resettlement represents hopefulness for a future that promises more than just getting by. Given the realities of early resettlement, refugees may be shocked, dismayed, and disappointed to learn that their energy must still go into simply trying to survive, making resettlement feel like a letdown. The sigh of relief that they have long been waiting to release continues to remain out of reach. As the one who often delivered the sobering realities of the USRAP to new arrivals, a caseworker in San Diego was aware that his professional role turned him into a "dream shatterer." Three years after his family's arrival in San Diego, Hafiz described how resettlement and welfare programs provided just enough assistance to be life sustaining without providing the support necessary to thrive. He said that it felt like "you will not get one glass of water, just only a little bit of water so you'll not die." Being spared death hardly felt like living.

Yara believed that had her family received an initial period of comprehensive support in the US, they could have found their footing, "because it's hard to find [ourselves] always struggling." If they had had a temporary reprieve from the insecurity that had begun six years earlier in Syria, it would have afforded them the opportunity "to build ourselves." In the absence of such stability, Yara's family had lived in an ongoing state of precarity since the Syrian War had upended their lives. A community service provider in San Diego was aware of the toll that this unrelenting stress caused as he worked to support Congolese and other refugee families. He remarked how on paper, refugees appeared to receive various forms of assistance, but once you pulled back the curtain, "you find that they have struggles; there is a heavy hardship." He remarked, "You're supposed to feel relieved when you get help. But you find, despite the help that they receive, people cannot sleep at night. . . . You find people who are overwhelmed with the situation. They don't know what tomorrow is going to look like; they [are] so, so worried about their life here." When refugees realize the different yet significant challenges that accompany resettlement, he said, "some of them say, 'I wish I could stay in the refugee camp, or even die from there, or even die in the conflict when I was running.'" For this community partner, this reaction revealed so much about the USRAP. He added, "You know, someone to choose death instead of life. That's means the hardship is horrible."

Refugees' mental and physical energy are once again consumed with matters of survival, using time and attention that could otherwise support cultural adjustment and language learning as well as recovery from past traumas. It is difficult to heal when meeting basic needs still feels tenuous. A Resettlement Agency health caseworker in Boise remarked that new arrivals "were definitely stuck on those bottom bar Maslows," referring to the lowest level of Maslow's hierarchy of needs, including food, water, and shelter. She noted that, as a result, it took several years after resettlement before refugees finally gained enough security to be in a position to begin prioritizing their mental health. She noted, "I think mental health is one thing you have to put on the back burner until people are more comfortable in the resettlement process."

Grace described initial resettlement as "wandering through the wilderness." Refugees may feel unmoored as so many aspects of their lives have changed, and previously simple tasks demand more energy. In a short period of time and with minimal assistance, they must gain employment, manage their finances, learn English, navigate public transportation, and attend to the needs of their children, who are enrolled in an unfamiliar education system. Refugees are dealing with these competing demands all while coping with the ongoing traumas of forced migration such as the loss of homeland, family separation, and the deaths of loved ones. Though resettlement resolves some of the immediate insecurities in refugees' lives, it does not automatically remedy lingering mental health issues, and the stressors of early resettlement may be felt more acutely for those who have already experienced significant trauma.

Even though refugees experienced greater relative hardship in the country of asylum, the struggles they face upon arrival are still considerable, and it is important to acknowledge them as such. Just because their lives are comparatively better than in a refugee camp does not mean that they are not also facing genuine—if quite different—difficulties. Six years after his arrival in Boise, Bastien reflected on how this comparison between life before and after resettlement can obfuscate the very real challenges that refugees encounter in the US. If he used life in the refugee camp in Tanzania where he grew up as his benchmark, the displacement of resettlement seemed less severe; yet it did not make the difficulties he encountered any less valid. He said, "If you can compare with where I came from, oh my God, it's very, very good. But then when you become in America, when you start living here, then you start getting those kinds of challenges here, you know? You can't compare with where you came from because you know how hard it is there, but [there are] the challenge of here, too." This comparison reveals all the ways that resettlement is difficult while also presenting an enormous opportunity. Refugees find themselves grappling with this comparative ambiguity. Though their situation has improved, it may nonetheless be disheartening in unexpected ways. The challenges and disappointments of resettlement are worth recognizing even when they are an improvement from prior struggles.

The nature of this comparison may also vary based on refugees' prior experiences, as all refugees do not have universal frames of reference. Just because someone is a refugee does not mean that they did not once lead a comfortable life. Consequently, aspects of their resettlement such as housing conditions, socioeconomic status, and neighborhood placement may feel inferior to what they once enjoyed. Abraham, a Sudanese father who had previously worked at a San Diego Resettlement Agency, noted how all refugees received inadequate benefits and services, but those refugees who had come from greater means had an even harder time squaring their expectations. He noted the particular difficulties of managing the expectations of such refugees who had once lived prosperous lives, as the reality upon arrival was far from the comforts they may have enjoyed prior to war, persecution, and forced migration. He wondered, "How do you manage that? That was a big problem."

Yet alongside these disappointments, there are nonetheless important gains that make resettlement difficult to categorize. Though Raphael's first three years in San Diego as a single parent of two young children were far from easy, resettlement had succeeded in meeting expectations about some of the issues most important to him as a father. Since their arrival, his children were attending school and focused on their futures. They felt safe. Raphael concluded that, at this point, resettlement "might actually be just around 85 percent [of my expectations], which is not bad."

TRAUMA AND LONELINESS IN EARLY RESETTLEMENT

The early resettlement period is about more than just checking off core services and meeting newly arrived refugees' material needs. A comprehensive approach to resettlement takes into account all the dimensions of a refugee's life, including psychosocial and emotional well-being. A Resettlement Agency staff member observed that "people take it for granted happiness, but . . . just because they are getting money, just because they are in a new country, just because they are in America, doesn't mean that they aren't dealing with an immense source of psychological trauma." In addition to major traumas, the displacing effects of resettlement permeate the mundane, making routine tasks feel unfamiliar. Grace remarked that she found the most difficult part of resettlement to simply be "trying to figure life out." Despite having always been comfortable preparing meals for her family, different ingredients and qualities of food disrupted her ease in the kitchen, "It made me feel like I didn't know how to cook, and yet I'd grown up cooking." A former Resettlement Agency staff member repeatedly saw her clients struggle with how overwhelming the accumulation of smaller challenges could be. She said, "When you get here, you're just confronted with a million different hard things. . . . And once the honeymoon stage wears off, a lot of them sink into a depression." Beyond expectations of security and material stability, refugees may experience new stresses to their emotional well-being when feelings of displacement crop up in unexpected ways.

As refugees seek to gain their bearings, resettlement can feel infantilizing. Despite being capable adults, refugees must relearn how to do basic tasks in a new country with different conventions and norms. Amara explained how her parents' inexperience with certain aspects of everyday life in the US, such as paying bills, likened them to children. She said, "Even though my parents were grown-ups, they were kids, because it's the first time we learned about bills." Refugees resettled after years in a refugee camp or constrained environments must quickly become proficient in competencies critical to their well-being in the US. Amara added that this knowledge deficit can feel degrading and humiliating. She wished people better understood the psychological impact of this adjustment, or as she called it, "the trauma part": "The psychological aspect is very overlooked. People just expect us to be grateful to be here. . . . Your sense of self is stripped when you're a refugee. . . . You're stripped of your personhood." Years of enduring poor treatment in a refugee camp or urban area take a toll. Amara noted that "with refugees, you're often looked at for the problem that caused you to be a refugee." Instead, she said, "you're a person, you went through that, but you're trying to move on." Warsame noted how insecure refugees feel when they arrive in a new place where they do not know the language, do not yet know how to get around, and have yet to develop a local social network. Because Rima's resettlement preceded the rest of her family as they awaited their pending cases from Iraq, she had to navigate this initial stage in San Diego alone. She told me, "I'm totally lost. . . . I'm not confident in myself when I was there. . . . I remember when I go to the bank or shopping, I was just afraid to talk." This initial period of adjustment is further complicated by other competing priorities, such as parenting, language learning, and becoming economically self-sufficient, all of which happen simultaneously and require significant mental and emotional energy.

By virtue of being in a new country and lacking the accumulated resources and familiarity they once had to resolve minor issues, refugees are put in a position where they must frequently ask for help. After a young Congolese man's bicycle broke in Boise, he had to seek out assistance from his caseworker. The repair was minor, and this young man made a point of noting how he could have fixed it on his own if only he had tools. Refugees also risk their dignity when they must navigate various forms of charity to sustain themselves and their families. As Kazem waited his turn to collect food at a foodbank in Boise, he made a self-deprecating joke about "being poor" that garnered some laughs from the other local residents awaiting bags of donated food.

As refugees go through the necessary motions of early resettlement, the effects of trauma may linger in the background. An Afghan single mother of three young children experienced a tragic loss prior to her resettlement, and she continued to suffer from anxiety several months after her arrival in the US. On one occasion she had difficulty recalling basic biographical information when she was asked questions at a social service office. Her caseworker told me that he would be talking to her and all of a sudden "she's gone, and her mind is somewhere else." Another Afghan single mother who had been in San Diego for several months could not recall her address, how much she received in monthly cash aid, or how much she received in monthly food stamps when asked by her caseworker. Though the caseworker had reviewed this information with her and was frustrated by her lack of attention, the woman replied, "My memory is bad because of things that happened." Trauma, stress, and the cognitive load of adjusting to life in a new country shape refugees' emotional well-being during this initial resettlement stage. Some may also be dealing with the aftereffects of the physical traumas that they or their family members have suffered, managing chronic pain or recovery from treatment and surgery, all of which complicate the adjustments of early resettlement.

Though Resettlement Agencies help connect new arrivals to counseling services, refugees may resist due to the stigma associated with mental health issues. Nour shared how she was reluctant to attend counseling sessions after receiving a referral at her first medical appointment soon after arriving in Boise. She explained that depression was understood differently during times of war. In comparison to life-threatening violence, mental health issues felt trivial. Though she did agree to attend counseling, she did not initially see the point. Grace had a similar experience. Despite her skepticism, she began to look forward to counseling sessions because in the midst of the loneliness of initial resettlement, it was at least a reason to leave her apartment and an opportunity to interact with someone. Given the inflexibility and time-consuming nature of the entry-level jobs that refugees are typically directed towards within months of arrival, counseling services may become unmanageable or feel like an additional burden. A Resettlement Agency staff member in San Diego who specialized in supporting clients with experiences of gender and sexual-based violence noted that one of her clients had access to specialized services as a survivor of domestic violence. However, this mother worked six days a week at an agricultural job thirty miles from her home, clocking eleven-hour days in addition to her lengthy commute. She was only paid for the time that she was in the fields, so attending appointments meant forgoing a full day of work.

Considering the enduring impacts of persecution, war, and forced migration, the displacement of resettlement can itself be felt as a form of trauma. A mental health professional in Boise explained, "I think [resettlement is] a huge trauma. And to anyone who's moved into another culture, you know how jarring that is. But to have these elements of you're moving from likely a camp setting or somewhere that was unsafe into what you thought was going to be safer. But you have a loss of community. So there's grief. You have suddenly a loss of a lot of your power with language, with just ability to navigate and all other systems. So there's a lot of grief and trauma in that process." In particular, this mental health professional noted how much more damaging it can be when social services are structured around ultimatums. She continued, "Then there's a lot that we do and have built into our systems that's inherently traumatizing too with our requirements. . . . You do this or we take your money, which takes your house, or you do this or we'll take your kids. And how traumatic is that? . . . So your safety as a human is threatened when your house is threatened, when your finances are threatened, when your kids [are threatened], right? That is trauma. And that's built into our resettlement process." Enforcing programmatic requirements through coercive "immoral proposals"[14] that jeopardize refugees' sense of security only increases feelings of displacement.

Though a refugee may have heard rumors about what life will be like in the US or have attended a few days of predeparture Cultural Orientation classes, what awaits in the days and weeks ahead remains unclear, including their physical safety in a new country and community. The week after a Congolese family of six arrived in San Diego, I joined a caseworker to help assemble furniture for the single mother and her five children. In the process of moving the mother's bed, we found a large kitchen knife hidden under her mattress. When refugees step off of the airplane in their resettlement destination, they must figure out how to calculate risk given so many unknowns. The night that Nina and Joseph's family arrived in San Diego, Nina made sure to ask her caseworker if they were safe in their new apartment and whether there was any violence in the community. A few weeks later, Nina mentioned that she was concerned by some of the behavior she had seen from other passengers on the bus. She asked if any of these people could be carrying a gun and, if so, how she could keep her young children safe while using public transportation. Despite enduring and new traumas, many refugees do consistently manage the numerous challenges that come with resettlement. As a Resettlement Agency staff member in San Diego put it, "They are sensitive and tender and fragile, but they are so resilient and strong. So don't underestimate [them]."

Following the relief of finally being resettled and as the steady pace of initial R&P services slows down, the early weeks in a new country can take on an unanticipated loneliness.[15] Contrary to other immigrants whose migration to the US is driven and facilitated by social networks,[16] refugees, especially those arriving as free cases, are often resettled in the absence of preexisting ties. Even for those resettled through a U.S. tie, typically a family member or friend whose resettlement preceded theirs, they are still arriving in a destination where they know only a few people who may also be recently resettled. While resettled refugees do have robust social networks upon which they rely for information and support elsewhere, they do not benefit from the same localized network dynamics that ease the initial settlement and incorporation of other migrants. As a result, resettlement may be followed by feelings of unwelcome solitude. A community partner in Boise noticed that initial resettlement services failed to fulfil the need for meaningful interaction. He explained, "What they are not getting is connection, and what they are not getting is friendship, and so, deep loneliness is setting in."

According to the benchmarks of the USRAP, Andre's resettlement had all of the hallmarks of success. The Resettlement Agency secured an apartment for him as a single case, and within his first month in Boise he got a job working hotel security. After a few months he was promoted to the front desk where he greeted guests and answered phones. Yet Andre struggled. He was among the first Congolese to be resettled in Boise, so there was no preestablished community to connect with or rely on. Andre was surprised by how little his surroundings resembled his assumptions of what a US city would look and feel like. He lived on a main thoroughfare, but people did not stop to greet each other. He was struck by how quiet it was and how alone he felt. "No neighbors saying hello. No one talks to you." His days took on a lonely routine. He said, "It was terrible. I would go to work, come home, and be alone and isolated." On top of the loneliness, he became the target of racist remarks by his colleagues and hotel guests, and he developed extreme stress and anxiety. He added, "Every time I go to work, I come back crying." In addition to receiving psychiatric care, he began participating in local sports and slowly made connections in his new city, which helped to counteract the pressures he dealt with on a daily basis.

The living arrangements secured by the Resettlement Agency as well as unfamiliar cultural norms can make refugees feel isolated. Pascal's family's first few weeks in Boise were characterized by loneliness. After moving into their apartment, they had expected their new neighbors to stop by to welcome them, but no one ever came. Instead his family spent their early days in the US reminiscing about the life they left behind. Pascal had been eager to meet new people and try out the English phrases he had been practicing in the weeks leading up to his departure from a refugee camp in Tanzania. He told me, "I was happy really to be in a new town, but, you know, the ground smelled different, water tasted very different, people were very different, and I wanted to go to meet people. . . . Then, a few weeks of being here, I didn't make friends, and didn't know anyone, and we were just ourselves in the house." They had arrived in February, so he figured that this solitude was in part due to the winter weather. Much to his disappointment, his family felt just as isolated as the seasons changed. Pascal continued, "The neighborhood was quiet—that's how I can describe it. . . . I was thinking it [was] just because it was cold. No, even in June, in the summer, I didn't see anyone outside." David remembered feelings of isolation when his family arrived in San Diego. He said, "Well, that first week, we were just in the house because we don't know anybody to go out, to hang out with. So, we did get a little bit lonely in the house."

With limited English proficiency and in the absence of close ties in Boise, Bastien confronted similar feelings of seclusion when his family was first resettled. "When I came here, too, there are a lot of challenges, because you don't know the language. So imagine you don't know the language, and you don't know anybody. How will I feel?" Though his family had the support of the Resettlement Agency, their caseworker did not always answer or return their calls, and Bastien knew that he was busy juggling the needs of other newly arrived families like his. Growing up in a refugee camp in Tanzania, Bastien used to regularly socialize with his neighbors and friends. But once in Boise, it felt like a "transformation of life." Without places for young people to congregate, everyone spent more time at home. People were busier, and over time, Bastien grew accustomed to being on his own.

Despite hardships in the home country or country of asylum, refugees may nonetheless have enjoyed a deep sense of community. Life in the US may feel particularly isolating and compartmentalized. Hafiz explained that "if you live in Afghanistan, you know more than one hundred families, and they are coming to your house. They're helping you. You can help them. But in the United States, I'm living three years in one apartment. Even I don't know my downstairs neighbor because they don't want the connection with you." Refugees with family or friends already in the resettlement destination may be surprised when their close ties do not offer the hospitality that would have once been customary in the home country. Hafiz had an uncle already in San Diego and was taken aback by his limited welcome. Hafiz said, "I thought when I am going there, my uncle will hug me. . . . When I found my uncle and aunt, only for five minutes he was very kind.

After that, he told me, 'You can go to your house.' . . . I don't want to blame them because the situation, the system is like that." The constraints of small apartments and occupancy limits combined with inflexible work schedules cause new arrivals to feel slighted by their own kin. With time, Hafiz came to understand the impossibility of providing the deep hospitality that new arrivals expected and yearned for. He said, "My brother-in-law came from Afghanistan, and he thought like me, right? . . . Because when they are coming, they're thinking you are sitting with them and laughing with them. I told them, 'Only Monday, Tuesday, I can sit. I don't want to lose my job for you.' So this is my life. So these are the things we thought before and they completely changed here." Even refugees with kinship networks in the resettlement destination are not spared from the loneliness of resettlement.

When I dropped off some paperwork for Jose, he was sitting outside of his father-in-law's home on a particularly secluded side street in Boise. He had been in the US for less than forty-eight hours, and he and his wife were spending much of their time with their relatives who had been resettled about six months earlier. Yet on that Friday afternoon most of the family was out. The adults were at work or English class and the children had not all returned from school. After I handed him the paperwork, Jose wanted me to stay and chat. He told me about how there were always people around at the refugee camp in Tanzania where he had lived. Now that he had made it to Boise, he sat alone in a folding chair in his father-in-law's driveway and saw no one.

THE RELIEF OF COMMUNITY SUPPORT

It can be challenging to make connections in a new country, particularly outside of one's language community, but it becomes an important way to combat the loneliness that often follows resettlement. It made all the difference when Pascal's family finally met some other Boise residents. He said, "Someone is noticing us, not feeling like we are just like an island among people." As outlined by the Refugee Act of 1980, refugee resettlement is intended to be a public-private partnership. While the public side of resettlement is highly standardized through federal resettlement services and Resettlement Agencies, the private side is unregulated, offering uneven support across and within resettlement destinations. In its most ideal form, private actors and community-based organizations offer crucial supplemental support that picks up where Resettlement Agency caseworkers have left off. Yet this type of ad hoc engagement and generosity of time and resources is unreliable and never guaranteed. Assumptions that private efforts will augment the formal resettlement program can leave families or whole refugee groups without important forms of support. When the ongoing Syrian War and early efforts to resettle Syrian families in San Diego were constantly in the news, local residents organized donation drives to provide goods to newly arrived Syrian families. Though this volunteerism bolstered assistance for Syrians, it simultaneously came at the expense of other refugee groups arriving at the same time who were overlooked. In one stark example, a Resettlement Agency caseworker in San Diego recounted how community members handed out toys to Syrian children whose families were temporarily housed in a hotel as newly arrived children from other countries of origin looked on. Regular cash donations may succeed in relieving the financial stresses of one family while others remain in precarious circumstances.

In particular, established co-ethnic communities in the resettlement destination can help to cushion the landing of new arrivals. Ethnic- and community-based organizations can offer tailored and much-needed support. A community leader in San Diego cofounded a local organization that sought to fill the gap between refugees' needs and the capacity of Resettlement Agencies. Whereas Resettlement Agencies close at 5 p.m. each day, his phone was always on. Indeed, our nearly ninety-minute evening interview was interrupted several times by phone calls from refugees in the community with questions, concerns, and requests for transportation. He noted that Resettlement Agencies instruct their clients to call 911 in case of an emergency during off hours, but "there are things for which you cannot call 911." He continued, "I think, really, you need to talk to somebody to know that somebody's there for you." This San Diego–based organization was one of a proliferating number of groups who were assisting refugees locally, including organizations that catered to particular refugee groups, providing culturally and linguistically familiar support. Others sought to make broad impacts through school-wide tutoring; still others made smaller touches by delivering care packages to newly arrived families. Given the high concentration of refugee-serving nonprofit organizations in San Diego, new arrivals were connected to additional outlets for assistance—either by their Resettlement Agency or by word of mouth that spread quickly within communities—which provided the services and contacts that help to expand a refugee's network in a new city.

In Boise, however, due to a combination of the recentness of particular refugee communities and the absence of concerted efforts to bolster and formalize refugee-led organizations, ongoing assistance remained largely within the Resettlement Agency. Refugees gained informal support through places of worship or their ethnic groups, but these associations were without the financial and organizational power that their counterparts in San Diego leveraged to support refugee families. The few refugee-led organizations that did exist in Boise felt like their potential was underestimated and that they were not considered full partners; they were left off of grant applications, which made them strapped for funding. Of the forms of community support that did exist in Boise outside of the Resettlement Agency, much of it came from religious volunteerism from nonrefugee residents. While these forms of "mentorship" or family matching did provide other avenues for assistance, they fell short of the more empowering organizational structures that supplemented formal resettlement services in San Diego.

CONFRONTING EXPECTATIONS

When refugees first land in their resettlement destination, they are afforded little ownership over many immediate and meaningful decisions that initially come to shape their lives. This chapter has focused on the early weeks in the US as refugees are put on a "conveyor belt of services" and become familiar with the terms and conditions of their resettlement. While resettlement has remedied many of the core hardships that previously constrained their lives and futures, refugees must confront new and unanticipated challenges that may clash with their expectations. Additionally, in the absence of familiar people and places, the resettlement process can feel both lonely and isolating. Resettlement Agency caseworkers play a consequential role during this period. Though their responsiveness has a direct impact on refugees' feelings of security, refugees' questions and needs may extend beyond standard business hours.

While resettlement may be a final and ultimately favorable displacement, newly arrived refugees must still undertake the arduous task of making a life in the US, a country in which they may never have anticipated living and according to a timeline over which they have little control. Once resettled, refugees are not simply "a closed case for whom solution has been found,"[17] as resettlement carries its own set of hardships to navigate. By moving away from the framework of resettlement as a solution and time of integration, I shift the focus to the complexities and contradictions inherent in the "structure of refuge" that shape refugees' first months in the US.[18] The pace of resettlement services as well as refugees' unmet expectations reveal just how displacing the early weeks of resettlement can be.

3

FAMILY

FIVE YEARS AFTER FLEEING to Jordan from Syria, Yara was resettled to the southwestern US with her parents and three younger siblings. Yara's aunt, a single adult, was resettled the year before, though she had been sent to Maryland. This aunt had begun the resettlement process with her mother, Yara's grandmother. Her aunt was approved first but was informed that the grandmother would soon follow. Yara explained, "My aunt and my grandma, they were together in the same file, and they just separate them, and they took my aunt to the United States, and now my grandma was by herself." When Yara's aunt inquired about the status of her mother's case, she was reassured, "She will follow you after a month." At the time of my interview with Yara, almost two years had passed since her aunt had arrived in the US. When I asked Yara if her grandmother was still in Jordan, she replied, "She died. . . . She passed away three months ago. She really wanted to come, and she was trying to come and see us, but she couldn't do that."

Yara continued, "My aunt was really depressed, too, this time, because it was the first time for her to be by herself." Though they had managed two visits since Yara's family arrived, the trips were expensive, and Yara's aunt struggled to adjust to life in a new country and city alone. Resettlement case approvals and subsequent destination decisions can seem counterintuitive, separating families and creating irreparable harm. Not only was Yara's extended family resettled to opposite sides of the country, but her grandmother was left behind in Jordan where she died awaiting reunification. This loss was particularly damaging for Yara's aunt who had to cope with the death of her mother and the challenges of resettlement alone, suffering a grief amplified by borders.[1]

Resettlement offered Yara's aunt legal status, security, and rights, yet it came with immense familial costs. The complications of forced migration and the unpredictability of resettlement can engender separation, which is all the more harmful when loved ones are lost in the process. Later in our conversation, I asked Yara what could have been helpful for her family when they first arrived. She replied, "I think the most ⌊helpful⌋ thing is understanding that there is a lot of family we miss. If we could be together, that would be also really helpful."

Research has identified the psychosocial and material benefits of familial integrity for immigrant and refugee families.[2] Not only does family support help ease the mental, emotional, and economic challenges of adjusting to life in a new country,[3] separations become a new source of hardship during this already difficult undertaking.[4] Thierry noted "all the stress and trauma that comes" when resettled refugees must endure separations, creating losses that may never be fully recuperated. He added, "What's the negative impact of that [separation]? It breaks families. . . . It breaks a lot of things." Family separation creates added stress, including the financial obligation of remittances,[5] as arriving refugees remain deeply connected to those left behind.[6] Separations mean not only that newly arrived refugees are without the material and emotional support of their kinship networks but also that they must build a life in a new country all while knowing that their loved ones remain in precarious situations.

This chapter explores the consequential ways that resettlement can alter refugee families and their sense of home. Resettlement unmoors when it disrupts key dimensions of familial life, particularly when refugees' kinship structures do not fit how US law defines a legitimate family and prior frames of reference for housing clash with assumptions about how refugees should live. Moreover, the displacing effects of resettlement may be experienced differently within the same family, adding new challenges to the task of parenting that create discord within households.

DISPLACING FAMILIES

There are numerous ways that the resettlement process reshapes refugee families. Research has demonstrated that family separation is detrimental to immigrants and refugees as they adjust to life in a new country.[7] This chapter's focus on familial life reveals the extent to which resettlement is disruptive, adding complicating layers of hardship to this already difficult undertaking. While some displaced families result from the complexities of forced migration, other instances stem from laws and policies.

When loved ones are left behind in countries of asylum, the assumed finality of resettlement along with logistical, economic, and legal barriers to reunification make separations all the more consequential. Musa was a newlywed when his resettlement was approved. Though he had applied for his wife to be added to his case, her case was still in process when Musa had to depart for the US. Musa reflected on his first six months in San Diego adjusting to life alone while waiting for news of his wife's case: "That was the worst part of my immigration because it double[d] the size of the normal hard time you are experiencing, because I was just married. It feels very bad if you just get married within few months and then you stay away from your wife. I was so kind of affected by that. I was honestly not feeling well at that time." For many refugees, a displaced family becomes a consequence of their resettlement, creating a difficult context for adjusting to life in a new community.

Making Existing Separations Permanent or Prolonged

Regardless of whether initial family separation at the time of forced migration is inadvertent or strategic, resettlement can add another factor that impedes hopes of eventual reunification.[8] Omari was a young child in the DRC when armed forces attacked his village, killing his mother. During his escape, Omari was separated from some of his siblings. For more than a decade, he lived in a refugee camp in Uganda with his brother and sister, not knowing that his other siblings had survived. Only after his resettlement to Boise did he learn through a network of contacts that his siblings were indeed alive. These contacts informed him that his siblings had come to the camp in Uganda looking for them, but Omari and his brother and sister were now more than eight thousand miles away. Omari had since reconnected with them through phone calls, but the distance that resulted from his resettlement denied them a regular presence in each other's lives after more than thirteen years apart. Though Omari had not known that he was leaving family behind when he departed for the US, the chaos of war and the complications of protracted displacement created a separation that was further cemented by his resettlement.

Idil's mother fled Somalia alone as a young woman, the only member of her family to seek refuge in Yemen. "When the war happened, my mom left by herself. So she basically got in a boat with some people and just came to Yemen. . . . So she had no one, no family." The circumstances of her mother's migration meant that after Idil and her siblings were born in Yemen, they grew up in isolation of their extended family. Idil added, "I've never really seen my family." Resettlement to San Diego years later offered greater safety and security for Idil's mother, now a single parent, and her children, but it also added more miles between them and surviving relatives who had ended up elsewhere in East Africa. When I asked Idil if any of her relatives had also been resettled, she replied, "No, it's only just us." Despite everything that resettlement provided Idil's family, it nonetheless further solidified the separation that had first split Idil's mother from her family years earlier, making an eventual reunion that much more difficult. Eight years after their arrival in San Diego, they continued to live without the support of family ties. When the complex circumstances of forced migration interact with the resettlement process, it can make earlier separations of necessity and survival permanent.

Sometimes persecution only affects one member of a family. In such cases, that person must separate themselves from their family in order to save their own lives. Targeted for his sexuality, Kazem was on his own when he left Iran for Turkey and pursued resettlement. The safety that resettlement provided was wrapped up in the sadness of knowing that his family would not be able to join him in the US. He remembered that when he arrived in the US three years earlier, he "felt a relief and lots of grief and sorrow." He continued by explaining why: "because of separat[ing] from the people that I knew, cause here I'm alone you know. I have nobody." He worried that if something terrible were to occur to him so far away, his family would never know what happened, "If I die, no one's going to tell my family. And there's no option for that for refugees who are single who are alone, that if they die, who's going to tell their family?"

Even when separations are eventually remedied, the precarity of refugees' circumstances combined with the bureaucracy of resettlement can prolong and complicate these separations in new ways, adding layers of struggle that disrupt familial dynamics. When Ashina's mother pursued resettlement in Kampala, Uganda, she feared that any mention of her husband would put his life in danger while he strategically remained behind in the DRC. Though Ashina's parents felt that conditions in the DRC had grown too dangerous for their six young children, her father stayed behind to continue working while the rest of the family sought asylum in Kampala, a strategic separation illustrative of the "new economics of displacement."[9] When the opportunity arose to pursue resettlement, Ashina's mother deliberately omitted her husband from the family's case. Once they were approved to come to the US, they had to leave for Boise without him, though they managed to arrange a brief and risky goodbye. Ashina's mother endured the early years of resettlement as a single mother of six, coping with the emotional and financial burdens of parenting in a new country on her own, just as she had done for several years in Uganda. While their separation had been Ashina's parents' decision, the opportunity for resettlement in conjunction with the ongoing dangers in the DRC created circumstances that complicated the possibility of a reunion, making daily life difficult in the intervening years.

Five years after their arrival in Boise, Ashina's family was reunited when her father was resettled following a complex process that at times had seemed unlikely to succeed. Though the family was relieved to be together, their long separation caused growing pains that took time to resolve. Ashina's father had missed seeing first-hand the years of struggle and sacrifice that his wife had endured taking care of their children, first in Kampala and then in Boise. His absence during the family's resettlement meant that he did not fully appreciate how high the stakes had been for his wife. As a successful businessman in the DRC, he had trouble adjusting to the conditions of a manual labor job in Boise. Ashina helped orient her father to the realities of the life they now lived, making sure he was aware of just how much he had missed.

She told him how her mother "had to learn how to ride a bike in the snow. . . . [to] get where she is right now. . . . and do all the things that she did while you were not here." She added, "We had to tell him. He doesn't know anything about it." Though Ashina's family was reunited, the strategic separation they had initially endured by choice was prolonged and complicated by resettlement, resulting in tensions that took time to overcome.

Creating New Separations

Even when families arrive in the country of asylum intact, the resettlement process can create new separations that become difficult to rectify. When only part of a family is approved, refugees are given the impossible choice of leaving without their loved ones or staying and possibly forgoing any chance at getting resettled. Given how rare resettlement is and how susceptible resettlement priorities are to political change,[10] turning down or delaying an approval is risky and the likelihood of future reunions is always uncertain. The Trump administration's 2017 travel bans and 2025 halting of resettlement stopped the approval of thousands of cases that had been at various stages of processing, upending pending departures and reunifications.[11] Shortly after the Trump administration announced that the annual resettlement ceiling for 2019 would drop to thirty-thousand arrivals, from a high of 110,000 two years earlier, an administrator of the San Diego Resettlement Agency lamented that this was "really very tough news to know how many family members won't be reunited as a result."

Rima was reluctant to abandon the career and life she had built as a young professional in Iraq, but the country's deteriorating security pushed her family to pursue resettlement. Leaving seemed like the only way to ensure their safety. But when Rima was notified of her approval to come to the US, the news was bittersweet. Her parents' and sister's resettlement cases were still pending. Not only did Rima worry about going to a new country while her family remained under increasingly dangerous and uncertain conditions, she was also a single young woman who had grown up with the cultural expectation that daughters stay with their parents until marriage. Leaving meant breaking these deeply rooted social norms. Despite her hesitation, Rima worried that if she tried to wait for the rest of her family's approval, she may lose the opportunity to ever go. She explained, "It's a big decision for me as a girl. I cried a lot, and then I feel like I have to do it because maybe if I said no, maybe I can't even go." Rima's decision was fraught and she felt pressured to leave alone regardless of her discomfort about it.

Rima's journey to San Diego was exhausting and stressful and included a thirteen-hour layover in Jordan during which she could not leave the airport. With so much time to think, Rima began to question her decision. She kept asking herself, "What did you do?" Rima had the support of extended family already in San Diego, yet she still felt very lonely after she arrived. Rima remembered how lost she was during those early months. She was insecure navigating the city as a single woman, and she worried about the judgment of her neighbors in San Diego. Everything felt new and different, and Rima lacked self-confidence as she tried to acclimate to her surroundings.

Refugees over twenty-one years old may get processed as single cases whose timeline becomes separated from the rest of their family. As occurred with Rima and with Yara's aunt, single adult children are often resettled as "split cases." This staggered resettlement can create new strains, both for the portion of the family resettled first and the members left behind. When Didier fled to Kampala with his mother and siblings, he became an important income earner and form of support for his family after his father disappeared, particularly given his mother's poor health. Didier's case was split, and his mother and younger siblings were resettled to Boise almost a year before Didier was approved. Not only was he left behind in Kampala without knowing if or when he would be resettled, his mother was without her son's assistance as she faced resettlement alone with her four youngest children in a city where she knew no one. In the year before Didier's approval and arrival in Boise, one of his siblings balanced high school with work at a fast-food restaurant to make ends meet while they waited for Didier to join them. Such separations create emotional burdens and practical challenges that complicate the process of resettlement. This practice of splitting cases assumes that unmarried children "age out" of their nuclear family at twenty-one years old, which carries both economic and emotional consequences.

One distinctive way that resettlement alters family composition is through the separation of plural marriage families. Because plural marriages are not recognized by the UNHCR[12] or US law, families with multiple spouses, typically multiple wives, must split in order to access this potentially life-saving opportunity. In such cases, the husband must have a resettlement case with one wife and their children as a nuclear family, while any other wives must have their own case with their children. Warsame explained how his family was in fact much larger than the one he had arrived with in Boise four years earlier. He had three wives: one who came with him to the US, one who had passed away before his resettlement, and one whom he had divorced "by mouth" for official purposes. She still lived in the refugee camp in Ethiopia with their children, and he sent them remittances. He added, "I hide it, because I want to come here. . . . But she's my wife." Though US immigration and resettlement policies are based on notions family unity, not all kinship structures fit how US law defines a legitimate family.[13]

Necessitating the breakup of plural marriages creates single mothers either in the resettlement destination or in the country of asylum, upending the economic and caregiving systems that they relied on for survival and denying parents and children the ability to remain together. The requisite fracturing of these families is illustrative of how the resettlement process engenders displacement, creating new forms of uncertainty, disruption, and vulnerability. Single mother families with young children are among the most challenging cases, given the USRAP's expectations of economic self-sufficiency and the meagre public assistance support available in the US. Because the timeline for processing resettlement cases varies so widely and not all cases are successful, these divided families may not be resettled at the same time, to the same place, or at all—separating them temporarily or permanently across borders.

In one instance, a mother and her children were resettled to Boise, while her husband and his other wife and children were resettled to Canada. In another instance, after a single mother arrived in San Diego with her six children, her caseworker inquired about her marital status. This woman shared that she had a husband but that he remained in the refugee camp in Tanzania with his other wife and their children. Her caseworker knew that her path ahead in San Diego was not going to be easy. In order to make their families fit the requirements for resettlement, these two mothers now faced significant economic challenges in the US. This practice of necessitating the breakup of plural marriages sets women up to fully assume economic and care responsibilities for their families for the first time in a country that offers minimal support.

A Congolese single mother in Boise with seven children under the age of ten years old struggled financially and emotionally. The Resettlement Agency later learned that she was not a single mother at all. Only after another family was resettled to Boise and the newly arrived husband began splitting his time between the two households did the Resettlement Agency learn that she was part of a polygamous family that had been separated and fortuitously reunited in the same city. A casework staff member noted how much this woman's demeanor changed after her husband, who at first said he was just her relative, arrived. "When she came, she was a mess, and then all of a sudden . . . they were hanging out together, and I was like, 'Man, she has really shaped up. That was a quick turnaround. That was amazing.' She had such a struggle, such a struggle when she first came. And then he got here, and of course . . . it was [her] husband. She was fine." Though the Resettlement Agency had to continue treating these two cases as administratively separate, staff adjusted their approach to supporting both cases once their relationship came to light. When family units split in order to access resettlement, women who arrive alone with their children enter an extremely tenuous situation. When plural marriages are concealed in order to pursue resettlement, reunions become complicated and unlikely.

The drawn-out timeline for processing and approving resettlement cases does not compensate for how families evolve over time. Despite the challenges of protracted displacement, refugees continue their lives.[14] In the years that pass between when a resettlement case is created and when it is eventually approved, new family units are formed, and others dissolve. Many refugees I spoke with noted how a prevailing fear of "spoiling" their resettlement case shaped the decisions they made while waiting in the country of asylum. In these instances, refugees worried that if they made updates to their file after it had been submitted, they risked undermining their case by delaying or even jeopardizing approval. Regardless of the validity of this concern, resettlement is "a coveted, golden ticket,"[15] and refugees awaiting resettlement function in a context of extreme uncertainty and precarity.[16] Refugees may make decisions based on incomplete or inaccurate information, as they do their best to strategize within this opaque and consequential system. Yet by withholding new information, the family units approved for resettlement may be incomplete.

In the six years between when Bastien's parents' resettlement case was opened and their family left the refugee camp in Tanzania for Boise, Bastien had gotten married, welcomed his first child, and was expecting his second. At the time of our interview, Bastien had not seen his wife and eldest child since he had been resettled five years earlier and had never met his youngest child who was born after his departure. He was still trying to find a way for his family to join him in the US. Bastien explained that the bureaucracy of camp management had made it difficult and potentially risky to combine his resettlement case with that of his wife and child.

When Bastien was approved for resettlement as part of his parents' case, he did not know if he would get another chance to leave the refugee camp where he had lived for thirteen years. He made the decision to go without his child and pregnant wife out of fear that if he stayed as part of a newly combined case, they might never leave at all. Like many refugees in similar situations, he assumed that it would be easier to bring his family once in the US. But Bastien's attempts at reunification had thus far been unsuccessful, in part because he had not mentioned them at the time of his approval. He had since taken DNA tests to prove his paternity of his children, a procedural obstacle intended to weed out fraudulent claims of family ties.[17] As he approached eligibility to apply for US citizenship, he hoped that this new legal status would carry more power to successfully bring his family to the US. In the meantime, he sent remittances through a mobile phone app to help his wife as she raised their children in the refugee camp. But time and distance wore on Bastien. He said, "It's not easy living like five years without having your wife. . . . So you don't have that hope. . . . But I still love them."

Such separations are harmful for both parents and children.[18] Not only did Bastien have to build a life in the US apart from his family, he did so knowing that they continued to struggle in the refugee camp he left behind. Even in the best-case scenario of reunification, his children will have nonetheless endured the harms that come from being apart for years. Bastien's choice to leave without his family was informed by assumption about the ease of future reunification. Though he exercised agency in his departure, it took place within a highly constrained and consequential context. While it is unclear whether amending a resettlement case already in the pipeline may jeopardize its progress, scholars have noted that, given the scarcity of resettlement, refugees in protracted displacement harbor the fear that complicated cases are less likely to be approved.[19]

Bringing Together Outdated Family Units

Outdated information in a case can also bring together estranged spouses who have long since separated. A Congolese couple's marriage ended after they had begun the process for resettlement. In the years that followed, the former husband and wife both remarried in the refugee camp where they lived, and the man had children with his new wife. Despite the change in their marital status, this ex-husband and wife never updated their case out of fear that they would lose whatever progress it had made, further delaying the possibility of resettlement. This former couple was eventually approved and resettled to a city in the western US. They had assumed that once they arrived, they would be able to send for their respective families.

A week after their arrival, the woman relocated to Boise to join a friend who had been resettled there, and she reached out to a Resettlement Agency for support. The Resettlement Agency caseworkers grew concerned when they learned the details of her situation. By claiming to still be married and failing to inform the US government of their new families, the casework staff concluded that they had likely committed fraud. It was unclear whether they could ever apply for their respective families to join them because doing so would expose this earlier fraud. Nonetheless, a Resettlement Agency caseworker empathized with their logic, "They wanted to keep their case. They didn't want to spoil it and put it back in a drawer." To make matters worse, all of the R&P funds allocated to support this couple's resettlement were tied to the ex-husband as the case's principal applicant. The woman's half of these per capita funds, a sum of $1,125, remained with the Resettlement Agency in the city and state that had initially welcomed them. Her portion of the case and funds could only be transferred to a Boise Resettlement Agency if her ex-husband moved as well. This woman arrived in Boise in need of assistance, but the Resettlement Agency was without the essential funds to provide it. Not only had resettlement separated two families, probably permanently, it also created obstacles that prevented this woman from accessing proper resettlement assistance.

The fear of "spoiling" a resettlement case highlights how vulnerable refugees feel they are to the whims of this potentially life-altering opportunity. When estranged spouses are brought back together by an approval, it can make the challenges inherent in resettlement that much more difficult for refugees and the Resettlement Agencies assisting them. When Resettlement Agency caseworkers in Boise were notified of the impending arrival of a young Congolese family, they began their usual preparations. They found an apartment, arranged for furniture, and coordinated a team of volunteers to shop for household essentials. Nothing about the predeparture paperwork implied the complicated nature of this case. When the family exited the arrivals terminal at the Boise airport late in the evening after a flight delay, their faces hinted at the fatigue from their long trip. They were driven straight to their temporary housing, given a brief home safety orientation, and left to settle in for the night.

Resettlement Agency staff returned the following day for their required twenty-four-hour home visit, which included plans for the family to sign a lease for their new apartment. It was during this home visit that the complexities of the case came to light. Though their paperwork showed that they were a family unit, the husband and wife were separated, had no longer been living together in the refugee camp, and were not on good terms. They had been brought back together by the approval of their resettlement case and had to endure close quarters during their trip from Tanzania to Boise, including a motel stay during an overnight layover in Los Angeles and temporary accommodations the previous night. The tensions between the mother and father became palpable the day after their arrival, and caseworkers speculated about a possible history of domestic violence. It was clear that the family could not live together, so the Resettlement Agency scrambled to locate last minute accommodations for the father. They also split the case administratively. These changes unfolded as the family was being enrolled in state-based public assistance programs, which triggered a child support case for the father.

For this family, the resettlement process exacerbated the messiness and stress that accompanied the dissolution of their marriage, pushing their fractured relationship back together and forcing them to divulge intimate details to strangers as soon as they arrived. The challenges that come with early resettlement were exasperated by the complex arrangements that were cobbled together following the disclosure of their separation—which made their initial days in Boise that much more displacing. These issues had ripple effects, which created additional obstacles for the Resettlement Agency staff assisting them. A Resettlement Agency staff member in San Diego noted that all of the financial and emotional stressors associated with early resettlement may make women reluctant to leave abusive relationships, keeping them in family units that are unhealthy for themselves and their children, particularly in the absence of the support of an extended family network.

Separation from Extended Family

The above examples demonstrate how the resettlement process reconstitutes nuclear families. Extended families are even more likely to experience separations. For many communities, extended family units are integral to well-being, yet the USRAP privileges the resettlement of nuclear families at the expense of larger kinship networks.[20] Separation from extended families was nearly universal for refugees who arrive as Special Immigrant Visa holders, or SIVs. These Iraqi and Afghan refugees qualify for resettlement because of their work for the US military in their respective countries, and only spouses and minor children can be included as part of the principal applicant's case. Extended family members are ineligible to pursue resettlement through the same pathway unless they have also worked with the US military. When SIVs leave Iraq or Afghanistan due to threats to their safety, they do so knowing that important family members, such as aging parents or adult children, will likely never be able to join them in the US.

Many SIVs I met cited how challenging this particular dimension of their resettlement was, both for the principal applicant who had worked with the US military and for their spouse, as coming to the US necessitated separation. Karam noted how his departure was made all the more challenging because he had grown up in a culture where extended kinship ties were especially strong and had always been a part of his daily life. He explained, "It was so tough, because we got separated from our family. We lived the whole life all together. I mean, we're kind of like a very family-oriented community back home. . . . We used also to live very close together, like in the same neighborhood, see each other, spend a week, the whole weekends together. It's our kind of like life there." He left Iraq to ensure his immediate family's physical security, but it came with the loss of this daily way of being. He continued, "All of a sudden, we got separated. It wasn't that easy to get acclimated here social-wise." Munir, a young father, described the same issues that came with removing himself and his wife from their close-knit families in Afghanistan. He said, "That was really hard for me, really hard. I mean, the way we all grow up, we all live together. I have five brothers, and they still live with my mom and dad." Given that Munir was the only member of his family to work for the US military, reuniting in the US was not an option for his parents or brothers.

Musa recounted how damaging this separation was for his wife who joined him in San Diego six months after his arrival. When his wife's case was finally approved, reunifying with Musa became the first time that she lived apart from her parents, let alone in another country. Not only did his wife struggle to build a home so far from her family, her unhappiness became a constant source of stress for Musa as he dealt with the challenges of resettlement. Musa and his wife sought to start a family together in San Diego, but his wife suffered a miscarriage, deepening her grief. Musa recounted: "She was just telling me that I cannot breathe anymore. I want to go back to visit my family." Given his low-wage job, they could not afford expensive airline tickets, not to mention the dangers associated with returning. When refugees experience family separations as a result of resettlement, numerous obstacles stand in the way of visits, including financial insecurity, risks to safety in the home country, and the challenges of returning to a refugee camp. At the time of my interview with Musa five years after his arrival, he and his wife had welcomed their first child and were making a life for themselves apart from their loved ones. They continued to save money in hopes of visiting Afghanistan.

A representative from a San Diego community-based organization that worked with SIVs, who are typically men, noted how difficult initial resettlement was for their spouses: "The wife comes here, and she has depression because she don't really go outside. They have to stay home with the kids, and they don't have as much of a community like they did back in Afghanistan. . . . I'd imagine it's very lonely there by yourself, not knowing the language." By virtue of the principal applicant's work with the US military, SIVs tend to arrive with strong English proficiency and a level of familiarity with US culture. But just because husbands have these skills does not mean that their wives will feel equally well equipped or comfortable. This community partner empathized with the situation these women found themselves in. He said, "I think that the SIV guys that I've talked to, I mean, I know it's hard on them, but I think it's probably much harder on the wives because you're taken away from everything that you've ever known, and the family and kids don't have grandparents here, and you're kind of forced to do it on your own." Though SIVs are not the only group that suffers separations from extended family, the program almost invariably results in transnational families, and so the experience was common for those who accessed resettlement through it.

Familial Integrity

Given the harms and stresses associated with separation, it is not difficult to see why familial integrity eases the burdens of resettlement and supports incorporation and financial stability, particularly for single parent families or families with extensive care responsibilities. Raphael, a single father, was resettled to San Diego with his two young children. After seventeen years in a refugee camp in Uganda, resettlement offered a brighter future for his young family, though it meant leaving behind his aging parents and his sibling's family in the camp as they awaited their own resettlement cases. Once in San Diego, Raphael tried to manage competing demands on his time as he cared for his young children, all while quickly beginning to work long hours in landscaping. A year and a half later, his parents' and sibling's cases were approved. Due to their tie to Raphael, they were resettled in San Diego.

With the family reunited, Raphael secured a larger apartment so that his parents could move in with him and his children while his sibling's family rented an apartment nearby. Raphael helped them adjust to life in a new country. At the same time, their presence in Raphael's life became transformative. He could finally attend evening English classes after work, a critical step in his plans to gain better employment in the future, a rare opportunity within a resettlement system that does not prioritize the development of skills.[21] He said, "When my parents came, it was just my favor." Not only did Raphael no longer have to worry about his family's security and well-being in the refugee camp in Uganda, their arrival provided Raphael with a sense of stability that had been elusive during his first eighteen months in the US. Reunification eased the displacing effects of initial resettlement and facilitated

Raphael's longer-term incorporation through caregiving support and English language gains in pursuit of upward mobility.

Not only does separation carry harmful consequences, keeping families together is protective against many of the stresses of resettlement, producing emotional and practical benefits that facilitate the programmatic objectives of the USRAP.[22] Though Raphael's family had the good fortune of being reunified, such reunions can never be counted on. One young Congolese man was fortunate to have his wife and baby reunite with him in Boise. In the four and a half years since his resettlement, he had returned to the refugee camp in Rwanda twice. Once to marry his wife and the second time to meet his child. His wife and child received news of their approval for resettlement during the second visit and joined the father in Boise soon after his return. As the young mother and baby exited the arrivals terminal at the Boise Airport, they were greeted by a large welcome party of friends and relatives. After the husband and wife embraced, finally able to live as a family in the same country, they paused together in the middle of the airport and shared a moment in silence. But they joy of their reunion was tempered by the fact that the husband had another child in the camp whom he had been petitioning for unsuccessfully. Given the scarcity of resettlement, it can take years before families are reunited, if at all. Resettlement is not a right; it is framed instead as a privilege for a select few.[23] Refugees in the resettlement pipeline have little control over the progress of their case,[24] making it impossible to assume with any certainty that they will be reunified with family members, let alone in the same destination. Though refugees may be assured that a case's approval is immanent, it is never guaranteed.

Unexpected Reunions

While forced migration and resettlement can disperse families, resettlement can at times also lead to unexpected reunions. Some refugees are unknowingly resettled in the same city as a family member or friend with whom they had previously lost contact due to the disruptions of war and forced migration. Because refugees may not know if these loved ones had survived, these serendipitous reunions are both remarkable and emotional. When a recently resettled Congolese family showed up at their first required medical appointment in San Diego, the interpreter waiting to assist them was the mother's childhood friend, resulting in a surprising and joyous moment amid the stress of resettlement. In another instance, Rosine's mother encountered a close friend at a church in San Diego early in their resettlement. After this woman had departed the refugee camp in Kenya where they all lived, Rosine's mother had no knowledge of what had become of her. This friend had already made it through the early stages of resettlement and offered Rosine's mother the reassurance she so desperately needed as they struggled to adjust, telling her, "Life soon will get better." After a Congolese family was resettled in Boise and began attending a local Congolese church, they ran into some extended family members who had long been resettled in Boise and whom they had not seen in years.

Tresor was shocked to see his uncle waiting at the airport to welcome his family to Boise. No one in Tresor's family knew that this uncle had been resettled, let alone in the same city. The Resettlement Agency had figured out their familial connection when preparing for the arriving case and, much to the surprise of Tresor's family, had arranged for the uncle to greet them at the airport. Tresor remembered how exhausted and overwhelmed they all were by the time they arrived in Boise after having traveled on multiple connecting flights through airports in which no one spoke their language. He recounted the relief at hearing Swahili as they exited the arrivals terminal, only to realize that their uncle was among the group waiting for them. He said,

We saw people from Africa [waiting] here at the airport. And at the time, there wasn't very many. So, we saw my uncle and we were like, "Oh my

God." We never thought we would see them again. . . . I think [the RA] found out that we were coming and then, maybe, they talked to him. I don't know how they did it. . . . So, we saw them at the airport, and we were like, "Dad, look! They're speaking Swahili." And he was like, "Yeah, I can hear them." We were all very excited, and we knew we were going to be okay when we saw them at the airport.

Though these moments of reunion are rare, they can momentarily relieve the alienating and displacing effects of resettlement.

DISRUPTING PARENTHOOD

In addition to navigating family separations, the displacing effects of resettlement are intensified for parents and caregivers. The responsibilities of parenting create particular challenges during early resettlement while the stressors associated with resettlement in turn affect caregiving. In concrete ways, parents may not be able to find the formula that their baby is accustomed to or diapers in the correct size. In more abstract ways, the uncertainties of resettlement may affect the social, emotional, and economic support that parents can provide to their children during this time of upheaval. A mental health provider in Boise elaborated on the relationship between trauma and caregiving. She explained, "I think one thing that we see a lot is that it's really difficult to parent when you have a really, really extensive trauma history and are dealing with active symptoms of PTSD. . . . So I think that's something that so many parents are trying to be a parent in the best way they can." Parenting and mothering in a resettlement context is challenging given the uncertainty, trauma, and absence of extended care networks associated with forced migration and resettlement.[25] Even before arriving in their resettlement destination, parents have managed and absorbed so much insecurity and stress in the processing and predeparture phases. Amara recognized that her parents had "normalized an otherwise abnormal situation for us kids." One consequence of displaced families is the increased strain on parents when they arrive in the US with no additional familial support. Refugees deal with all the challenges that come with parenting but do so in an exceptionally difficult context.

For parents of infants, the dislocation of early resettlement can make the material demands of caring for babies feel overwhelming as they try to procure essentials all while dealing with the myriad other complications of early resettlement, including long appointments and settling into new accommodations. Grace's baby was eight months old when her family was resettled to New England in the early 2000s. By the time their flight landed, she felt nauseous, having spent most of the trip from Kenya to the US rocking her baby in airplane aisles or mixing bottles of formula. She recalled how meeting her child's basic needs felt impossible in those early days. Getting formula and diapers required navigating an unfamiliar and confusing bus system, only to arrive at the store and face shelves of unfamiliar brands. She explained that "it was such a discombobulating [experience]. . . . I needed diapers. I needed wipes. I needed formula. [I] couldn't figure out the formula." Her husband would venture to the store while Grace stayed home with the baby, but without a cell phone, he could not consult her when he did not recognize any of the available options. The daily challenges of adapting to a new environment are thus amplified when caring for children. Though refugees with young children are eligible for the WIC program to supplement their children's nutritional needs, enrollment takes time, and parents need resources as soon as they step off of the airplane.

In the early weeks of resettlement, Resettlement Agencies typically provide diapers to families with young children. However, the availability and range of sizes depend on donations. When Joseph and Nina arrived in San Diego, their toddler was still in diapers, yet the Resettlement Agency's stock was limited to infant sizes. Nina and Joseph had a particularly tight budget shortly after arrival due to high housing costs that tied up most of their R&P funds. When they inevitably ran out of the supply of diapers they had brought with them less than two weeks after their arrival, Nina had to fashion a homemade diaper for her child in order to make it through a long day of appointments. The family had already used up their pocket money, and their caseworker was reserving the remainder of their funds to cover their second month of rent. Their caseworker was frustrated that the Resettlement Agency had not put more effort into securing diapers in a range of sizes. He needed to ensure that they could pay their rent, so he recommended potty training as the solution.

Before parents have been oriented to public services and transportation in their resettlement destination, they must rely on the responsiveness of others when a child gets sick. Learning how to navigate the US medical system takes time, and families may not yet have had their first postarrival medical appointment before a child falls ill, leaving them unsure of how and where to access proper care. When I joined the housing orientation for a Congolese single mother of three the morning after her family had moved into their new apartment and less than a week after their arrival in Boise, the mother shared at the end of the orientation that her baby had had a fever all morning and needed help. Simply getting her baby to a doctor was a multistep process: I called her caseworker who then informed the medical caseworker who arranged for the baby to see a doctor later that day. Grace remembered how uneasy this system of securing appointments made her feel when she was faced with the urgency of a sick baby: "In many hospitals in Kenya you don't schedule an appointment with the doctor, you just show up. So this whole thing of my baby's sick now but you'll see her next week didn't quite make sense."

Regardless of prior use of and level of comfort with out-of-home childcare, parents must often rely on daycare providers for their young children in order to comply with the workfare requirements of both resettlement support and public assistance. Even before refugees begin working, resettlement-specific and general public assistance programs require that all adults of working age participate in job readiness activities and English classes. Consequently, parents of children under five years old are obliged to begin using daycare providers, particularly in the absence of extended kin networks. While there was an exemption for one parent, typically the mother, when a child was under one year old, financial necessity often require employment anyway, especially for single parents. Though public assistance programs in both San Diego and Boise help to cover the cost of daycare for low-income families, entrusting an infant or young child to an unfamiliar system of care in a new country can be distressing. Both cities had numerous at-home daycare providers from refugee backgrounds or who spoke the same home language, which helped alleviate some anxiety, though it was not always possible to find a provider with an opening who could offer the comforts of a shared culture or language. For example, at the time of my fieldwork, there were no Rohingya daycare providers in Boise even though there was a small community of families from this minority group.

In order for a Ukrainian family in Boise to continue receiving financial assistance, the mother had to begin attending required classes and could no longer stay at home full-time to care for her youngest child. The mother protested against this requirement, arguing that her child was "too sweet and kind" to be cared for outside of the home. The Resettlement Agency was having trouble finding a Ukrainian-speaking provider to ease the transition. If this family wanted to receive their remaining cash aid, keeping the child at home full time was not an option. Despite what parents may believe is best for their children, the resettlement program imposes caregiving arrangements.

As an alternative to long days with childcare providers, Resettlement Agencies counsel two-parent households with young children that an effective employment schedule may be for one parent to work a day shift while the other works a night shift. While this strategy may function on paper, it creates significant strains on parents and their children. Such was the case for a Congolese family in San Diego with three young children. The father worked weeknights from 5 to 10 p.m., commuting ninety minutes to his janitorial job only seven miles away. The mother worked full-time as a hotel housekeeper, with weekday and weekend shifts, managing a similarly prolonged commute due to their reliance on public transportation. When their youngest child was baptized during a Sunday service at their community church, the mother was notably absent during the ceremony as she worked her regular weekend shift.

The early days and weeks of resettlement can also be trying for expectant mothers. A young Congolese woman was very early in her pregnancy when she was resettled to Boise with her husband and young child. She suffered from bouts of morning sickness as she sat through long meetings in unfamiliar offices, excusing herself when the nausea became too much. The intense schedule of appointments and paperwork during a refugee's first few days in the US does not allow for predictable moments of rest and recuperation. As I drove this family home from a meeting at the Resettlement Agency one week after their arrival, I had to pull over a couple minutes into the drive when the mother began vomiting into a plastic grocery bag. The physical symptoms that commonly accompany early pregnancy made this woman's resettlement experience all the more draining.

Moreover, the prospect of giving birth in an unfamiliar medical system can feel unsettling, particularly given language barriers. A Boise hospital tried to address this issue with interpreted tours for pregnant refugees so that they could gain familiarity with the surroundings prior to labor and delivery. But when advice standard within a US context is foreign, it may instill new fears at an especially vulnerable moment. When an Afghan mother was in the hospital delivering her sixth child a few months after her arrival in San Diego, she and her husband were given the standard warning not to let anyone but a nurse take their baby out of the room, creating sudden fears that someone was going to kidnap their newborn.

Before children are enrolled in school, parents must simultaneously care for and keep young children occupied while gaining their bearings in a new country as they jump on the "conveyor belt of services." Children have to tag along for full days of back-to-back appointments, sitting in waiting rooms and small offices while their parents attend to paperwork and program enrollments. Grace was unprepared for how jetlagged she would feel at the beginning. She said, "Nobody talked about jetlag. . . . There was a jetlag to where all of a sudden you're sleepy and you need to sleep right now, but you have an eight-month-old. So that's not going to happen. So I developed this headache." Four days after Bonheur's family of four arrived in San Diego, he told me, "Time goes too slowly here." They were all still adjusting to the eleven-hour time difference between Kampala and San Diego. Exhausted by the end of the afternoon, they would all fall asleep and find themselves wide awake in the early hours of the morning. Bonheur was overwhelmed by the prospect of keeping his young children entertained in their one-bedroom apartment for two weeks before they could start school, especially given the noise complaints they had already received from their neighbors. Similarly, an Afghan father worried about the noise complaints from his downstairs neighbors. He did not know how to avoid the disturbance when his five jetlagged children woke early and began playing in their two-bedroom apartment. Given the location of their housing, there was nowhere to take them when his neighbors complained.

When children begin school and parents are still familiarizing themselves with their new surroundings, they may take time-consuming precautions to safeguard their children. Idil's mother went to great lengths as a single parent to ensure her young children's security. Every morning, Idil and her mother would walk the three youngest children to their elementary school, and then the mother would accompany Idil to her middle school, nearly a mile away before returning home. In the afternoons, Idil's mother would repeat the process, walking to both schools to get her children at the end of the day. Idil remembered that "she wouldn't allow us to walk by ourselves. I think she was kind of scared. She didn't know the environment. She wasn't really aware of what was going on. So she didn't feel safe until she walked us to school and walked us back."

As has long been the case for immigrant youth, children become more quickly rooted and acculturated in the US through school, peer groups, and the media.[26] In the wake of resettlement, parents may struggle with these changes, as they never aspired for their children to grow up in the US; instead, a series of circumstances had brought their families here. Among the many losses caused by forced migration is the inability for parents to raise their children ensconced in the culture and community of their own upbringing. As their children settle and adapt to life in a new country, parents may feel like they lack fluency in the culture that their children navigate with greater ease. Toussaint explained that resettlement was never the desired outcome for his family; it was simply the least bad option. Within the context of their forced migration, returning to the DRC was impossible due to continued violence and remaining in Tanzania with refugee status meant a life without freedom. As a parent, he mourned the fact that his children were changing in a new country that was so far from the one he left behind. Toussaint said, "It's hurtful to us. It's painful to us. . . . We practice American culture, but we cannot practice it in full. And now we are losing our country." Witnessing this cultural loss among his children deepened the wounds of having involuntarily lost his homeland. As with many immigrants, refugee parents worry about what happens when the pull of American culture becomes stronger than their traditions and authority.

In addition to the linguistic and cultural barriers that reshape the relationship between parents and their children, parents feel stripped of authority when they are cautioned soon after arrival that certain types of discipline are illegal in the US. Central to this warning are US laws concerning child abuse. In a Cultural Orientation class in Boise, the instructor informed a group of newly arrived refugees, "If it's bad enough, children can be taken away and you can go to jail. You need to learn new ways to discipline your children, other ways to teach them right and wrong. Have discussions with your children. You are all learning together and need to respect each other differently." These messages equate using the "wrong" type of punishment with incarceration or the loss of one's children. Regardless of how refugees are used to disciplining their children, such warnings instill fear among parents. More effort goes into telling parents what not to do than informing them of what is acceptable. Moreover, such admonishments rely on the implicit assumption that all refugee families necessarily use physical discipline. At a meeting of community leaders in Boise, a Congolese pastor voiced his frustration with these generalizations. He said, "People think if you're from Africa, it's 100 percent physical violence. Not all families in Africa do this."

Another Congolese community leader in Boise noted the outrageousness of suspecting that refugee parents would mistreat or harm their children considering everything they had gone through in order to get their family safely to the US. He shared an example of one Congolese family whose children were removed from their home and placed into foster care following reports of abuse. "These parents escape with their children as bullets are flying. They don't throw their kids away then. Then they come here and have their children taken away." Warnings from Resettlement Agencies and cautionary tales within communities about consequential and unfamiliar laws can make refugees apprehensive about how to parent without risking the integrity of their family.

These messages about discipline get reinforced with youth at school and through peers, and the threat of reporting child abuse can become weaponized against parents. Parents worry that their children may report them if they are too strict, and so they back down when conflicts arise. At a community meeting in Boise on issues facing refugee youth, a young Iraqi man shared how his uncle spent two days in prison after his cousin called 911 in the heat of a minor dispute. He said, "She had been told in school that she had authority." In order to avoid confrontations or breaking the law, some parents take a step back as their children exploit this newfound control. A member of the Boise Police Department was aware of how parents with limited English proficiency assume that "if the police showed up, they would only listen to their children anyway."

Grace echoed how this threat of child protective services looms over refugee parents. She said, "Our kids go to school and they're told, 'If your mom spanks you, you need to call 911.' We live in fear of 911 because you're told, 'Don't spank your kids.' We're told the don'ts, but we're not told the dos." While parents internalize early on that they cannot use physical punishments, they are not simultaneously provided with what the acceptable alternatives are, creating a vacuum of parental authority that some youth will abuse. During a casework meeting in Boise, the staff recognized how much resettlement complicates parenting. One caseworker noted, "From the minute they get here we take away the parental power. They've been parenting one way their whole lives, and then, boom!"

Grace noted how difficult parenting became amid all of the other challenges that come with resettlement. She said, "I'm busy trying to make sure we have a roof over our heads, food in the fridge, clothes that you have to keep buying. . . . So in the midst of that you have kids who are getting on social media. You probably don't even know what social media is and your kids are on social media. And you just feel so unprepared to be a parent in this culture." With so much focus on helping parents avoid a catastrophic error, they are not equally supported with strategies for success. When it came to light in Boise that some elementary school students from refugee backgrounds were using school computers to watch pornography, it served as an example of the vast technological gaps that can quickly develop. Parents in the refugee community were shocked by what these young children had become adept at searching for. As a result, a community partner who worked with refugee youth noted that young people are "navigating a pretty nasty world on social media with no guide."

Advice that effective parenting is achieved by simply spending more quality time with children falls flat for refugee parents whose energy is exhausted by their family's survival in a new country. Hafiz worked as a family liaison in local schools and pointed out that refugee parents are provided unrealistic advice given the realities of low-wage employment. He told me how during a district meeting, a parenting specialist espoused the merits of deeper parental involvement. Hafiz noted how given the schedules of his six children, they seldom had time to connect during the week, and on weekends, he drove for Uber to supplement his family's income. He noted the hypocrisy of telling low-income families to make more time for their children when their time was spent fulfilling strict welfare requirements to make ends meet. The economic demands of resettlement combined with workfare requirements sap parents' time and energy, further complicating the task of parenting. A service provider who worked with refugee families in the Boise School District noted how "things start to make sense when you get to know the parents, their work schedules, their struggles."

DISRUPTING HOME

Housing is foundational to ensuring that resettlement provides refugees with stability and security in their new communities. Regardless of the type of housing refugees are accustomed to or had to endure in countries of asylum, the transition to a new home takes time, particularly when it is not of their choosing. A housing caseworker in Boise knew that it was impossible to predict which clients would struggle and which would settle in with ease. When two single mothers arrived in Boise around the same time—one Congolese woman from a refugee camp whose case had been flagged due to significant trauma and one Iraqi woman from an urban area—this housing caseworker's assumptions about who would need more intensive support were quickly proven wrong. Much to her surprise, the Iraqi mother needed significantly more handholding as she settled in, while the Congolese mother took to her new surrounds seamlessly. As this contrast in adjustment played out, this housing caseworker noted how frequently she had to adjust her expectations about how clients would fare.

Securing housing is one of the fundamental tasks carried out by Resettlement Agency casework staff, as so many other dimensions of initial resettlement rely on a permanent address, such as school enrollment and job placements. For one caseworker in San Diego, concerns about finding housing for arriving cases was the stress that he brought home with him in the evenings. Despite his confidence about carrying out other aspects of his job, securing apartments involved so many variables outside of his control. Given the financial limitations of R&P funds, caseworkers typically seek out the least expensive apartment that still meets federal regulations for "safe, decent, and sanitary" housing and is within legal occupancy limits given the case's size. Other factors such as proximity to the Resettlement Agency and public transportation as well as the willingness of landlords to rent to newly arrived refugee tenants shape housing placements. Caseworkers noted that some landlords would rely on legal means to discriminate against newly arrived refugees, requiring proof of income at three times the monthly rent or not accepting third-party checks for rent, including those furnished by the Resettlement Agency.

Occupancy guidelines and the cost of housing differed between San Diego and Boise, shaping accommodations in each city. Landlords in San Diego typically followed a "two plus two" policy, meaning two people could sleep per bedroom and an additional two people could sleep in the living room. In real terms, these regulations meant that in San

Diego, a one-bedroom apartment could house up to four people, while a two-bedroom apartment could house up to six people. Any cases of seven or over needed three or more bedrooms. Boise had lower occupancy limits—set at "two plus one" (two per bedroom plus one in the living room)—though some landlords preferred to keep occupancy down to only two per bedroom. Given financial limitations that stem from high rental prices in San Diego, families are generally housed at maximum occupancy. In San Diego, a family of four was typically placed in a one-bedroom apartment, while in Boise, a family of four would have two bedrooms. Consequently, refugees arrive in housing that is both cramped and rudimentary. Amara remembered that her family's first apartment in Boise "had no personality at all, and it was just the tools that you needed" to live. Not only must caseworkers find housing that does not exceed a case's available R&P funds, but they also must ensure that their clients can afford their monthly rent once their financial assistance ends and they are employed in low-wage jobs. Casework staff must simultaneously satisfy federal and local housing regulations while also ensuring that rent remains affordable. A former employment specialist in Boise noted that not doing so "is setting them up for failure."

In the best-case scenario, a caseworker will have secured an apartment shortly before a case's arrival, and caseworkers go to great lengths to make this happen. In the worst-case scenario, it can take weeks or even months to locate housing that meets the case's size and budgetary requirements. For different reasons, large families and single cases are particularly challenging. As a former employment specialist in Boise asked, "What do you do with a family of eight and ten in such a tight housing market, and with such limited financial resources?" For families of nine or more members, it may not be possible to find an apartment within occupancy requirements; at times two adjacent units in the same complex might be necessary—but this was rare to find. Even so, complications arise if the family redistributes themselves across the units in ways that do not correspond to the lease. Because single cases cannot afford a studio or one-bedroom apartment on their own, Resettlement Agencies must seek out and negotiate roommate arrangements, which take time. With each newly assigned case, casework staff must put together pieces of a puzzle that seldom fit. When there are delays in finding housing, new arrivals are placed in temporary accommodations, such as hotels, which are both costly and disorienting.

Though the quality of housing that I saw throughout my fieldwork consistently met the basic "safe, decent, and sanitary" guidelines, caseworkers knew that apartments were suboptimal. A caseworker in San Diego felt like the living conditions in the complexes where the Resettlement Agency typically placed clients was "really bad." He continued, "They go in these places where there is like rats, roaches, dirty apartments. I mean, they're livable," but, he added, "it makes them really sad, really depressed." Better apartments within the same budget existed, but they were too far from the services, organizations, and public transportation upon which new arrivals must rely. Particularly in cities like Boise with limited public transportation, housing options are constrained by sparse bus routes.

A staff member in Boise remembered how shocked she was when, shortly after she began working at the Resettlement Agency, she visited an apartment complex that housed numerous refugee tenants. "I also remember being appalled. . . . I remember being like, I can't believe we are okay with conditions like this in Boise. I didn't even know it existed. . . . I had such a hard time because I could not believe that they would let people live in those conditions." This apartment complex was particularly inexpensive, and financial constraints at times necessitated inadequate housing. A journalist in San Diego who covered local stories on resettlement noticed that "housing quality is the first to be sacrificed when it comes to affordability."

Poor quality housing can become hazardous for families with young children. When Nina, Joseph, and their four young children moved into their second-story two-bedroom apartment on the night of their arrival, it became evident that the property management company had not completed all of the preparations after the previous tenants moved out. The window in the bedroom shared by two of their children had no screens, sharp nails could be felt through the carpeting in the living room, and bugs were visible in the kitchen. Despite the caseworker nudging the property manager on several occasions, it took two months before the repairs were addressed. Grace remembered how unsafe their apartment was for her eight-month-old daughter when they were first resettled in New England. "Don't even get me started about the apartment. Somebody moved out in the morning, and they put us back there in the evening. It hadn't been cleaned, hadn't been vacuumed, nothing was done. So I remember, you know, obviously you're looking at the carpet. My daughter was eight months old, so she was crawling, and I'm seeing pins and I'm seeing needles and I'm seeing things that she can pick up and put in her mouth."

Ultimately families were housed in arrangements that many people would be uncomfortable moving into, especially considering family size. Though crowded apartments were particularly prevalent in San Diego, discontent over housing size was also common in Boise. Moreover, important details about a case may only emerge once a family arrives, after the caseworker has secured their housing. For example, the caseworker for Bonheur's family of four arranged for them to live in a one-bedroom apartment and set up two adjacent double beds in the bedroom, one for the parents and one for the two young children. Only after the family landed did the caseworker learn that Esperance was several months pregnant, which would soon make them a family of five in this small apartment. Similarly, a casework staff member in Boise spent months trying to find housing for a Congolese family of seven, eventually securing them a three-bedroom apartment. News of the wife's pregnancy shortly after their move-in created renewed stress for the Resettlement Agency staff, as this baby would put the family over the legal occupancy limit for their home.

Throughout this process, clients are seldom given choice in determining where they will live. Casework staff in both San Diego and Boise recounted to me how earlier attempts to let clients view and select apartments were unsustainable. A housing caseworker in Boise joked that doing so had made her "a real estate agent for refugees." But housing decisions made by Resettlement Agencies matter, as families often find themselves in these initial apartments long term. When living paycheck to paycheck, it is difficult to accrue enough savings to afford the security deposit needed for a better and larger apartment. Landlords may also require proof of income that exceeds the monthly rent, an impossibility when refugees are barely making ends meet.

As a result of several concurrent factors in 2016 and 2017 in San Diego, such as rising housing costs and a dramatic increase in the city's refugee arrivals, including many large families, caseworkers were put in a position in which they had to stretch the rules to make housing work. As large families of nine or more arrived, it was virtually impossible to secure apartments in City Heights or El Cajon that could accommodate the family's size without exceeding their budget. Consequently, caseworkers were compelled to devise strategies amid the significant constraints presented to them. They were under extreme pressure to move clients who had already spent weeks in hotels into permanent housing, while knowing that more cases were on their way. Some caseworkers came to agreements with landlords or property managers to exceed standard occupancy limits. In such instances, signed lease agreements omitted the names of young children, producing a "papereality" that gave the appearance of following regulations.[27]

Ultimately, this practice of knowingly excluding tenants' names from the official lease caught up with the Resettlement Agency when a local news agency exposed the practice and characterized it as neglectful casework rather than crisis management. The San Diego caseworkers felt attacked and blamed for something that seemed uncontroversial given the variables that shaped housing in San Diego. This public revelation resulted in negative attention and scrutiny, hitting the San Diego Resettlement Agency in its Achilles heel. Following significant intervention and review by the Resettlement Agency's national office and the federal government, which one caseworker said felt like an FBI investigation, new paperwork requirements were uniformly put into place in Resettlement Agencies across the country. From that point on, all tenants' names were required on lease agreements, and caseworkers had to provide written justifications in case files for why a particular apartment was selected, as if there were actually enough supply to allow caseworkers to choose from among multiple available units. When I began my fieldwork in Boise, the casework staff lamented the added burden of paperwork that this incident in San Diego had created for them. One housing specialist in Boise complained about "paying the consequences" for the issues that had unfolded in San Diego. Not only was the San Diego Resettlement Agency reprimanded, but all Resettlement Agencies were penalized with additional paperwork requirements. Moreover, the root cause of the problem was not addressed, making the task of finding suitable apartments even harder. The only tool available to the San Diego Resettlement Agency was the refusal of large cases, which would instead get routed to cities with more affordable housing like Boise.

In Boise, it often took longer for casework staff to find suitable apartments, resulting in long hotel stays that caused the Resettlement Agency to overspend significantly beyond their clients' allotted R&P funds. In one year, the Boise Resettlement Agency spent over $30,000 on hotel stays for new arrivals. In light of this persistent challenge, a local affordable housing organization worked in conjunction with Resettlement Agencies to create a stop-gap solution called Welcome Housing. What began with local residents renting out their accessory dwelling units (ADUs) to newly arrived families at an affordable rate while they awaited permanent housing transformed into the purchase of three two-bedroom, one-and-a-half-bathroom condo units near the Resettlement Agency, which could each sleep up to nine people. These condos offered temporary housing at much lower rates and were more comfortable than lengthy hotel stays. Additionally, the organization's staff was well versed in resettlement and offered their own housing orientation to new arrivals to ensure their comfort and safety, remaining on call should needs arise during their stay. The model was financially sustainable because the units were rented out as Airbnbs when they were not needed by the Resettlement Agencies. This local solution helped to alleviate some of the disorienting challenges that come with temporary housing. Other programs, such as grants from Airbnb to cover the cost of short-term rentals, also worked to ease difficulties in the Boise rental market. Temporary options, however, come with their own complications, such as delaying the process of settling into a permanent home. Additionally, Airbnb units were spread throughout the city and public transportation was not always accessible.

Affordable housing for low-income families can address many of the challenges that newly arrived refugees face. For the few families I met in San Diego and Boise who had successfully made it off the years-long waiting list for Section 8 housing, vouchers allowed them to live more securely. The Boise Resettlement Agency managed to secure a low-income apartment for a single Ukrainian mother and her child at $348 per month, but this was considered a miracle. In San Diego, the wait for affordable housing can take ten years. A property manager in San Diego joked that the quickest way to get Section 8 housing was to move to Nebraska, where residents could get off the waitlist in only six months—at which point the family could bring their voucher back to San Diego.

In the absence of affordable housing, refugee families, like other low-income families, risk becoming unhoused, particularly when they no longer qualify for resettlement assistance. Resettlement Agencies do their best to support extended clients, but they do not have the dedicated staff time or the resources to do so on a regular basis. During my fieldwork in Boise, the Resettlement Agency scrambled to support three families who were about to lose their housing, including one large family whose apartment building was scheduled for demolition. Alternatively, community members will take in people who have been evicted or can no longer afford their rent, resulting in hidden homelessness within refugee communities. A former caseworker and employment specialist in Boise whose family also arrived through the USRAP explained, "They live with relatives so that way they can help each other. And you find cases where there's like ten people in a house, and sometimes it's not legal, but they can't do anything else."

In both San Diego and Boise, caseworkers worked tirelessly to cultivate and maintain a rapport with the finite number of property management companies and landlords who were accommodating to the financial and logistical constraints of early resettlement. Consequently, new arrivals are often housed within the same apartment complexes. Though it may seem beneficial to house new arrivals in the same apartment complexes, the tensions associated with refugee-producing conflicts can spillover from the home country into the resettlement context. When refugees arrive in the US, the conflicts that were at the root of their forced migration may be displaced with them. Regardless of whether fears in the resettlement destination are perceived or real, they impede the feelings of safety and security that are supposedly afforded by resettlement. An Afghan man in San Diego explained to me that the Afghan community does not speak across ethnic lines, even when living in the same buildings. Similarly, there were several instances throughout my fieldwork in which Congolese arrivals expressed concerned about how the ethnic divisions that had propelled war in the DRC might transfer to their new communities. War can create refugees from opposing sides of a conflict, and resettlement does not erase histories of violence between the groups. Because the USRAP categorizes all refugees from the DRC as Congolese, official records obscure the complicated histories and diverse ethnic groups that make up this refugee population.

Resettlement Agency staff who were not Congolese were often ignorant of these dynamics and risked putting newly arrived refugees in situations that felt compromising. A Congolese community leader in San Diego remarked, "That's where culture and issues come. . . . [The Resettlement Agencies] just consider them refugees." He explained how two newly arrived Congolese families who had been housed in neighboring units in San Diego could not greet each other as a result of lingering hostilities from war. He added, "These conflicts go on and on and on and on." A Congolese community leader in Boise explained that "people came divided by [a] history of social rifts, political turmoil back home, the trauma. . . . They were here living in a similar apartment complex, but they cannot even talk to one another." For example, whenever Nina and Joseph's caseworker encouraged them to connect with the Congolese community in San Diego, Nina was quick to show her disinterest, responding that they did not need the Congolese community; the Resettlement Agency was their family now. She also specified that she wanted to find a daycare provider for her youngest child who was not Congolese.

In several instances, these fears and apprehensions surfaced through housing placements. A Congolese single mother in Boise was uneasy about moving into a particular apartment complex that housed many other refugee residents. While this family was in their country of asylum, the woman's husband was killed after neighbors informed on him, which had generated in her a general mistrust of other refugees. Another newly arrived Congolese family in Boise was apprehensive when they learned where they would be moving. This family belonged to an ethnic group that had suffered a particularly brutal massacre at the hands of other Congolese, and they felt unsafe at the prospect of having Congolese neighbors. Yet in spite of their reluctance, both families ended up moving into these apartment complexes. After the second family objected, they were presented with a coercive proposal: They could either move into the complex where they felt unsafe or lose the $400 deposit that the Resettlement Agency had already put on the apartment. The Resettlement Agency staff needed to get this family housed and wanted them to sign the lease, regardless of their concerns. As social work scholar Yeheskel Hasenfeld writes, "[W]orkers use their power resources to influence the behavior of their clients, and these power resources therefore become the major tools in shaping the helping process."[28] Though refugees' apprehensions tend to dissipate with time, clients' fears are secondary to the caseworkers' need to secure housing. While refugees may eventually feel safe in their home, it is not without first enduring increased anxieties about their family's security.

DISPLACING FAMILY, DISRUPTING HOME

When refugees exit the airport arrivals terminal at their resettlement destination, the meaningful changes that their families have undergone may not be apparent. This chapter shows how family and the stability of home are central to refugees' well-being. The complexities of forced migration along with narrow definitions for how US law defines a family can create painful separations that may be difficult to remedy. Some refugees arrive having made the seemingly impossible choice of leaving behind loved ones so as not to lose the rare chance at resettlement. As refugees undergo the many challenges of early resettlement, they may also be contending with difficulties at home or with family who have been separated by borders. Resettlement uproots and restructures key dimensions of refugees' familial lives.

Newly arrived refugees are often enduring complicated and uncertain separations all while trying to build a home in a new and unfamiliar place. Temporary housing, crowded apartments, or unease with new neighbors can make it difficult to feel settled and safe. Benchmarks of incorporation such as employment and educational outcomes obscure less measurable yet deeply meaningful aspects of refugees' lives, including familial dynamics and residential security.

4

WORK

THE DAY AFTER NINA AND JOSEPH landed at the San Diego Airport with their four young children, their caseworker and I arrived at their apartment at noon for their twenty-four-hour home visit. We had left this Congolese family of six around 10:30 p.m. the previous night to settle into their new home. As we sat around the kitchen table in their sparsely furnished two-bedroom apartment, their caseworker walked them through the alarming economics of resettlement. While this family of six was allocated $6,750 in Reception & Placement (R&P) funds ($1,125 per person) from the federal government, only $580 remained after their caseworker had secured their housing, cell phone service, furniture, household goods, and some food prior to their arrival the previous evening (see table 5). Nina and Joseph had been in San Diego for a mere sixteen hours before they had to face the harsh reality of their financial situation. Their caseworker explained that this R&P funding was the budget to help them

TABLE 5
Nina and Joseph's Reception & Placement spending prior to arrival

Expense type	Expense amount
First month of rent	$1,385
Last month of rent	$1,385
Security deposit	$1,000
Monthly water fee	$100
Housing application fee ($30 per adult)	$60
One month of cell phone service and activation fee (for donated cell phone)	$40
Furniture (4 beds, futon, kitchen table and chairs)	$1,244
Household goods (linens, cookware, etc.)	$480
Groceries	$133
Hot meal upon arrival	$43
Checks for pocket money ($50 per person)	$300
Total	$6,170

resettle and was not for them to keep. These parents were concerned about how little remained. This family of six had arrived in San Diego from a refugee camp with one small suitcase, two backpacks, and no other funds or means of support. Their caseworker explained that they would soon be enrolled in public assistance programs through which they would receive about $900 per month in food stamps, about $1,100 per month in cash aid through the CALWorks Program (California's TANF program), and Medi-Cal health insurance (California's Medicaid program).

Though their status as refugees meant that they qualified for these various forms of public assistance, their level of cash aid would not be enough to cover their rent, making immediate employment a necessity. Their caseworker tried to reassure them that the Resettlement Agency would provide employment services, but they would need to take any available job. While it would not be dangerous work, it might not be ideal or near their home. With little grace period to acclimate, this family was jolted by how the USRAP propels refugees into the labor market. Less than a day after arriving in the US, they were given no choice but to obtain employment as quickly as possible. Nina voiced fears about her family's financial future. At one point during the home visit, her eyes began to well up with tears. She spoke about how hard life had been in the refugee camp and how happy she was with their apartment. She did not want her children to lose this new home. Their caseworker chose not to mention that their finances could have been worse. When he secured their apartment, he succeeded in negotiating down their rent, which had originally been set at $1,425. Despite their precarious situation, their caseworker tried to reassure them. He told Nina and Joseph that after new families arrived, he often thought to himself, "Oh my God, how are they going to be able to make it?" But he was not worried about this family. He was confident that they would do well in San Diego.

Alongside the many adjustments of resettlement, refugees confront a stark economic reality soon after landing in the US. This chapter focuses on how the disorientation of unmet expectations and fast-paced services is further compounded by the pressure of immediate employment and the stresses of financial insecurity. Though a Resettlement Agency staff member in Boise recognized the significance of R&P casework, she noted just how central employment was to the US model of resettlement. She explained, "Casework is the backbone. . . . But at the same time, everything hinges on employment." The R&P period is short, and for cases like Nina and Joseph, R&P funds may not stretch beyond initial set-up costs. While resettlement provides access to longer-term forms of refugee-specific and general assistance, cash aid levels fall short of monthly expenses by design in order to incentivize employment. A community partner in San Diego who worked with SIV families saw how this reality played out, "The job stuff is obviously a pretty big deal. . . . Nothing else really matters because there's going to be a financial struggle the whole time."

The Refugee Act of 1980 established that the objectives of resettlement are "to achieve economic self-sufficiency among refugees as quickly as possible" and "ensure that cash assistance is made available to refugees in such a manner as not to discourage their economic self-sufficiency."[1] This legislation therefore defines a successful resettlement according to the dual goals of early employment and economic self-sufficiency. These policy priorities motivate the services provided to refugees as well as the economic conditions that come to shape their lives. Prior research has identified that forced migration creates "displaced livelihoods" for refugees.[2] This chapter reveals that refugees' livelihoods continue to be displaced even after resettlement, as their vocational ambitions and hopes for financial stability are once again disrupted after arriving.

The USRAP's principal objectives of early employment and economic self-sufficiency create insecurity in distinct yet complementary ways, subjecting newly arrived refugees to harms that are consequential to their well-being. Prior studies have documented that financial instability characterizes US resettlement, yet none isolate the ways in which the goals of early employment and economic self-sufficiency contribute to the outcome of poverty.[3] This chapter untangles how and why refugees like Nina and Joseph are resettled into poverty as well as the consequences of this approach for their well-being. This chapter shows how the necessity of early employment steers refugees into low wage occupations, while the objective of economic self-sufficiency uses poverty-level income as its benchmark of success. This economic precarity trickles down within families to youth, at times disrupting their educational and career ambitions. Though refugees do immediately receive forms of assistance unavailable to most other groups of migrants, these benefits come with strict terms and conditions that shape refugees' incorporation in important ways.

Though new arrivals in both San Diego and Boise faced financial insecurity, when and why they arrived at this outcome was influenced by local factors.

EARLY EMPLOYMENT

One way that welfare state policies can shape the relationship between society and the economy is when relief programs allow for decommodification such that an individual's well-being is not dependent on active participation in the labor market. In these cases, the state recognizes a standard level of economic rights disassociated from employment.[4] Decommodification is curtailed in liberal welfare regimes through means tested benefits and workplace contributions, tying support to employment rather than making it a right.[5] While scholars typically study decommodification by examining what happens when people transition out of the labor market and into social welfare programs, the case of the USRAP inverts this process. Refugees begin with public assistance and are quickly transitioned off it and into the labor market. Intended to prevent welfare dependency, specialized workfare programs for refugees and ubiquitous narratives of self-sufficiency encourage immediate entry into employment at the expense of language learning and strengthening transferable skills.[6] While refugees do have access to a variety of social services upon arrival, these assistance programs are motivated by the goal of labor-market incorporation. The USRAP takes refugees through a process of *commodification*, in which their well-being is contingent on employment. Newly arrived refugees are pushed into the labor market and quickly weaned off social service support, discouraging the use of federal and state support early on.

From the moment refugees arrive in the US, resettlement services are predicated on early employment, which shapes the nature of refugees' interactions with their Resettlement Agency and other service providers. Many refugees are unprepared for the fact that the USRAP sets them up for this process of commodification, as they are quickly pushed off time-limited welfare programs into employment. The financial conditions that greet refugees upon arrival can be jarring. After learning about the limitations of his and his wife's resettlement assistance, Haidar, an Iraqi man in Boise, became preoccupied about what would happen should he fail to quickly become employed. Thinking back to his arrival five years earlier, he said, "This was horrible because I was afraid if this three month[s] will finish, [the Resettlement Agency] cannot help me. . . . I have to find a job and that time, it was really hard for me because I was thinking if I don't have job, what I have to do, how I'll pay the rent because this will be a responsibility." With the help of the Resettlement Agency's employment services, Haidar secured a janitorial position four months after his arrival in Boise.

An employment specialist in Boise explained just how unaware refugees may be of the financial realities of US resettlement. He said,

> There are these expectations that arise when a refugee arrives to the United States, where they assume they're going to have a house that is ready for them, they're going to have a car, they're going to have some sort of a stable life. And then when they don't have that it's a huge shock, when they realize how much of cultural shift that it is, and how the economic conditions here are so fast paced, and propel people to constantly work, work, work. It's something that takes time for them to actually understand and realize that yes that I am in a safer place, and I am in a place where I can be free, but they also start realizing what the cost of those freedoms are.

Because the R&P funds allocated to each refugee may not stretch much further than initial set-up costs, immediate employment becomes imperative for refugees to meet their basic expenses.

The pressure to begin employment commodifies refugees into a particular segment of the labor market. Refugee-specific and general cash aid programs, with the exception of SSI, are time-limited workfare programs that require the active pursuit of employment. Additionally, because cash aid alone is rarely enough to cover expenses, the priority of Resettlement Agencies is to get their clients a source of income as quickly as possible. They are typically directed towards entry-level occupations, such as hotel housekeeping, janitorial work, dishwashing, or factory work. Even if these jobs are poorly remunerated or offer few opportunities for upward mobility, Resettlement Agency staff become confined to this approach, as it is the best way to ensure that their clients gain some income before the ticking clock of formal resettlement services ends. Didier, who arrived in Boise as an ambitious twenty-two-year-old, joked that Resettlement Agency employment specialists "think all of us have qualifications to become a janitor." He continued, "When you first get here, the first job they give you is a janitor, and then you have to find your way out. So, it's tough." Though Didier was initially placed in this occupation at a hotel, he did manage to get out. Six years later, he was completing his bachelor's degree in engineering at a four-year university.

In addition to being quickly obtained, entry-level jobs were also accessible to refugees who arrived with limited English proficiency and minimal formal education. A former employment specialist in Boise shared that, practically speaking, job placement options were narrow for these new arrivals. He said,

It's really hard to hire somebody that doesn't speak English. . . . It was difficult finding places where people had to work without talking. . . . So, a lot of restaurants, housekeeping. . . . Some of the clients were even illiterate. They can't read or write. So, it's kind of hard to find a job for somebody that can't speak English, that can't read, or that can't write.

Refugees typically begin English classes soon after arrival, though it can be challenging or impossible to continue attending once employed. The USRAP is based on the presumption that language learning and cultural integration will take place on the job.[7] But since refugees are hired in positions that do not require English proficiency, it is difficult to imagine how employment might provide meaningful opportunities for language learning. When I asked Ma Htet if her parents had the chance to learn English in the seven years since their resettlement to San Diego, she replied bluntly, "No, they don't. They work."

Consequently, refugees are typically directed towards minimum wage, manual labor jobs where they earn salaries at or below the poverty line. A former employment specialist in Boise explained how difficult it was to break the news to refugees who arrived thinking they would be taken care of only to inform them that they were actually being "resettled into poverty." Another former employment specialist in Boise recognized the weight of these early employment decisions, as they carried lasting consequences. She said, "I think it is unfair that [we] send people here to live in poverty and stay in poverty because we know that poverty in this country is systemic and it's cyclical and it's really hard to climb out of." Despite the much-needed income that these types of jobs offered, they also came with a loss of agency, as new arrivals felt like they had no hand in shaping their trajectories.

Not only are entry level jobs more easily obtained for refugees with limited English proficiency and varying degrees of formal education, Resettlement Agency employment specialists develop relationships with certain employers over time, creating a reliable pipeline for future job placement. These jobs are paid at or slightly above minimum wage, which at the time of fieldwork was $7.25 per hour in Boise and $11.50 per hour in San Diego. While a meat packing plant just outside of Boise provided a more lucrative option at $12 per hour plus overtime, it was not without risks. The work was physically demanding and dangerous. A former client lost use of one of his arms when he was injured by a machine that had not been turned off properly. An employment specialist explained how they only make referrals to this factory after they "talk to the client about what it will do to their body."

Even if the work is not dangerous, refugees may still be placed in jobs for which they are physically unfit. Like many new arrivals, a young Burundian mother in Boise was first place in housekeeping work which quickly took a toll on her body. Her husband told me, "She never had [in her] life [done] hard labor. . . . Honestly after one month she wasn't able to walk. She couldn't even carry the baby anymore." Such manual labor jobs are even more problematic for refugees with chronic health conditions or disabilities that are not severe enough to exempt them from employment. A former employment specialist in Boise explained how alternatives did not exist for less able-bodied refugees. She said,

> When you don't have a lot of formal education, you don't speak the language, you don't understand the culture, you have a lot of trauma affect your mental health, and then on top of it you have physical health issues, where you can't walk, . . . you can't lift a lot, your back is just messed up from everything you've gone through. . . . There was close to no options for them. So some of them just had to push through.

Some of her clients ended up in dry cleaning jobs that were a poor match for their health. She noted how the quick pace, unnatural body movements, heat, and unrelenting noise of this occupation made it particularly difficult for refugees who were not in peak physical condition. Some quit and risked ending up in a homeless shelter.

Refugees over sixty-five years of age or with a disability qualify for SSI. But many health issues were not considered severe enough to qualify, and so these clients were also compelled to take on manual labor jobs. A man in his early sixties from the Central African Republic arrived in Boise with several medical issues and was awaiting news about whether he needed surgery. He was informed by a Resettlement Agency staff member that if surgery was not necessary, "we'll have to talk about employment." A medical caseworker in Boise explained that "it's a hard conversation to have" when "people who really are medically sick" do not meet the threshold for SSI. She understood the adverse consequences of employment for these clients, who are "probably going to have to be in a physically demanding job, which obviously doesn't help the medical condition." Some refugees obtained a doctor's note in hopes of being exempt from physically demanding work. Unfortunately, for refugees with limited English proficiency, other employment options rarely existed. In one instance, a Congolese woman in Boise gave her employer a doctor's note saying that she had to be placed on "light duty" for her hotel housekeeping job. Her hours and income suffered because there was not enough light work for her to do.

Another Congolese woman in Boise presented a doctor's note to her Resettlement Agency employment specialist explaining that she could not continue her hotel housekeeping job due to the pain in her legs and feet. The employment specialist was frustrated by the lack of available alternatives. As a single mother, this client needed to maintain a paycheck and the Resettlement Agency did not have jobs that were less physically demanding. This employment specialist added that clients believe these notes are a "golden ticket" to less strenuous work, but in reality, the choice was between manual labor or homelessness.

When Etienne, a single Congolese man in Boise, was reluctant to begin work given his ongoing recovery from a serious illness, the Resettlement Agency presented him with three options: begin employment to afford rent, stay as someone's houseguest to delay employment, or go to a homeless shelter. Though the Resettlement Agency staff managed to provide him with a couple of weeks of temporary accommodation through creative shuffling of client housing, he began a hotel housekeeping job soon after despite ongoing medical treatment. Such refugees live with extreme precarity given that so much hinges on their employment in manual labor jobs. A Resettlement Agency staff member in Boise explained, "If you're not well and you're not feeling well, then you're not going to be able to work; you're not going to be able to pay rent. It's just such a domino in every other factor of life in the resettlement process."

The health of the economy also shapes the labor market into which Resettlement Agency staff must place their newly arrived clients. During moments of economic downturn, employment specialists go to extreme lengths to get their clients employed, putting them in even more challenging and less sustainable work conditions. Throughout the Great Recession, it became increasingly challenging to secure jobs within the city of Boise. As the county unemployment rate reached 9.5% in January 2010, the low-wage labor market grew too competitive for new arrivals to get hired.[8] As a result, Resettlement Agencies cast a drastically wider geographic net and began busing their clients more than fifty miles away across state lines to work agricultural jobs in eastern Oregon. In order to ensure that their clients had an income, employment specialists would drive them to Oregon at dawn to work and bring them home to Boise in the evening.

Even in a strong labor market, transportation becomes an added challenge, and early employment cannot be understood outside the context of local public transportation infrastructure, an understudied yet critical component of refugees' daily lives. Refugees often end up with long commutes, either due to the distance between affordable housing and employment opportunities or due to poor public transportation systems. Newly arrived refugees do not typically have the funds, time, or experience to obtain a driver's license and car, making them reliant on public transportation, bicycles, or other people. A former employment specialist in Boise knew just how important transportation was in the equation of placing clients in their first job. He said, "The more complex it becomes for a person, the more you are setting them up for failure, so you have to reduce those barriers to employment. You have to make sure that they can get to work."

At the time of my fieldwork in Boise, most city bus lines ended service between 6 p.m. and 10 p.m., and they either did not run on Sundays or did not run at all over the weekends, creating insurmountable challenges for refugees who worked in occupations that regularly required evening and weekend shifts. The Resettlement Agency would often set clients up with bicycles, but these commutes became difficult during the winter months. Others would cobble together rides from those in the community who did own cars, but they were beholden to someone else's schedule. For example, in addition to the hotel housekeeping job she worked during the day, a Congolese single mother in Boise began working a second job in the evenings doing cleaning and maintenance work at a large building downtown. Though she could take the bus to begin her 7 p.m. shift, buses no longer ran when she finished around 11 p.m. She told me how much she suffered trying to get home at night, as she was reliant on other people for rides that would get her back at 2 a.m. or 3 a.m.. In response to this type of issue, the city of Boise began offering subsidized Lyft fares to low-income residents who otherwise relied on public transportation to get to and from work. Soon after taking on her second job, this mother began getting a ride home for a $3 flat rate as soon as she finished her shift, a significant improvement for her well-being.

Transportation posed challenges in San Diego for different reasons. Given the geographic size and spread of the city and county as well as the substantial distances between the neighborhoods where refugees lived and where they worked, commuting added significant time to the workday. A single mother of five who worked a hotel housekeeping job from 2:30 p.m. to 10 p.m. had to take multiple buses to travel approximately ten miles to her job. This journey added an hour and a half onto each end of her shift; she would leave her home at noon and return at midnight. This exhausting schedule caused reverberations that affected her whole family. Her children had to attend an after-school program and then, in the evening, be looked after by a childcare provider.

Others were placed in jobs in Carlsbad, California, a city more than forty miles north of El Cajon where new arrivals were typically housed. Amusement parks, hotels, and agricultural industries in Carlsbad reliably hired newly arrived refugees, but transportation was a major obstacle. Employment specialists would do their best to facilitate carpools with other clients who had cars, but these arrangements involved risk. After an Afghan single mother of four and her daughter were hired for full-time hotel housekeeping positions in Carlsbad, the Resettlement Agency connected them with another refugee who made the same forty-five-mile commute from El Cajon. The mother and daughter each paid him $10 per day for rides to and from work. However, when the man's car broke down several months later, this mother and daughter found themselves without a ride. The Resettlement Agency tried their best to find replacement transportation at the last minute, but nothing came through. The clients informed their supervisor of their predicament, but after not showing up to work for three days, they were both fired.

Initial employment prospects are seldom better for refugees who arrive with strong English proficiency and professional backgrounds, and prior research has shown that, despite variation in occupational background, refugees resettled in the US have comparable economic trajectories.[9] In such cases, unmet expectations about continuing one's career trajectory in the US can make resettlement feel degrading, as refugees experience deskilling though initial job placement. One Afghan man who had previously worked for a major international organization had been cautioned by a relative not to come to the US, as this relative felt like he still had nothing to show for all of his efforts a decade later. After moving forward with the resettlement process despite this warning, this Afghan man began working the overnight shift at a 7-Eleven convenience store in San Diego, earning $1,500 per month, one-third of his prior salary. With rent at $1,800 per month, this job did not even cover housing costs for his young family. The urgency of an income filters such refugees into the same low paying, easily accessible jobs, and they risk getting stuck in these occupations.

Firas knew how difficult it was for his father to go from being a successful medical doctor in Iraq to working for minimum wage in Boise. He said, "I am feeling so sorry for my dad. From a college teacher with a PhD, a doctor owning his own business, to a laundry [job]. Just imagine." A former employment specialist in Boise was aware of how disheartening this new reality was for many of her clients. She said, "I think expectations with highly skilled workers was definitely one of the most difficult devils to work through. Breaking people's hearts over and over again like that, just was so hard." Some clients may arrive with skills that go unrecognized, especially if their employment took place within a refugee camp. During the seventeen years that Raphael lived in a camp in Uganda, he spent five years working for the World Food Program and six years working for the UNHCR. As Raphael explained, "there is no more difficult job than giving more than 43,000 refugees food." When I met him in San Diego three years after his resettlement, he was still working in landscaping.

The sting of deskilling is particularly acute for those who supported the US military, often as interpreters, in Iraq and Afghanistan and arrived through the Special Immigrant Visa (SIV) program. Given that SIVs gain access to resettlement as a result of their employment with the US military, most arrive with university degrees and advanced English proficiency. What is more, their work in Iraq or Afghanistan was considered both prestigious and highly skilled. For SIVs, it can be especially challenging to reconcile the status of their prior positions with the realities of low-wage employment once in the US. Not only did they risk their own and their families' safety for the US government, but it can also feel as though the skills they demonstrated in these highly regarded and well-paid positions in their home countries all of a sudden become irrelevant in the context of the US labor market, creating a sense of betrayal and disillusionment.

One woman founded a program in Boise for highly skilled refugees after growing frustrated by this situation. She said, "How do we give people pathways out of poverty? . . . I really decided I can't come to work anymore if I meet doctors and teachers and businesspeople, and I'm like, 'Oh, okay. We got you a great job. It's so good. You're going to be washing dishes.'" It was often challenging to convince clients of the merits of entry-level work. Employment specialists emphasized the value of gaining experience with US workplace culture to give undesirable jobs more value. They also used the promise of subsequent career-development assistance to make entry-level work palatable, framing it as a temporary necessity.

"Survival jobs" were sold as the first step in rebuilding careers, even though the latter was not guaranteed. Yonas explained that rebuilding one's career in the US was easier said than done, as refugees fall into a trap of deskilling. He said,

> I have seen some people get back to their profession, but very few. . . . When they came here, they are supposed to provide, and they don't have time to go through that process [of recertification]. . . . It's time consuming and you'd rather just go to work and afford to support your family. . . . And later on in a few years you don't have the energy and the need and the courage to go back to that. There are really few that get back into career and work in their profession.

Familial obligation and programmatic expectations make quickly earning a paycheck more important than working towards reestablishing a career. Once these refugees have found their footing, a combination of inertia and exhaustion prevent them from turning back to their former professions. Despite having the backgrounds and skills for career advancement, quotidian obligations stand in the way of the lengthy process of recertification. The long hours, low wages, and time-consuming commutes associated with manual labor jobs created insurmountable obstacles for upward mobility.

A Resettlement Agency staff member in Boise recognized that aspirations of career growth often went unrealized. She said, "They assume that if they work hard enough that they can get out of that, but I don't think that's true. I mean, it happens, of course. People always beating the odds, . . . but it's not the majority. Where there's a huge portion of people who get stuck in low-medium economic standing." Barriers to upward mobility often came as a surprise. She continued, "I don't think people know that there's less mobility than they think because they've been promised the American Dream." A representative of the Boise city government recognized this reality. She noted that after new arrivals end up in their first entry-level job, "there's no clear path forward." She felt like Resettlement Agencies and other service providers in Boise succeed at delivering initial services to refugees but struggled to offer opportunities for longer-term progress and advancement. Similarly, a religious leader in San Diego observed that the same issue held back several of her congregants who had come through the USRAP, some over a decade earlier. Despite the desire for advancement, they found themselves in the same positions as when they first arrived, back when "the immediate needs [were] so pressing." As a result, she said, "you start to hear and see deeper layers of both frustration and just some structural things that prevent them from making the steps" either to "a slightly better job" or "a really better job."

Even a "slightly better job" can go a long way in creating stability and satisfaction. The mother and daughter in San Diego who had lost their hotel housekeeping job in Carlsbad when their transportation fell through were subsequently placed in jobs at an automotive manufacturer. They had since gained enough English proficiency to meet the employer's requirements. At this new job, the single mother and her daughter, as well as one of her other children, earned a more stable $13 per hour plus overtime pay for work that was less physically strenuous, only a couple of miles from their home, and allowed more opportunities to practice their English. In every respect, this new job was an improvement, which offered greater security and peace of mind.

Constantly pushing new arrivals into entry level work wore on the Resettlement Agency employment specialists tasked with meeting job placement deadlines for client after client. A former employment specialist in Boise explained, "Getting a client a job that they didn't expect they would have is really shitty. And being the person that they perceive as placing them in that situation, when you have no other choice and they have no other choice. You have nowhere else to go that you know of." Assistance programs come with contractual conditions that require refugees to take the first job opportunity available, and refusal results in the termination of cash aid. This former employment specialist knew that while her clients could technically turn down a job, doing so meant "they're choosing a crisis, and you being the face of that." Witnessing this process unfold on a regular basis "definitely, like, takes a toll on your soul. . . . When you check in a couple of weeks, and you can see them wearing housekeeping on their face and the weariness of how hard they're being pushed and the way they put their hands on their backs. And you know that you played a role in that. . . . It starts to really take a toll on you. Because you feel like you're putting them in this position. That you were a cog in that system." Though manual labor jobs were rarely avoidable, another former employment specialist in Boise drew the line at potentially hazardous work. She reasoned that if she would never do a particular job, she could not expect her clients to, even if it is the first job available.

While the majority of refugees I met in San Diego and Boise followed the typical employment trajectory into low-wage work, there were exceptional cases—people who secured professional-level employment or started their own businesses. Many first worked "survival jobs" before finding positions with more prestige. These refugees did successfully translate US-based job experience and English-language gains made in entry-level positions into an asset for upward mobility. Others underwent the long process of professional recertification, earned advanced degrees while working, or pivoted careers. Regardless of how it was achieved, upward mobility required time, dedication, and a tremendous amount of work.

Haidar earned a bachelor's degree in his native Iraq and worked in a family business before fleeing first to Syria and then to Turkey after the Syrian War began. Haidar's first job in Boise was as a janitor where he benefitted from a colleague who helped him practice English at work. Of this gesture of support he said, "I will never forget." After three months, Haidar moved up to a more favorable cleaning position. Seven months later, he was promoted to supervisor. He had since participated in one of the Resettlement Agency's career development programs and found work with a large international shipping company. Sometimes these atypical pathways resulted from being the right person at the right time. Gerard, a Burundian father, had worked as a teacher in the refugee camp where he lived for nineteen years. Though his first job in Boise was on an assembly line, he made his qualifications known to the administration of the school where his child was soon enrolled. Little did he know, the school was in need of a liaison for refugee families. Before long, he was employed by the Boise School District. These people recognized that they were the exception, not the rule.

Both the San Diego and Boise Resettlement Agencies offered career development and vocational training programs to extended clients like Haidar who had been resettled years earlier and had reached some degree of stability in an entry-level position. These programs facilitated the acquisition of technical skills or certifications, such as forklift operation, long-haul truck driving, or hospitality. Typically these programs benefited those who already had a professional background in their home country, leaving behind less formally educated clients who were more likely to get stuck in manual labor jobs. Yet one promising program at a Boise hospital offered in-house English classes to create opportunities for internal promotion. Refugees would initially begin in cleaning positions, and over time English-language gains coupled with on-the-job training provided a feasible pathway for career growth and promotion throughout the hospital system.

Both the San Diego and Boise Resettlement Agencies offered extremely popular courses for at-home childcare certification. Funded by the Office of Refugee Resettlement, this program was often utilized by women who already had extensive childcare experience, offering a vocation that felt like a better fit than manual labor. The program also increased the number of at-home childcare providers within refugee communities, filling a need for other working parents who preferred to have their children cared for by co-ethnics or at least someone who spoke the same language. These at-home providers could better accommodate the childcare needs of parents who worked evening or overnight shifts. This certification program was highly sought after, as working as a childcare provider paid well enough to help bring families out of poverty.

Gaining employment at Resettlement Agencies or other social service organizations was a way for some refugees to break out of the cycle of entry-level jobs, as their migration experience and linguistic and cultural backgrounds were an asset. Refugees are hired as Resettlement Agency caseworkers, employment specialists, interpreters, and support staff. In this sense, the USRAP creates jobs for refugees in the social work sector.[10] Abraham, a Sudanese father, was trained as a veterinarian and worked in temp jobs when he arrived in San Diego. Following a position at a hotel, he became a caseworker at a local Resettlement Agency. Though these positions are considered more highly skilled and carry more status, they are not necessarily well paid.[11] One caseworker from a refugee background in San Diego joked that he was earning the same salary as when he used to work at Burger King.

Regardless of professional background, some refugees asserted their agency in the face of a system that discourages claims-making and resisted the ways the USRAP sought to commodify them.[12] Acts of noncompliance, however, subject refugees to disciplinary measures by the Resettlement Agency and other social service providers. Refugee-specific and state-based programs of cash aid come with terms and conditions that require participation in job readiness activities. By not attending required English or employment classes, refugees risk punitive actions. Upon enrollment in benefits, refugees sign an agreement to take the first job opportunity available, and acts of non-compliance carry real consequences. Because services beyond the ninety-day R&P period were contingent upon participation in employment programs, turning down a job offer put employment specialists in the difficult position of terminating assistance. A former employment specialist in Boise explained that "some women just flat out said no [to a job], and you're like, 'Okay, we'll help you as much as we can, but also by turning down a job, unfortunately, legally, I have to stop helping you.'" An Iraqi engineer in San Diego recounted that one month into his employment program, his employment specialist found him a position at a 7-Eleven. Though he was open to the job, he wanted to postpone employment by a couple of weeks while he figured out how to get his children to school. His employment specialist sanctioned him for refusing the job, cut off his remaining cash aid, and sent a letter informing the county welfare office. When he went to the welfare office in hopes of enrolling in benefits, they turned him down because he had been sanctioned for refusing the job offer. He was left to find employment without the safety net of financial support in the interim.

The USRAP's inflexibility and coercive approach to employment plagued many of the Resettlement Agency's employment staff who had to enforce these disciplinary policies on a regular basis. One former employment specialist in Boise struggled, "It's patronizing in structure. . . . There is a power dynamic that is really, really hard. It's really hard to make these conversations productive." Despite her misgivings, she felt cornered by programmatic requirements. She added, "You should never be instilling fear in a population from a Resettlement Agency perspective. But we're forced too; like, the government forced you to. I'm just saying, 'Look at the contract.' . . . That instills fear." She noted how this dynamic between clients and the employment special- ists who make decisions on their behalf was disempowering and "put clients back into that recipient position." She confessed, "There will be moments with certain cases, like, this makes me want to quit my job. It makes me feel problematic." Resettlement Agency staff become the enforcers of this punitive approach to workfare, which can strike a pa- ternalistic tone as newly arrived refugees try to establish themselves in a new country. Like other forms of humanitarian work, implementing the USRAP means accepting the unfavorable aspects of the job.[13]

ECONOMIC SELF-SUFFICIENCY

While the need for early employment pushes refugees into low-wage occupations, the goal of economic self-sufficiency ties the USRAP to the US welfare state. According to the US Office of Refugee Resettle- ment, "Economic self-sufficiency means earning a total family income at a level that enables a family unit to support itself without receipt of a cash assistance grant."[14] In other words, self-sufficiency means earning enough income to meet monthly expenses without cash aid, though a refugee can still receive food stamps or Medicaid health insurance. In most states, the threshold to no longer qualify for cash assistance is well below the poverty line. So despite its implications, the USRAP categorizes families as self-sufficient even though they might still be economically insecure. Refugees' economic stability is hindered by this definition. When the measure of a "successful" resettlement is tied to the benchmarks of a retrenched welfare state that perpetuates eco- nomic inequality, it sets refugees up to exit the resettlement program while still living in poverty.

Comparing the income threshold to qualify for cash aid in San Diego and Boise with a living wage that covers all basic needs, such as housing, transportation, food, healthcare, and childcare (see table 6) demonstrates

TABLE 6

Monthly income limit for TANF cash aid in San Diego
and Boise vs. monthly poverty wage and living wage

	Family size	Income limit, 2018/19 (at time of fieldwork)	Income limit, 2022	Poverty wage, 2022	Living wage, 2022
San Diego	2	$1,082	$1,324	$1,452.25	$7,798.50 (1 adult + 1 child)
	3	$1,342	$1,641	$1,830.05	$9,664.94 (1 adult + 2 children) $7,280.33 (2 adults + 1 child)
	4	$1,592	$1,947	$2,207.84	$13,148.27 (1 adult + 3 children) $8,314.93 (2 adults + 2 children)
Boise	2	$309	$309	$1,452.25	$5,682.51 (1 adult + 1 child)
	3	$389	$389	$1,830.05	$7,048.11 (1 adult + 2 children) $5,550.80 (2 adults + 1 child)
	4	$469	$469	$2,207.84	$9,403.26 (1 adult + 3 children) $6,549.01 (2 adults + 2 children)

SOURCE: Poverty wage and living wage data from the Living Wage Institute via https://living wage.mit.edu/counties/06073 and https://livingwage.mit.edu/counties/16001.

how refugees can continue to live in poverty despite technically achieving the Office of Refugee Resettlement's criteria for a successful resettlement. For example, though the poverty wage for a family of four in San Diego is $2,207.84 per month, that family must earn below $1,947 per month to qualify for cash aid through the Temporary Assistance for

Needy Families (TANF) program.[15] These income levels stand in stark contrast to a living wage in San Diego County, where a family of four comprised of one adult and three children would need to earn $13,148.27 per month while a family of two adults and two children would need to earn $8,314.93 per month, revealing the gulf that exists between the USRAP's definition of self-sufficiency and a true living wage.[16] This notion of self-sufficiency as constructed in relation to cash aid qualification is even more shocking in Boise where a family of four must earn below $469 per month to qualify for TANF.

One former employment specialist in Boise found the definition of self-sufficiency to be misleading. She explained, "I just get stuck on us letting people [live] in poverty and not doing much about it. I think one thing that I would change that is really tangible to me is the idea of self-sufficiency. . . . Because the idea that if someone makes their bills and has zero dollars left over is self-sufficient, that is ridiculous." Self-sufficiency also obscures how refugee families achieve this economic goal and the costs of maintaining it. In order to support his family, Warsame, a Somali father, worked two jobs in Boise. During the day, he earned $11 per hour with a carpet and floor cleaning company and during the evening shift, he cleaned a nursing home for $13 per hour, leaving him with three to four hours of sleep per night. Like many refugees, Warsame also sent remittances to family left behind in a refugee camp in Ethiopia. The added economic strain of remittances becomes another obstacle that keeps refugees from getting ahead.

When refugees are technically self-sufficient but have no savings, progress becomes impossible, leaving them feeling stuck despite having had a "successful" resettlement. Yara was frustrated by how her family's life had stagnated in San Diego one year after their arrival. She said, "When we came here, it's just like, okay, we have to work. . . . We're really willing to work. We want to work. . . . But then you're in the same place. Like you're not moving. You're just working to pay the rent, and that's it. You're not doing anything else to improve yourself."

Yara's family of six was getting by on the combined income that she and her father earned. They wanted to move from their two-bedroom apartment to a small house with a garage so that her father, a skilled artisan, could set up a carpentry workshop to supplement the income he earned driving for Uber. But with no savings, the family could not afford the security deposit needed to rent a new home, and the cash from their current apartment's security deposit was inaccessible until they moved out. They felt trapped. When refugees are just making ends meet each month, they are unable to demonstrate the proof of income required by many landlords. For larger families like Yara's, two incomes were not always enough.

Refugees risk getting caught on this treadmill, which seldom leaves the time and resources for growth.[17] Ramin, an Afghan father in San Diego who arrived through the SIV program, had previously worked with the US military and the UN in Afghanistan and found employment on an assembly line following his resettlement. Despite his background and aspirations for the future, supporting his family had left no time in the two years since his resettlement to pursue opportunities for advancement. He told me, "I can't [think] about my education directly, because I am thinking about rent." A caseworker in San Diego observed this pattern unfold with many of his clients. He said, "They're basically living the same life as they were at the beginning, trying to figure out how to collect enough money at the end of the month to be able to pay their rent, and there is no savings for them. No thinking about anything extra, because they cannot afford it." By the standards of the USRAP, the outcome of subsistence is considered successful resettlement.

A community partner who worked with SIVs saw how much this reality weighed on families, which tarnished the opportunities presented by resettlement. He explained, "All of them are happy to be here . . . to have some safety and, you know, the ability to kind of try and start their lives again." Yet at the same time "a lot of it feels like a ton of weight on their shoulders because of cost of living, and how am I going to ever get out of this? Is it always paycheck to paycheck? And that might even be stretching, because a lot of times their paycheck doesn't even cover their bills. . . . I know that's a pretty big weight on them." Before they arrive, people have expectations of stability and simple comforts, yet "some of them are ten [people] to a two-bedroom apartment, and then they struggle finding a job."

Moreover, when families are barely getting by, they have no cushion to absorb unexpected expenses, putting them one emergency away from financial crisis. This precarity was particularly salient in Boise due to restricted eligibility for Medicaid, which left many adults uninsured after their eight months of Refugee Medical Assistance (RMA) ended. On top of everything else that refugees must deal with upon arrival, Resettlement Agency staff in Boise would advise their clients to undergo any medical procedures or surgery within their first eight months to ensure that it was covered by insurance. Even during the temporary RMA period, Resettlement Agency staff in Boise had to warn clients that the cost of an ambulance was only covered for life-threatening emergencies. Otherwise, a call to 911 could end up costing them thousands of dollars. This detail is both confusing and worrisome for new arrivals who have been told to call 911 if they need help. When a caseworker raised this issue with one of his clients who had been in Boise for several months, the client was taken aback, asking why they had been told to call 911 if it was going to be so expensive. He wanted to know how he was supposed to get to the hospital if he was injured. His caseworker told him that if he was not badly hurt, he should find another way to get to the hospital.

If someone gets injured on the job, she would likely qualify for workers' compensation, but off-site injuries have no financial recourse. A Resettlement Agency staff member explained how devastating such accidents could be, given the lack of a safety net in Boise: "An injury off the job that affects your ability to do your job is a nightmare. . . . That's when you're screwed." The tenuousness of refugees' financial situations leaves them in fear that they will not be able to bounce back from a crisis. Remi was fired from his first job on an assembly line after nine days because he had not known to check his voice-mail; his supervisor had been leaving messages on how Remi could improve. Without an income, Remi wondered, "How am I going to survive now?"

The objective of self-sufficiency is inculcated soon after refugees arrive through tools such as a service plan, family budgets, and Cultural Orientation. During a Cultural Orientation class in Boise, the instructor told a group of new arrivals, "learn how to become self-sufficient. This is different than showing up and expecting everything to fall in your lap. You have all the resources to do it. . . . Our goal is to get you to the place where you're self-sufficient." The following day, she further moralized about this programmatic goal, "There are some things Americans admire, like being independent and self-sufficient." After completing Cultural Orientation, refugees take an assessment to verify that they are equipped with the basic knowledge for their lives in a new country, such as where the closest grocery store is located, how to keep children safe at home, and which medical issues require a trip to the emergency room. There are also questions that promote financial independence. Clients are asked, "Once your financial assistance ends, how will you make money?" and "What are two things you can do to become employed?" Messages promoting self-reliance are omnipresent once refugees arrive in the US, which all work towards laying a foundation for self-sufficiency.

Because of the US welfare state's reliance on means-tested benefits, progress is illusive. Whenever refugees' earnings increase, their benefits decrease, leaving them no better off. Rather than feeling stable, refugees who do achieve economic self-sufficiency may instead feel abandoned. When successful resettlement is measured against a bar set by the US welfare state, it belies all the ways that refugees continue to struggle. Just because refugees can meet their bills does not mean that they have gained financial security. Employment and means-tested benefits that maintain self-sufficiency levels allow for little more than survival. Hafiz explained what this survival mentality felt like three years after his family's arrival. He said, "You cannot enjoy the life in America. You cannot, because you are like engine, machine. You should work."

Nonetheless, self-sufficiency is still out of reach for far too many refugees. Former and extended clients continue to ask their Resettlement Agency or community-based organizations for emergency rental assistance. A caseworker in San Diego did not know how some of his former clients managed to make their rental payment each month, getting by with an ever-changing combination of low-wage work, public assistance, and charity. Others leave bills unpaid, either because they do not have the funds or because of barriers to understanding what the bills are and how to pay them. A Resettlement Agency staff member in Boise noted how medical bills often become an issue when, after eight months, many adults become uninsured. She said, "There are families that I have talked to about the bills they can't pay, then all of a sudden, they are getting a call from a collector." Not only was it disorienting that, at month nine, bills they once did not have to pay all of a sudden become their responsibility, medical bills do not always arrive as a lump sum, creating confusion over separate payments for different components of the same medical service.

Refugees do not end up in these situations because of a lack of motivation or desire to become financially stable. Yet given what they are up against, some refugees still struggle to make it work. A Resettlement Agency staff member in Boise explained that refugees "are trying to do everything they can to make ends meet. But the price is just too high and they're still $200 short." An educator who worked extensively with refugees noted that "they're up against so much more than even just an impoverished family." She repeatedly saw how much parents struggled. She said, "Our families need this like super, super long runway to just get to the low-income status, you know, because they're just so far behind in so many other areas." It took significant work for some families to even make it to a place of self-sufficiency.

Because of the employment barriers faced by some adults, youth often become indispensable to helping their families achieve self-sufficiency. While young children are immediately enrolled in school and adults are expected to gain employment, some older adolescents face competing priorities. For those arriving in their late teens, earning enough credits for a high school diploma in a couple of years may be difficult, particularly when they have limited prior formal education or English proficiency. From a financial perspective, these older youth can be a valuable and often necessary source of income for their families, especially in single parent households or in families where manual labor jobs are too physically strenuous for parents. A caseworker in San Diego had seen this reality unfold for many of his clients, "It's always those [kids over 18] who take on the most burden." A former employment specialist in San Diego referred to young people between the ages of sixteen and twenty-four as the "lost generation." She elaborated:

> I think a lot of responsibility ends up falling on that age group. . . . [The family] needs another source of income. So, then it's up to the oldest child who didn't finish school. So, they kind of just get stuck on supporting the family. . . . And then employers prefer the eighteen or twenty-year-old than the sixty-year-old man. And that's the heartbreaking part: that they just then have the weight of the family's success on their shoulders. That population kills me, because . . . all they want to do is study, but also catching up to the level of what they missed. . . . If you're 18 and you have

all of these education gaps, . . . it's really hard to catch up and you can't do it while you're working.

Despite dreams of gaining an education and learning English, some youth instead bear the burden of their families' economic stability. Those who manage to balance high school with employment often encounter obstacles at school. They do their best to satisfy dueling demands but risk falling asleep in class after working an evening shift or being labeled as truant. During a meeting about refugee youth, an employee of the Boise School District attributed poor attendance and tardiness to students' laziness and carelessness without acknowledging all of the other barriers that they faced, such as working nights, getting younger siblings to school, or not having alternative modes of transportation should they miss the bus. Resettlement Agency staff did their best to explain to schools that these young people were trying to be the very best students they could under the circumstances. While some managed to earn a diploma, others dropped out.

Esin, a young Afghan woman in San Diego, was the only member of her family of four who could work. Her younger sibling was enrolled in school and her older sibling had an incapacitating illness that required constant supervision yet did not qualify for SSI. While their single mother cared for the oldest, Esin became solely responsible for her family's economic wellbeing. As I drove Esin to her first day of work washing dishes for $11.50 per hour at a restaurant twenty miles from her apartment, she told me how she was "crazy about school" despite only having had one year of formal education as an eleven-year-old. Though the job was good, she desperately wanted to improve her English. Yet she had no choice but to take full responsibility for her family's economic stability. She was singlehandedly keeping her family afloat. The USRAP's economic self-sufficiency imperative stands in the way of the ambitions of young, motivated refugees like Esin, whose incorporation was shaped by low-wage employment rather than school. The primacy of work in these young people's lives has consequences for their language acquisition, educational attainment, and career pathways.[18]

Despite the odds, some youth managed to make the impossible work. Pascaline and her sister both worked the overnight shift as home healthcare providers in Boise so that they could be full-time college students during the day. Their mother's poor health kept her from working, so it was up to Pascaline and her sister to support their household. They had managed to secure low-income housing, which helped, but they still had to cover their reduced rent and other expenses while managing classes. For other youth, dreams that had once been deferred were eventually achieved with time and persistence. Nour was twenty years old when her family arrived in Boise. She was part way through college when she fled Iraq, but as the only one in her family who could work, she had to put her education on hold. She began working as a cashier three months after her arrival, but she eventually graduated from college with a degree in engineering and was pursuing a career in her field eight years later.

For economic reasons, Resettlement Agency staff may push young clients in a direction that runs counter to their educational and career ambitions. Some youth managed to resist the pressures to abandon high school, but it took effort and persistence. Education was important to Patrick, who arrived in San Diego at the age of seventeen. After having spent fifteen years growing up in a refugee camp, he was eager to focus on high school. He felt unsupported by both the Resettlement Agency and the school administrators who tried to convince him not to pursue his studies. By the time the school year began, Patrick had already turned eighteen. "At the beginning, it started out [a] little scary, like, 'Oh you are not going to finish it; your age is already [too old]; you know, you are supposed to finish high school when you are eighteen, and you don't speak English.'" A friend from the refugee camp who had previously been resettled in the US came to visit Patrick shortly after his family arrived. This friend encouraged Patrick to trust his ambitions. Patrick recounted, "[The Resettlement Agency] said I had to get a job. . . . Like the people here, they decide for you, you know?" He did not want to miss the opportunity to further his education, so he enrolled in high school despite the advice he was receiving to the contrary. After successfully graduating, Patrick was working an overnight shift to contribute to his family's finances while also taking college classes part time.

THE DISTRESS OF ECONOMIC INSECURITY

Beyond the practical challenges of covering monthly expenses, the speed with which refugees must begin employment and the reality of their financial precarity after arrival have harmful repercussions that can be damaging to newly arrived refugees' mental and emotional well-being. Several of the employment specialists I interviewed in San Diego and Boise noted that if they could change one aspect of the USRAP it would be lengthening the time frame before which refugees must earn an income. Even for families in Boise whose R&P money stretched comparatively further than in San Diego and covered several months of rent, immediate employment was imperative to begin saving money for future months when a salary alone would not meet their basic expenses. One former employment specialist in San Diego explained, "I just don't think employment can be pushed so quickly. . . . Everything is bombarded at the same time. In the eyes of the government to think that someone who doesn't speak English, has never lived outside of a refugee camp, to [have] the expectation that they'll be completely independent and self-sufficient [in], let's say, eight months. . . . is ridiculous."

By the time refugees are resettled in the US, they may have experienced persecution, war, violence, torture, family loss, and drawn-out migrations—all of which take a toll on their well-being. Resettlement does not undo the years of trauma they have endured; nor does it negate the costs associated with periods of protracted waiting.[19] Though refugees arrive with ambitions and skills,[20] it is important to acknowledge that the realities of early employment and economic self-sufficiency are experienced in relation to their forced migration, adding another layer of displacement to their resettlement.

Kazem knew the fragility of his mental state well enough to know that he could not remain at the home-healthcare job his employment specialist had found for him shortly after arrival. Kazem arrived in Boise alone, carrying with him the enduring weight of the emotional and physical abuse he had suffered as a young man in Iran. He fled when it became clear that he would likely be imprisoned. He had too much anxiety to work alongside other people, and he told me that Resettlement Agencies should not put depressed people in depressing work. He wished employment services would consider refugees' mental health before placing them in jobs. Reflecting back on the short time he spent as a home-healthcare provider, he said, "I needed care giving for myself. . . . I said, 'Man, I am feeling sad. This person makes me feel so demotivate[d]; I can't help it no more.' So, I left the job. . . . Emotionally I couldn't take it." He ultimately quit his first two job placements.

Three years later, Kazem was barely getting by, and ongoing financial insecurity further strained his mental health. He said, "I have to always think about money. So, I don't like it. It directs me to dark ways. I tell you, it's drove me to think of suicide. . . . I can't take it sometimes." He told me how he felt like he was resettled from one hole in Turkey only to be put into another hole in the US, where he suffered from "economy stress and job stress." He added, "I don't feel any safe[ty] of my situation. I always worry about my food, about my work.

So, I have to be in this stress of not having the regular needs of my life. . . . They put me in a bigger hole, you know, but what can I do?" Never did Kazem fathom that after finally reaching the US he would have to worry about hunger or homelessness. Kazem reflected on the US approach to resettlement, "I don't know why they take the refugees here in the first place anyways. [If] you want to give them a miserable start, just don't take them. . . . They think they are coming here to be fine, and it's a different world."

Some new arrivals are overtly distressed by how little support they receive, how quickly they are pushed into employment, and the insecurity of their financial situation. A former employment specialist in San Diego confessed that she wondered whether the USRAP was ultimately doing more harm than good. While her supervisor reassured her that resettlement at least provided safety, she still asked, "Are we retraumatizing them . . . now [that] there's. . . . another struggle because they can't pay rent?" She worried that the unintended consequences and harmful practices related to employment outweighed the positive dimensions of resettlement.[21] Several of the employment specialists I interviewed noted that the speed with which refugees are pushed into the labor market was indeed traumatizing. One former employment specialist in Boise noted a "lack of kindness" in the process. She wished the USRAP offered "more time, more grace." She added, "I think the initial resettlement period is way too short. I think it sends people into a panic. I think its traumatizing for people." Another former employment specialist who had worked for a different Boise Resettlement Agency elaborated about how this trauma unfolded on a regular basis:

So many of the things we did, I know we retraumatized people. . . . For some people it creates a freeze reaction where they aren't able to forget. And so that was really hard too as we had people where they're having more mental health issues come up. . . . Being empowered to heal from trauma, you need choice. And all of your choice is literally stripped away from you, and you're once again put in a situation where someone else is controlling your situation. . . . And that's not a very empowering situation. It's a very unhealthy situation for everybody.

A mental health provider in Boise explained how prior experiences with trauma, or "something that threatens your core well-being," change how people react in subsequent situations. She described how after experiencing a major trauma, stressful but otherwise manageable events are experienced as if they, too, endanger one's core well-being. Refugees may develop post-traumatic stress disorder after surviving war, violence, or torture.[22] Once they are resettled in the US, refugees like Kazem encounter the stressors associated with poverty, such as financial instability and housing insecurity, which may trigger a trauma response.[23] Making ends meet becomes a monthly struggle for newly resettled refugees as they work to cobble together sufficient funds, what Gowayed has called "living as a math problem."[24]

It was the fifth of the month, and Esin was late in paying her family's $1,250 rent. She had reached the end of her landlord's five-day grace period, after which her family would incur a penalty. Esin's caseworker convinced the Resettlement Agency finance office to quickly cut the next RCA check for Esin so that she could pay rent by the end of the day. With the check in hand, I drove the family to the bank so that she and her mother could each cash checks. Next, we went to a local market to purchase a $1,250 money order for the family's rent. Esin first asked the cashier to charge $500 from the family's EBT card that stored the TANF cash aid that they received for her younger sibling. Esin then stood in front of the cashier counting out the bills from the cashed checks. She was $60 short. Esin began to panic and recounted the cash. She looked through her purse and pulled out smaller crumpled bills that had been tucked away in different pockets. She guessed that only about $40 of TANF benefits remained on the EBT card. As Esin grew more anxious, the cashier figured out that they had a TANF balance of $70. Esin charged the $70 and paid the rest in cash, putting the leftover bills into her purse. She let out an audible sigh of relief once she had paid for the money order in full.

For many refugees, initial resettlement becomes characterized by economic insecurity and an absence of agency. When refugees first arrive, they lack options and the control to shape the trajectory of their lives in a new country. Decisions are made on their behalf based on the principal goals of early employment and economic self-sufficiency. The mental health professional in Boise noted that this lack of agency makes the USRAP inherently traumatizing. She recognized that service providers felt trapped into perpetuating this dynamic: they "feel like, 'That's my responsibility to ensure you're okay and . . . the only way I know how is to take the control from you and do this for you and force you into this role.'" As I accompanied an employment specialist and his client to a job interview for a hotel housekeeping position in Boise, I asked him about the particularities of the case. He replied that while he would like to learn more about his clients before finding employment, he did not have the time. What mattered was where they lived, if they could get to the job by bus, and if they had any language or literacy barriers. The employment specialist's priority was to secure an income for this single mother of seven, despite knowing little else about her.

Structural factors put Resettlement Agency staff in situations where they are overworked, underpaid, and have limited alternatives at their disposal.[25] They are intimately familiar with the consequences of the USRAP. A caseworker in San Diego told me, "Basically, we put them in danger. That's how I feel." A former employment specialist in Boise reflected on her experience, "I mean the agency workers are burnt out. They're tired because they're constantly having these crappy conversations. They're underpaid. . . . And then you're having these horrible conversations, like, 'Hey, I might just have to let you go and not help you. So don't become homeless.' It's just a hard situation for everyone involved, and particularly the people who come as refugees." Alongside the lingering traumas of war, displacement, and difficult journeys, refugees arrive in the US only to confront the stressors of deskilling, housing insecurity, and poverty.

STATE-BASED WELFARE: DIFFERENT EQUATION, SAME OUTCOME

Though all arriving refugees receive federally standardized services, welfare benefits are set by each state. Differences in public assistance levels and eligibility determine the ongoing financial support that refugees receive. State-based policies also shape the environment within which Resettlement Agencies support their clients, affecting how they approach the allocation of limited resources. Most studies of resettlement have examined a single geographic case, which can obscure how state-based differences effect the economics of resettlement. California and Idaho sit at opposite ends of the spectrum of state-based approaches to public assistance in the US, and local differences shaped how each Resettlement Agency enrolled clients in programs and the options at their disposal. Though newly arrived refugees in both San Diego and Boise experienced poverty and economic insecurity, a different combination of factors contributed to this outcome, including cost of living, minimum wage levels, and the generosity of state-based public assistance. Refugees in both cities ultimately arrived at a precipice of financial instability, but how and when they got their differed between sites.

One way in which resettlement destinations vary is cost of living. Though public assistance levels may be comparatively higher in more expensive cities like San Diego, the per capita R&P funds allocated by the federal government for each arriving case are set at $1,125 regardless of the resettlement destination. This sum of money carried a notably different value in San Diego and Boise. As illustrated with Nina and

Joseph's case, their family's R&P funds were nearly exhausted before they had even landed in the US. Given the lower housing costs in Boise, R&P funds offered newly arrived families a larger buffer. While Nina and Joseph's two-bedroom apartment cost $1,385 per month for their family of six, a Congolese family of seven in Boise paid $999 per month for their three-bedroom apartment. When cases in Boise approach the end of their ninety-day R&P period, the Resettlement Agency had a practice of sending leftover R&P funds to the landlord as down payments on future months' rent, temporarily making housing even more affordable. R&P funds stretched notably further in Boise, offering arrivals a longer runway before which they needed to begin earning an income.

Despite all the advantages of San Diego as a resettlement destination, a caseworker believed that the cost of housing made it an unsuitable place to send refugees, particularly those without family ties in the community. Even after relocating their operations from San Diego to El Cajon due to its lower rent, this caseworker felt like they were still setting clients up for financial vulnerability. Though public assistance levels were more generous in California, they nonetheless fell short of monthly expenses, creating a particularly urgent need for employment as soon as refugees arrived. This caseworker confessed, "I would be really happy to see the end of settlement in these big cities. It's not fair for the family. . . . They're basically putting you in danger of being homeless."

Refugees who arrive in San Diego are enrolled in one of four assistance programs. Because R&P funds do not provide meaningful support beyond the first month, caseworkers are quick to enroll their clients so as not to delay their cash aid. With the exception of SSI, the cash aid associated with these programs is contingent upon the active pursuit of employment. Regardless of program enrollment, all arriving refugees qualify for the Supplemental Nutrition Assistance Program (SNAP) and Medi-Cal health insurance, as long as they are below a certain income threshold.

Particularly vulnerable cases, such as single parent families, would be unable to get by in San Diego without CalWorks, California's TANF program. When Rosine's family arrived eleven years earlier, her mother had to figure out how to support her five children on her own. When I asked Rosine what the most important form of support was when her family arrived, she said, "The most helpful, I think, welfare. Since my mom was a single parent. And during that time I remember minimum wage was $7 and that's what she was getting an hour. And she had to pay rent and try to feed us. So it wasn't easy." Still, sometimes the combination of Rosine's mother's income from her cleaning job at a nursing home and welfare assistance fell short. In such cases, their Resettlement Agency caseworker would give the family her own money to meet their bills. The local economics of resettlement in San Diego meant that the Resettlement Agency had to refuse large cases whose housing needs would be prohibitively expensive.

Because of San Diego's high cost of living, refugees typically make ends meet with a combination of earned income and public assistance. When that is not enough, a caseworker in San Diego explained that some refugees have to resort to illegitimate tactics, such as selling a portion of their food stamps or renting out their unused parking spot at their apartment complex. He explained, "They don't do it because they just like to do that. They're basically forced to do those things to get enough money to cover their rent." Later in our conversation he added, "When they come to the point that they have to sell their food stamps to make money . . . [it] goes for the cost of living." Refugee families in San Diego survive through a delicate balance of low wage employment and public assistance. When a family has two full-time incomes, they will likely have met self-sufficiency requirements by exceeding the income threshold to qualify for cash aid. Yet achieving this benchmark does not always translate to stability. It is important to note that state-based public assistance in San Diego only provides an ongoing safety net for refugees with minor children, leaving adults without children or with adult children without comparable assistance.

While the cost of living in Boise was comparatively more reasonable, lower wages coupled with a nearly nonexistent public safety net set refugees up for a similar state of financial insecurity. Refugees arriving to Boise also reached a precipice of economic instability, but they had a runway of a few months before they got there. At the time of my fieldwork, housing prices in Boise were increasing at a concerning rate, yet rent was still more affordable. However, public assistance levels in Idaho are among the most meager in the country.[26] Moreover, despite Boise's welcoming city-based policies that supported refugees, Resettlement Agencies operated within a state that was at times vocally hostile to resettlement.

Given the delicacy of resettling refugees within this political context, families were deliberately kept off Temporary Assistance for Families in Idaho (TAFI), Idaho's TANF program. Both Resettlement Agencies and the Idaho Office of Refugees were wary of the political optics of refugee families regularly accessing public assistance. Instead, the Idaho Department of Health and Welfare in conjunction with the Idaho Office of Refugees created an alternative TAFI program, which provided a separate track administered by the Idaho Office for Refugees for select cases of refugees with minor children in need of specific and time-limited support, including emergency rental assistance, which covers the cost of rent for a maximum of four months within a twelve-month period. Like other workfare programs, this support comes with mandatory job search activities.

A representative from the Idaho Office of Refugees explained, "We were trying to keep the refugee population off of the state's TANF dole. . . . like that would look bad." She noted not only that refugees' use of public assistance might appear unfavorable to the state's predominantly Republican government but also that the Department of Health and Welfare did not feel adequately equipped to support refugee families. As a result, refugees resettled in Boise with minor children have no equivalent of the CALWorks TANF Program available. The longest duration of cash assistance available to those resettled in Boise is eight months after arrival, after which they must apply through their Resettlement Agency for special emergency funds, which requires approval by the Idaho Office of Refugees following a thorough application process. A Resettlement Agency staff member explained how they were seldom able to help all of the families who needed support. She said, "We have our backs against a wall, and our clients have their backs against a wall."

The meager assistance landscape in Boise affected how the Resettlement Agency managed its resources. Though R&P funds are nationally standardized, Resettlement Agencies have the option of withholding up to $200 per client in order to create a discretionary flex fund to support other clients in particular need. The Boise Resettlement Agency consistently took this approach in order to build up an emergency reserve. Each new arrival benefitted from $925 to support their initial resettlement expenses, while the Resettlement Agency retained $200 for a flex fund. In the absence of a public safety net, the Resettlement Agency had to become a welfare office for its own particularly vulnerable clients who had nowhere else to turn to. A Resettlement Agency administer noted, "The scarcity of resources means that somebody's coming in. We're scratching our head how to cover it." Whereas extended clients who had exceeded the initial R&P period with minor children in San Diego could always reenroll in the county's CalWorks program, families in Boise would return to their Resettlement Agency. The unfriendly political environment in which the Boise Resettlement Agencies operated also resulted in a stricter emphasis on client compliance, as Resettlement Agencies could not risk actions that put the program's future in jeopardy. This emphasis on compliance created ripple effects that heightened the monitoring of client attendance at English or job readiness classes, resulting in the issuing of warnings or sanctions should clients not follow through with program requirements. Resettlement Agency staff also went to great lengths to keep clients employed in jobs even if it was going badly, so as not to lose their paycheck. A former employment specialist explained, "You would desperately try to keep people in jobs that they were continuing to make the same mistake and you're putting it back together."

Considering the scarcity of funds in Boise, clients typically had to already be in a crisis before they received support, both for emergency rental assistance and for use of the flex funds. Some clients were instructed that becoming homeless was an alternative path to unlocking certain forms of assistance. The absence of a safety net in Boise meant that the Resettlement Agency was constantly finding temporary stopgaps. The precarity created by the lack of public assistance in Idaho was further exacerbated by restricted eligibility for Medicaid, as many adults were left uninsured at the end of the eight-month Refugee Medical Assistance period. A former employment specialist explained why their Boise clients consistently had such high self-sufficiency rates compared to other resettlement destinations. Because of the "ticking time bomb" of no more than eight-months of support, "they have no other choice." Resettlement Agency staff in Boise did their best to help clients achieve self-sufficiency, but it came at tremendous costs. She continued, "What is the effect of the lack of state assistance? . . . The answer is trauma in my personal opinion."

"RESETTLED INTO POVERTY"

Despite benefitting from programs of relief, refugees arrive in their resettlement destination only to confront economic insecurity. This chapter reveals that the speed with which refugees are pushed into the labor market combined with poverty-level wages as the threshold for success means that refugees are being resettling into the working poor. Before they can gain their footing in a new country and community, refugees learn the distressing reality that their well-being depends on immediate employment. As an extension of the US welfare state, the USRAP sets newly arrived refugees up for a process of commodification in which they are swiftly transitioned off financial assistance and into the labor market. As a result, refugees are funneled into low-wage manual labor jobs, which keep them living at or below the poverty line. Families live paycheck to paycheck and at times must patch together inconsistent forms of charity simply to meet their monthly expenses, putting them one crisis away from homelessness. The instability of economic insecurity shapes the experience of refugee youth, many of whom arrive with strong educational aspirations. As their families struggle to make ends meet, young refugees forgo or delay their ambitions in order to support their families.

When resettlement assistance is informed and shaped by a national approach to welfare that is both punitive and stratifying, newly arrived refugees encounter harms that are damaging to their financial and emotional well-being.[27] Resettlement Agencies are not in a position to rectify the inequality produced by the USRAP. Resettlement Agencies find themselves near the end of a chain of compliance monitoring, and so they assume a disciplinary role towards their refugee clients. Just as Resettlement Agency staff are monitoring refugees, Resettlement Agencies are being monitored by state-level offices, their national headquarters, and the federal government. Resettlement Agency staff operate under daily conditions of crisis management where they are bound by constraints that limit their discretion.[28]

5

TRUST

HELENE, A CONGOLESE MOTHER of five in Boise, arrived at
the Resettlement Agency on check day to pick up her family's next Transitional Refugee Assistance (TRA) check for
their upcoming rental payment. Four and a half months
after their arrival in Boise, this monthly check of $999 for
their three-bedroom apartment would soon come to an end.
Helene's husband, a former school headmaster, had recently
begun working in a warehouse for $9 per hour, and Helene,
pregnant with their sixth child, was starting her first day of
work that afternoon. The TRA program, the Refugee Cash
Assistance Program managed by the Idaho Office for Refugees, covers rent for up to eight months or until a case
achieves economic self-sufficiency, whichever comes first.
That morning, Helene met with one of the Resettlement
Agency staff to sign for the check, which had already been
made out to their apartment's property management company. Since several receipts in the family's case file had not

yet been reviewed and signed by either Helene or her husband, the staff member used the meeting to walk through the outstanding documents with Helene. In an effort to promote transparency, clients are required to sign whenever the Resettlement Agency spends money on their behalf, including checks for rent and receipts for any initial expenses covered by the R&P funds used to secure and furnish housing.

This staff member began with a $300 Walmart receipt for household items, such as pillows, clothes hangers, and an alarm clock, among other goods. Through the assistance of an interpreter, Helene contested these charges, stating that her family had not received any items from Walmart. According to Helene, the Resettlement Agency had only provided them with mattresses and a couch. Friends of theirs who had previously been resettled to Boise had helped them get the other items they needed for their new home. Sensing tension, the staff member pivoted to an $857 receipt from the four nights that the family had stayed in a hotel before moving into permanent housing. Helene signed the hotel receipt without hesitation but continued to dispute the Walmart receipt, particularly the $196 that had been spent on mattress covers. As she pushed back, the interpreter explained to her that it was Resettlement Agency policy to purchase mattress covers for every bed to protect against bedbugs. Despite her reluctance, Helene signed the receipt. The staff member then presented Helene with another Walmart receipt for kitchen supplies, towels, and more mattress covers. Helene interjected, "these mattress covers keep coming and coming. How many mattress covers?" Recognizing the delicacy of the situation, the staff member stepped away to find the housing specialist who had helped prepare this family's home.

The housing specialist joined the meeting and immediately pulled out supporting documentation from the family's case file. She explained to Helen,

Sorry this came as a surprise to you. Maybe this wasn't explained clearly enough. When you come, [the Resettlement Agency] is told by the governing body that we will supply all the things to make a home with the R&P money. I know this sounds crazy because you should choose, but they standardize it, and they make this list. You and I talked a lot through this process. I asked what your community could provide and gave you this list. They moved everything into the apartment for you. When I came over, I went through everything and marked down what was provided, and I got everything else from Walmart or from donations. I tried really hard not to spend money I didn't need to spend, but I followed the rules. I'm the same. When I go to Walmart, I think, "What did I buy?!" This is what we provided, and I brought it to your house. I know your moving in was a long process, and I'm sorry for that. Did that help clarify? We don't want you leaving feeling bad. I know a standard family of seven would have cost a lot more. If you're okay with that, you can sign.

Not only did this housing specialist try to clarify the purpose of R&P funds, colloquially referred to as "welcome money," she also deliberately passed off any culpability onto the Department of State's Bureau of Population, Refugees, and Migration (PRM), the federal office that manages the initial R&P program. The Resettlement Agency was just following the rules, even if they seemed counterintuitive. Before signing, Helene asked if they had any R&P money left, which had originally been a sum of $7,875 for their family of seven. The Resettlement Agency staff member informed her that none remained. Regardless of any lingering doubts she may have had, Helene signed the receipts and left with her rent check. Once Helene was out of earshot, the staff member let me know that the Resettlement Agency had actually overspent beyond the allotted R&P funds on this family's initial resettlement. He had decided not to mention it to Helene out of fear that it would only complicate the situation.

When this housing specialist prepared Helene's family's apartment, she had to follow the housing supply checklist (see table 7) mandated by the federal government for new arrivals. A former employment specialist in Boise noted that clients were not only upset to learn that they

TABLE 7
Housing supply checklist

Furnishings	
	Mattress(es): twin/double
	Box spring(s)
	Bed frame(s)
	Set of drawers, shelves, or other unit for storage of clothing
	Kitchen table
	One kitchen chair per person
	Couch or equivalent seating in addition to kitchen chairs
	One lamp per room unless installed lighting is present
Kitchen items	
	One place setting of tableware per person (fork, knife, spoon)
	One place setting of dishes per person (plate, bowl, cup)
	Pots/pans, including saucepan, frying pan, and one baking dish
	Mixing/serving bowls
	One set of kitchen utensils
	Can opener
	Baby items as needed
Linens and other household items	
	One towel per person
	One set of sheets and blankets for each bed
	One pillow and pillowcase for each person
	Alarm clock
	Paper, pens, and/or pencils
	Light bulbs
Cleaning supplies	
	Dish soap
	Bathroom/kitchen cleaner
	Sponges or cleaning rags and/or paper towels
	Laundry detergent
	Two wastebaskets
	Mop or broom
	Trash bags
Toiletries	
	Toilet paper
	Shampoo
	Soap
	One toothbrush per person
	Toothpaste
	Personal hygiene items as appropriate

SOURCE: Adapted from the International Rescue Committee Supply List

did not get welcome money in cash as expected but that it had already been spent on items that they neither wanted nor felt they needed. She gave the example of clients who found the purchase of double shower curtains with inner liners and outer curtains to be a waste of money. A caseworker in San Diego has had to decline clients' requests to return items purchased from the list. These federal guidelines create a difficult situation because the parties involved in the immediate transaction have little control. Caseworkers are required to purchase items that their clients do not get to choose. A Resettlement Agency administrator recognized that it was problematic that clients do not "see, choose, or touch" their R&P funds and that "we're buying a bunch of stuff in their name."

This chapter reveals how a combination of regulations, implementational decisions, and unmet expectations create dynamics in which clients begin to lose trust in the Resettlement Agencies that welcomed them. The scarcity of resources within Resettlement Agencies puts caseworkers in a position where they feel the need to maintain control over finances so as not to put their clients in crisis. Yet when Resettlement Agency staff become the custodians of refugees' financial assistance, new arrivals are denied ownership over decisions consequential to their initial resettlement. Though clients like Helene may ultimately sign documents, case files belie refugees' ongoing doubts about whether R&P funds were used appropriately or whether they benefitted from them in full. This dynamic fosters a reluctant dependency in which acquiescence does not always indicate confidence.

This chapter centers on the role of trust throughout the resettlement process, as clients reevaluate the trustworthiness of their services providers and as Resettlement Agency staff assess the truthfulness of their clients. Given the "asymmetrical relationships"[1] characteristic of humanitarian programs, decisions over the use of limited funds create conditions that are particularly disempowering and disaffecting for new arrivals. Regardless of their intentions, Resettlement Agency staff control the distribution of resources, rendering their clients dependent upon them for their basic needs.[2]

Bastien shared with me that even though he mistrusted the Resettlement Agency's administration of his family's R&P money, he felt pressured to sign the requisite documentation, as he was under the impression that the Resettlement Agency would withhold his remaining assistance should he refuse. He signed out of duress, not in agreement, and continued to harbor the conviction years later that his caseworker had withheld a portion of his family's money. He explained that he felt like he had no choice, "if you don't sign, you know, they will not give you the last check, maybe to pay the bill. So then you become in dilemma. You don't know what to do. . . . So you're upset. So then after that, you are focused working. After that, you know, after, you forget your debt. Life goes on." Because Resettlement Agencies hold the purse strings to refugees' much-needed financial assistance, trust gives way to reluctant dependence when refugees lose faith in how their welcome money is spent.

A Resettlement Agency administrator in Boise was very familiar with this dynamic; she noted that the need for a signature on every transaction came "from a controls perspective" yet amounted to "a little bit of theater." She was aware of how much clients feel compelled to sign, because "they know they'll be penalized if [the signature] isn't captured." She knew that new arrivals often assume, "If I hope to get what remains, I'm forced to sign this anyway." A mental health provider in Boise was concerned with how often the resettlement process defaulted to the use of signatures and paperwork. She said, "I think it's really common for us to new Americans to put paperwork out and say, 'Sign this.' I really dislike that because I wouldn't want that to happen to me either." The control of essential resources is fundamental in shaping the relationship between providers and clients in social service organizations. Social work scholar Yeheskel Hasenfeld notes, "The power of the agency is reinforced by the fact that clients must yield some control over their own fate to the agency when seeking help from it."[3] In the early months of resettlement, matters of survival are tied to the resources and information controlled by their Resettlement Agency. New arrivals must navigate a delicate balance between compliance and claims making. As the realities of early resettlement diverge from refugees' expectations, the accumulation of interactions like Helene's risks eroding refugees' trust in the people tasked with helping them.

The USRAP requires a certain amount of faith from refugees as they arrive in a new country and find themselves reliant on their Resettlement Agency and caseworker for food, shelter, resources, and information. Refugees are coming to an unfamiliar place where they have few to no preexisting social ties and limited or no financial resources, creating material and logistical circumstances that produce dependence. Constrained by limited options and reliant on the programs available to them, refugees must entrust their future well-being in the USRAP. However, over time, unmet expectations, disappointments, and imposed limits eat away at refugees' trust, making them wary of their caseworker and the decisions being made by their Resettlement Agency. Yet given the power imbalance between refugees and service providers and the extent to which new arrivals must rely upon their Resettlement Agency for support and resources, refugees' misgivings have practical limitations. Despite their ongoing dependence, refugees may become suspicious of the service providers who are making the decisions that shape their resettlement, which takes place within a system that limits choice and compels compliance. As refugees' assessment of the resettlement process evolves over time, unsatisfactory encounters diminish trust.

Concurrently, Resettlement Agency caseworkers are appraising their refugee clients. As refugees deviate from the trope of the "good" or "acquiescent" refugee, Resettlement Agency staff may begin to become distrustful of what their clients tell them and question clients' deservingness. The situations that breed mistrust, both on the part of Resettlement Agency staff and newly arrived refugees, are inherent in the structure of the resettlement program and stem in particular from the management and distribution of financial assistance. In a high stakes environment of resource scarcity, caseworkers manage limited finances within strict institutional guidelines while refugees assert their agency and test the boundaries of claims making. Though similar dynamics existed in both San Diego and Boise, the absence of a public safety net in Idaho led to administrative decisions within the Resettlement Agency that made the preservation of trust particularly challenging.

A PRESUMPTION OF TRUST

The resettlement process assumes a significant amount of trust from refugees before they even arrive in the US. Once refugees have an open resettlement case, they give their future over to a system that filters them through a long, drawn-out, and impenetrable bureaucratic system in the hopes of gaining security for themselves and their families.[4] When they are approved for resettlement, refugees board an airplane, often for the first time in their lives, for a country with an unfamiliar language. During predeparture medical processing, refugees may be required to take medications without fully understanding their purpose. Yara recounted that one of the steps that her family had to go through before departing Jordan involved taking pills, yet no one in her family knew what they were for. Even her young siblings had to do it in front of staff to prove their compliance. Shortly before their departure, refugees are provided with a flight itinerary, which may terminate in an unfamiliar destination where they know no one. During a trip that can last several days, refugees are told that someone will guide them at each layover, as they may not be able to effectively communicate in connecting countries and airports.

When refugees eventually reach their resettlement destination, they must trust that someone from the Resettlement Agency will be at the airport to greet them, transport them, and provide them with food, shelter, and assistance. In particular, those designated as "free cases" are arriving in a city where they likely have no social network. Their well-being depends on their travel going as planned, since they may be without money or a cell phone. The stakes are high, and refugees have no choice but to trust that someone will be waiting for them across the threshold of the airport arrivals terminal. So much of their immediate safety and security rests in the hands of a stranger. It is not difficult to understand the relief on some refugees' faces when they finally arrive in their destination. When an Iraqi single mother slowly made her way down the long corridor towards the arrivals exit at the Boise Airport with her young son clinging to her side, her face and shoulders visibly relaxed when she realized that the small group waiting just beyond the glass doors was there to welcome her.

Refugees are expected to arrive having confidence in this bureaucratic system despite potentially prior experiences to the contrary. Many refugees will have encountered corruption in their home country, country of asylum, or during the resettlement process.[5] An Afghan man explained that corruption had infiltrated the approval process as his family awaited resettlement in Pakistan years earlier. When their case stalled in the country of asylum for several years, they eventually learned that it had likely been "sold." The family was then introduced to a man who claimed to have UNHCR connections and charged thousands of dollars to help refugees move their cases to the top of the approval list. This family could not afford his services, and soon after, they learned that he had been caught for his fraudulent business swapping out the photos of approved cases with those of his paying customers, guaranteeing their speedy departure. In recounting his family's experience, this man noted how prevalent this sort of corruption was in urban areas. Sociologist Bram Jansen was told of this same practice of "selling" files during his research in Kakuma refugee camp in Kenya.[6] A Congolese community leader in San Diego recounted that in Uganda, "there's a lot of bribe, there's a lot of corruption. . . . It's a messed-up system." Refugees may thus enter the resettlement process with exploitation and corruption as their frame of reference.

Once refugees successfully make it through the resettlement process and arrive in the US, their Resettlement Agency caseworker takes on an exceptionally critical role at the beginning, particularly for free cases. The caseworker is a lifeline during the first few weeks, and refugees have no choice but to rely on this stranger. Especially during the initial days, the caseworker is a refugee's source of food, money, shelter, transportation, and information. Fortunately for Nina and Joseph's family, their caseworker was both experienced and prepared. After their evening arrival in San Diego, he took them to the furnished and stocked apartment that he had set up earlier that day. Joseph and Nina knew no one else in San Diego, and, like many refugees coming out of years spent in a refugee camp, they had no financial resources. This family of six had arrived with two backpacks and one small suitcase containing only a couple changes of clothes for each family member. Once their caseworker showed them around their new home, they had a warm meal to enjoy at their kitchen table and freshly made beds to sleep in that night.

However, not all refugees benefit from a reassuring welcome, and the system in which refugees place their trust can betray them. Grace's failed resettlement from Kenya to New England in the early 2000s prompted her family to relocate to Boise less than a month after their arrival. The caseworker assigned to Grace's family was inattentive and largely absent during their first weeks in the US. The housing provided had been substandard, and they were left to their own devices to procure necessities for their baby. Though the Resettlement Agency helped them obtain a food stamps card, the family was without instructions about how to get to the grocery store. This family of three arrived in early winter, and the changing weather added to the inhospitality of their reception.

Reflecting back on her early days in the US, Grace said, "The thing that was really, really disheartening is the lack of support from the agency there. . . . We had issues with the house. . . . It felt like it was one thing after the other." Asking for help was unreasonably difficult. She added, "We didn't have a phone in the house, so I had to keep going to a pay phone to call anyone, to get in touch with anyone." When I asked what she would have done in an emergency without a phone easily accessible, she responded, "We would have had no idea what to do." Less than two weeks after their arrival, Grace thought to herself, "I'm done. I cannot do this." Another refugee in a neighboring apartment building offered her own family's experience as a cautionary tale. She told Grace, "You guys need to get out of here. . . . If you guys have somewhere else to go, go." This neighbor even purchased a calling card for Grace, instructing her to "call and find out where else you can go." Luckily, Grace's sister was in Boise and helped connect the family with a local Resettlement Agency. Her sister paid for their flight with the money she had been saving to travel to New England over the holidays. But many others like Grace's neighbor are left without an alternative and must cope with poor conditions and deficient service provision.

In the weeks that follow a refugee's arrival, caseworkers and other Resettlement Agency staff move their clients through the "conveyor belt of services" that comprises R&P assistance. Given the highly standardized nature of services and the resource-scarce environment within which Resettlement Agency staff operate, new arrivals may find that service providers make decisions on their behalf and provide recommendations contrary to their wishes. As refugees get their bearings in their new surroundings and move beyond the early days of jet lag and disorientation, a subtle tug-of-war develops between what Resettlement Agency staff believe is best, what refugees want for their lives, and what the USRAP expects of each party. Critical issues such as housing arrangements, employment, educational pursuits, and, most importantly, finances become flash points of contention. With time, refugees gain information, expand their networks, and rationalize their experiences, all of which can contribute to an erosion of trust in the resettlement process. As refugees begin to doubt the decisions being made on their behalf, a latent tension builds between clients and Resettlement Agency staff, even if refugees must continue to depend on them out of necessity. Refugees nonetheless find moments in which to voice their discontent, asserting their agency within a program that affords them limited control. As clients begin to deviate from the trope of the acquiescent client and the grateful refugee, these attempts at claims making and securing resources may damage their reputations with Resettlement Agency staff.

LOSING TRUST

When I asked Patrick what would have been helpful for his family when they were resettled in San Diego eight years earlier from a refugee camp in Tanzania, he noted that refugees are excluded from so many of the early decisions that affect their lives, such as where they live and how their R&P money is spent. He felt like his family's initial resettlement failed to take into account their preferences. He explained, "I don't think it's fair to decide for you what you want. They should ask you what you want." Later in our conversation he elaborated, "They never told us [that] we are going to spend your money. . . . They never asked us, 'What do you guys want to do? This is how much money you have.'" Years later, Patrick was still bothered by not having been consulted about where his family of nine, which included his parents and their seven children, would live. On the night of their arrival, their caseworker brought them to the three-bedroom apartment that had already been secured for them, but Patrick's family did not feel safe there. On their second night in San Diego, someone was shot in one of the neighboring units. This was not the life that Patrick's parents had envisioned for their family after finally leaving the refugee camp where they had spent fifteen years. Patrick added, "We had no option [to move]. We didn't have an option for basically a year. . . . We didn't know how to look for an apartment. We told them we don't want [to live] here, but nobody even cared." They had to wait out their twelve-month lease before relocating.

For Patrick's family and others, housing quality and neighborhood placement are a particular source of disillusionment. In an effort to avoid costly hotel stays, caseworkers do their best to secure housing before clients arrive. This need to quickly procure an apartment in advance of a case's arrival means that casework staff choose where and how their clients will live without getting their approval first. Given the numerous factors that caseworkers must weigh in housing decisions, they favor the cheapest apartment that is within occupancy limits for the case size, that is reasonably accessible to public transportation and the Resettlement Agency, and that meets basic standards of cleanliness and safety. Initial lease agreements are typically six to twelve months. As with job placements, housing quality reflects the low-income standard of living into which refugees are resettled, which may clash with their expectations given their prior frames of social class and standards for acceptable housing. A caseworker in San Diego recounted how distraught some of his clients were when he brought them to their new home for the first time. He recalled how one client objected to her "suffocating" apartment, telling her caseworker, "I need something with open air or I'll die. Why did you bring me here only to die? You should have let me die in Syria instead." Given the financial constraints imposed by the resettlement program, refugees are put in a position where they are expected to sign a lease despite their dissatisfaction.

Caseworkers consistently work with minimal resources and time when setting their arriving clients up with housing that meets federal requirements. It is their responsibility to ensure that their clients are housed, and at times casework staff get carried away with the prescriptive nature of their position, not only making decisions about where their clients will live but also about how they will live. To ensure that housing remains affordable once resettlement assistance ends, it is standard practice for bedrooms to be shared. Moise, a young Congolese man, was resettled in Boise from a refugee camp in Tanzania a few weeks before the rest of his family's case was approved. Because he was over twenty-one years old, Moise had been processed separately as a split single case and was the first of his family to receive approval and travel to Boise. When news came that the rest of his family would join Moise, the Resettlement Agency's casework staff secured housing for what would soon be a family of eight. Given the difficulty of finding large apartments, the family needed to be split between two neighboring two-bedroom apartments. Though five could legally live in a two-bedroom apartment in Boise, the Resettlement Agency proposed dividing the family evenly so that four members would live in each unit. Prior to consulting with Moise, the housing staff had already mapped out how beds would be distributed and who would sleep in each bedroom. In one unit, Moise would share a bedroom with two others, a teenager and another adult, while his mother would sleep in the other bedroom. The remaining four family members would share the other unit.

Moise came to the Resettlement Agency for a meeting with a casework staff member in anticipation of his family's arrival, and she presented him with this housing plan. Moise disputed the arrangements, insisting several times that putting three people in one bedroom was too much. He argued that even "in Africa" it was too cramped to have three adults in one bedroom. He added that perhaps these sorts of close quarters were normal in a hospital or a jail but not in a home. Moise protested that the Resettlement Agency was making intimate decisions on his family's behalf, and his frustration intensified throughout the meeting. At one point he pushed back, saying that the Resettlement Agency "does things without asking us and makes decisions for us." He wanted to wait for his family to arrive so that they could discuss and decide on the living arrangements together. Determining not only where Moise's family would live but also how they would live made Moise feel left out of consequential decisions regarding his family's new life in Boise. Moise asserted himself and his preferences, questioning the choices being made.

Beyond housing, expectations around the management of financial resources plays a significant role in eroding refugees' trust in their Resettlement Agency. Because it is common for refugees to arrive in the US without any savings or monetary resources, R&P funds are essential for meeting their needs—including rent, furniture, utilities, household goods, and some food—during the first few weeks of resettlement. Federal R&P funds are allocated to the Resettlement Agency on a per capita basis, providing $1,125 for each refugee arrival to cover initial set up expenses until the client is enrolled in a refugee-specific or general public-assistance program and begins employment. Despite rumors and refugees' expectations about the purpose of R&P money, in practice refugees only receive a small portion of these funds as discretionary cash in the form of "pocket money." This money is generally capped at $50 per person at a time (such as $300 for a family of six) to cover any minor expenses that might occur shortly after resettlement. Beyond the pocket money provided to them within twenty-four hours of arrival, refugees may see little more of their R&P money as cash.

Most arriving refugees are aware that they will be provided with financial assistance during their resettlement. Information about support, both accurate and erroneous, circulates within refugee camps and urban areas and gets transmitted by previously resettled family and friends. Rosine, a young Congolese woman whose family was resettled to San Diego from a camp in Kenya, told me, "A lot of times people used to have high expectations, like when you get to America you will never have to work for the rest of your life. You will get free money every month." An Afghan man in San Diego explained how the stark juxtaposition between conditions in the country of asylum and the US can initially make refugees feel like they have arrived in "paradise," creating first impressions that travel back to loved ones awaiting resettlement. When his family arrived in the US, the poor housing that had been available to refugees in Pakistan made everyday items such as carpeting, a refrigerator, a stove, and furniture seem like luxuries. Amid limited and selective information, rumors of free money and images of paradise take hold in countries of asylum.

The predeparture Cultural Orientation program provided to refugees shortly before travel to the US risks inadvertently reinforcing these perceptions. Beyond providing refugees with basic information to help prepare for resettlement, these classes also shape expectations. The curriculum is not destination specific, and according to some of the Resettlement Agency casework staff in San Diego and Boise, it can contain inaccuracies, creating or fortifying unrealistic expectations that are betrayed upon arrival. As the USRAP is made up of many complicated, interconnected programs, which differ across states and even within the same city, misunderstandings can occur easily. The classes may contain outdated information or be taught by instructors who are unknowingly perpetuating falsities. A Resettlement Agency staff member in San Diego with a refugee background shared that his family received predeparture Cultural Orientation from an instructor who had never been to the US and thus could only rely on the information that had been provided.

Yonas echoed this observation: "The orientation was given by people who had never been to the United States. They would tell you information, and the documents and books that they use are very old. When you come here it doesn't match. It's totally opposite. That's what most people get confused." Likewise, Thierry explained, "The people that do orientation, sometimes they've never been in America. They really don't know anything about what life looks like in America. So what they do is they will feed you these dreams and hopes and feeling like you're going to be working in diamonds." He noted that Hollywood images stand in as refugees' frames of reference, not neighborhoods like City Heights. These ideals coupled with incomplete knowledge of the purpose of R&P funds creates an environment susceptible to misinformation. Thierry continued, "When I come like that and you're my case manager, first of all, I know that you have money for me. If you're a case manager that does not really address the issue properly on how it works, that refugee has lack of trust."

A Congolese community leader in Boise shared that these "twisted and different" perceptions created by predeparture Cultural Orientation generate confusion among refugees when they arrive, which can quickly transform into disillusionment. A caseworker recounted how such misunderstandings can escalate. After a Somali family's nighttime arrival in San Diego, their caseworker took them to their prepared apartment. The father refused to stay, insisting that this was not his home. Following much late-night arguing, the caseworker took the family to a hotel so that her supervisor could resolve the issue the following day. When this man had seen images of a home during predeparture Cultural Orientation, which is intended to give refugees an idea of the types of accommodations that exist in the US, he was under the impression that the home he had been shown was the very home that was waiting for his family in San Diego. When his caseworker brought his family to their apartment, he had been trying to inform her that they had been taken to the wrong home. In addition to housing, any mention of specific sums of money during predeparture Cultural Orientation sets refugees up for confusion and disappointment. Bastien explained, "In the seminar, they told us, 'You guys will get to the America. They will give you. . . . kind of, like, $1,000 to help yourself buy those kinds of stuff.'" Ambiguous information or improperly informed instructors risk reinforcing inaccuracies and solidifying unrealistic expectations. Maxime noted that much of this conflict revolved around poor communication. He explained that, given what they had been told, refugees arrive and "think you have money but you're just being stingy, you know?"

When refugees arrive with specific notions of how much money they should receive, they may quickly feel as though they have been cheated, creating a domino effect that wears down their trust in their Resettlement Agency. Rather than giving clients a sum of $1,125 per person upon arrival, caseworkers are responsible for carefully budgeting and managing this money to cover initial expenses during the first several weeks, otherwise their clients may not have enough money left by the time their next rental payment is due. During one of the check day meetings in Boise, three Congolese brothers came to the Resettlement Agency to receive the monthly assistance that comes with the first four months of the Matching Grant employment program. One of them inquired about the status of his R&P funds. He said, "About our welcome money, until now we didn't get [it]." The caseworker presented the brothers with a detailed ledger that documented how their R&P money had already been spent on rent and other necessities. She said, "Did we deliver furniture? We bought household items. . . . We need to use R&P money to pay the first month of rent." In an effort to quickly dispel the rumors that circulated about welcome money, she added, "This idea that R&P money is welcome money that we give to you is misleading. You probably heard from others that [the Resettlement Agency] will give you money." After the meeting, as she and I discussed the exchange, and she acknowledged that there is "always an issue of clients not trusting money."

Over time, PRM has grown increasingly strict about the handling of R&P funds, the documentation associated with its spending, and most importantly, how much of it can be given directly to refugee clients in the form of checks for cash. Previously, in the absence of such rigid guidelines, Resettlement Agencies had more discretion regarding the distribution of these funds. A caseworker in Boise explained that they used to give clients a check for any leftover R&P funds at the end of the ninety-day R&P period. When this practice came to light in an audit, they were told to stop giving clients so much cash. Instead, the Boise Resettlement Agency sends any remaining money to the client's landlord as a down payment on future rent, or, occasionally, they will provide clients with prepaid gift cards to stores like Walmart or Target. Figuring out what to do with leftover R&P funds was less of an issue in San Diego. Since housing was so much more expensive and property management companies required an additional month of rent upfront along with the first month of rent and a security deposit, caseworkers in San Diego rarely had excess money to distribute.

Unfamiliar with these increasingly strict federal regulations, many refugees arrive under the impression that this money is theirs to use. Typically, however, only a few hundred dollars of R&P funds will ever pass through the client's hands as cash. Given that caseworkers must manage these funds and prioritize them for critical expenses such as rent, the doling out of pocket money often creates tension between caseworkers and clients—more specifically, it can become infantilizing for refugees who must ask for and justify requests for money that can only be provided in small increments. Six days after Jose's family of three arrived in Boise, he asked his caseworker for $300. The caseworker responded that he first needed to know what the money would be used for. Jose explained that he simply wanted to have some cash available as he had already spent the initial pocket money that his family had been provided the previous week. Caseworkers are put in a position where they become conservators and gatekeepers, requiring refugees to ask permission for funds that they thought belonged to them. As a Resettlement Agency employment specialist observed, "Anytime that you are dealing with a person's finances, there is going to be scrutiny on the person who is making those decisions."

Postarrival Cultural Orientation is one tool used to correct false expectations about the purpose of R&P funds. During a Cultural

Orientation class in Boise, the instructor explained to a group of new arrivals, "When you first arrived, the money used comes from the federal government. . . . IRC can't legally give you the money to resettle yourself. It's used for pocket money, a meal when you first arrive, furnishings. Legally some things have to be new, like beds and mattresses. Kitchen items, a deposit and rent, cleaning supplies, hygiene items, utensils, and basic food. . . . IRC is required to purchase and provide these for you, including a car seat and bus pass." Moise was growing suspicions of the use of his R&P funds nearly two months after his arrival and spoke up during the class. He said, "When I compare what the agency bought for us, I'm not convinced the money was all spent for me. What happens to the balance left?" The instructor replied, "It's a good question. . . . Sometimes IRC has to dip into emergency funds for one person. Sometimes when there are many people in the family some money is left over. IRC can't keep it but can pay rent in the future. Say $100 is left. They would apply $100 to the next rent or power bill. Your caseworker keeps a budget, and you have the right to see that."

Beyond adhering to strict federal regulations, caseworkers retain their clients' R&P funds in an effort to safeguard their well-being given the economic precarity and resource scarcity of early resettlement, as there is little margin for error. Because the budget for newly arrived refugees is so tight, any misuse of R&P funds or other forms of cash aid may result in a client falling short on rent soon after arrival. In San Diego, a few hundred dollars in remaining R&P funds could be the difference between affording the second month of rent or not. In Boise, R&P money is conserved to supplement future rental payments, particularly for single-mother families who may struggle to get by on one low-wage job. Nina and Joseph's family of six only managed to make their second month of rent because their caseworker had held onto the $580 in leftover R&P funds, which, when combined with their first disbursement of TANF cash aid, covered the cost of their apartment with only days to spare. Regardless of caseworkers' intentions, this practice of assuming management of their clients' money is based on the presumption that newly arrived refugees cannot manage the funds themselves. This belief that refugees cannot be trusted to manage resources themselves undergirds much of the international refugee assistance regime.[7] Instances in which clients do quickly spend R&P money further reinforce this notion.

These safeguards fell through for a Pakistani family of four in San Diego when it came time for their second rental payment. Very little R&P money remained after their caseworker secured their apartment and purchased the bare minimum in household goods and furniture. The family was reliant on their remaining R&P funds and first installment of TANF cash aid to cover rent until one of the parents gained employment. By the time their rent was due, their caseworker learned that they did not have enough money. It came to light that during the prior weeks the family had spent a shocking $250 on local transportation. Their caseworker learned that they had been taken advantage of by an Urdu speaker in the community who had offered rides to the family at an extremely inflated rate. Not only was their caseworker upset that this family was short on rent, but she was also frustrated because she had been especially careful about preserving as much of this family's R&P money as possible while setting up their apartment, knowing just how tight their finances would be. Because caseworkers are responsible for keeping their clients housed, especially so early in their resettlement, they are put in a position in which they feel they must assume control and management over R&P funds and other financial benefits, as there are few alternatives should the money be spent elsewhere.

The use of R&P funds for initial set up costs combined with caseworkers' efforts to protect those funds means that welcome money largely bypasses the hands of their refugee clients. Caseworkers purchase furniture and household goods on behalf of their clients, often before they have even arrived, and, in Boise in particular, rent is paid for with checks that have already been made out directly to property management companies. While this practice of managing clients' money is intended to be for their benefit, it leaves refugees with little involvement in basic financial transactions or confidence in how their funds are being spent. Patrice, a young Congolese man, was still unsure what had happened to his family's R&P money when they resettled in Boise eight years earlier. He told me, "the people that came before we came, they say when you get to the United States, there's money that they give you to help you out. . . . They call it welcome money. But then we came here they never gave us that welcome money. So, the agency . . . they spent it on something else, I don't know. Because they told us they bought couches and bunk beds and stuff like that, but then when you calculate everything and the money we were supposed to get. The money doesn't come up." Caseworkers act as the custodians of what refugees believe to be their money, managing it in ways that run counter to their expectations.

In spite of refugees' perceptions about not fully benefiting from what was allocated for them, in reality, Resettlement Agencies often over-spend on clients' initial resettlement. Particularly when there are delays in securing permanent housing, caseworkers must rely on hotels until a lease is signed. Even short hotel stays can quickly add up and deplete R&P funds, especially for single cases and smaller families. Though a caseworker in San Diego managed to secure housing for a young single Iranian man four days after he arrived, the four nights he spent in a hotel used up more than one third of his R&P funds. In one extreme example, a family resettled to San Diego stayed in a hotel for more than a month during an especially busy period of arrivals, costing the Reset-tlement Agency $8,000 beyond the family's allotted R&P funds. A for-mer caseworker in Boise explained that these hotel stays were at times necessary, but they only further fueled clients' suspicions about the mis-management of their assistance. This former caseworker said, "People would be put in hotels. . . . and those are expensive. And yet we don't have any other funds to pay for that, and helping people understand that can get extremely challenging and could add another layer of mistrust on." Upon learning that their R&P money had been spent on their hotel stays, she said that clients would question their caseworker's judgment, asking, "So why didn't you just put me in a house if you knew that I was coming? Why didn't you find a house for me?"

Alphonse, a Congolese community leader in Boise, elaborated about how this dynamic unfolds, "With the money that they get from the federal government, they've been paying the hotel for those refugees—some of them spending three months at the hotel. And once they get their own place, [the caseworkers] say, 'No, we have no money left. Only $500, whoops.'" He explained how in trying to rationalize their circumstances, new arrivals may wonder, "How come you're accepting people to come and you don't prepare for them?" He noted, "The breach of trust is there," which ultimately leaves refugees thinking "No, I don't like them. They took my money." Not only are clients upset that they did not receive their welcome money as expected, they also feel like they are suffering the consequences of their caseworker's unpreparedness. In reality, it is a matter of luck whether a case gets permanent housing immediately or must endure lengthy and costly hotel stays. The federal funds provided to support resettlement are highly standardized, yet actual experiences differ according to numerous variables that are out of the hands of new arrivals and sometimes even of their caseworkers.

Though caseworkers are required to maintain transparency by keeping detailed records and receipts, some clients continued to mistrust the process. A former employment specialist in Boise shared the challenges of explaining the fine print of resettlement assistance to new arrivals—a challenge that she found took at least eight months of "consistency, transparency, and repetition" to overcome. But despite continued efforts by Resettlement Agency staff, some clients walk away from their resettlement services convinced that their caseworker withheld, or even stole, some of the R&P funds. Patrick felt like the

Resettlement Agency that had helped his family operated more like a business than a social service agency and had not been forthcoming about his family's R&P funds. He told me, "They will just steal your money and everything, and they don't give you a receipt." A Congolese community leader in Boise surmised that some of this suspicion resulted from the types of expenses that were commonplace in US rental transactions but could be unfamiliar to some refugees, such as security deposits or an additional month of rent used as a guarantee for tenants without credit histories, both of which used up large portions of R&P funds. It can be difficult to fathom how so much money can disappear so quickly.

Other clients accused their caseworker of "eating," or misappropriating, their money. A former caseworker and interpreter in Boise from a refugee background explained how unfulfilled expectations about R&P funds led people to this conclusion. She said, "We were very transparent about: 'This is how much you've received in your welcome money.' . . . I think the picture in their head is that they'll come here and everybody will be handed their money, and, you know, go play with it. . . . But it's the same money that we're using to rent a house, and the deposit, and get furniture for the house, and all of a sudden people will say, 'The case manager ate our money.'" She noted just how irrational this explanation seemed from the perspective of a caseworker, adding, "Why would I jeopardize my job, my life, my reputation by eating your money?" Yet she understood how intractable the issue had become: "It's a whole thing of just the way the picture is painted. So, I know that we were very transparent, and we would share and would have the receipts and everything. . . . If there's any money left over you'll give it to them and say, 'Hey, this is what is left over.' But I've interpreted in cases where people are saying, 'No, they ate our money. This is how much we're supposed to [get].'" In some instances, claims about not receiving what one was owed may be less about anger over missing dollars than an expression of overall dissatisfaction and disappointment with how the process has unfolded.[8] Trust suffers when circumstances make refugees question whether Resettlement Agency staff are working in their best interests.[9]

Didier still believed six years later that he had been cheated out of his R&P funds. Since his arrival, he had become a leader in Boise's Congolese community and worked closely with local Resettlement Agencies. Despite his proximity to and familiarity with the resettlement process and service providers, he was resolute that his caseworker had withheld funds. He recounted,

> I don't know what they do with the money. . . . They give you nothing in the end. And I'm like, you [are] supposed to give me this money. And then at the top of that, I need help. . . . But no, that money never even showed me, you never see the money. I was lucky that my mom was aware of it, and she guided me. I got half my money. All my friends who came here, nothing. I remember [my friend], I kept telling him the same thing and after that he told me he got $75 out of the $900.

Even with intimate knowledge of the work of local Resettlement Agencies, Didier held on to his conviction that casework staff were deceiving new arrivals.

This notion that clients do not receive all of their welcome money and that caseworkers withhold R&P funds circulates within communities, further fueling suspicions. Once a community member plants seeds of doubt, it can be difficult to regain a client's trust. A caseworker in San Diego explained how after a family of seven was warned by someone that they were being cheated out of money, it shaped all subsequent interactions. No matter what their caseworker did, the family was convinced that he was personally profiting off their resettlement. After one Congolese family learned early in their resettlement that a friend also lived in San Diego, their caseworker told me that this news was both good and bad. While this friend could be a form of support, he could also be a source of misinformation.

Five days after a Congolese family of eight was resettled in San Diego as a free case, they informed their caseworker that they had a relative in California. They wanted to move out of the three-bedroom apartment that their caseworker had secured and furnished for them ahead of their arrival so that they could join this relative. The clients asked their caseworker for their money, explaining that they preferred for their relative to help with their resettlement instead. Their caseworker was caught off guard as the family had seemed content with their new home only days earlier. During this exchange, their caseworker grew noticeably frustrated with her clients' sudden change in tone, at one point interjecting, "Money? I have no money!" Later in the day, this caseworker speculated that the relative had likely vilified the Resettlement Agency, causing their sudden change in demeanor.

Shortly after a Congolese single mother of three was housed in an apartment complex that was home to several other Congolese families, her neighbor warned her that the Boise Resettlement Agency "ate" all of the welcome money that her family of ten was supposed to have received, believing many months after their resettlement that they had been cheated during the resettlement process. A casework staff member later informed me that in reality the Resettlement Agency had spent about $6,000 beyond that case's allotted R&P funds. This newly arrived single mother shared her concerns about her neighbor's warning with an interpreter who tried to dispel any doubt and clarify how her R&P funds were being spent.

Andre, who, more than a decade earlier, had been among the first Congolese refugees to be resettled in Boise, explained how a preexisting community in the resettlement destination can at times complicate the task given to Resettlement Agencies. Because there was no Congolese community to welcome him, he was not exposed to such advice and rumors. He noted that efforts to connect new arrivals with other refugees can backfire when people share negative experiences. He said, "Now you are learning everything you need to learn from these Congolese that were here, that have experience with the [Resettlement Agency] before. If these Congolese had a bad experience with the [Resettlement Agency], guess what? They want to tell you all the bad stuff."

Yonas explained how refugees come to understand the resettlement process based on their individual experience, which does not account for changes in the cost of housing over time, the irregular availability of donations, or the use of hotels on a case-by-case basis. He said,

> Now refugee[s], they will stay in [a] hotel for two weeks. Hotels are an average of $50 to $150 a night. . . . That money will go away, and they will ask where the money go, and they will show them on paper. But that's not going to make sense. Those things are really an issue to understand, and of course creates confusion and mistrust between the agency and the refugee.

Federal R&P funding has undergone only a few significant increases over the past two decades despite the constant rise in the cost of living. Yonas noted how much the value of R&P funds in Boise differed ten years earlier. Those resettled earlier may suspect that more recent arrivals are not receiving all their R&P funds simply because they received more during their own resettlement. The circumstances of each case are unique, yet this variation sews doubt about the credibility of Resettlement Agencies.

Henri noted that unmet expectations about resettlement may engender mistrust of other resettled refugees, particularly when new arrivals feel like they were misled to believe that life in the US would be easy. He explained,

> You're coming here and you have this whole mindset and vision that Americans are going to be like that, but then once you get here, it's not like that, so you have those kind of depressed notion and feeling. . . . So you begin to distrust people, even the people within your own community. Stop trusting because you're like, 'Oh yeah, they lied to me. They told

me it was going to be like this, but it's not like that.' So yeah, there is a lot of distrust.

Though the USRAP is a highly standardized program, each case has its own particular characteristics that affect services and levels of financial support, such as family size, number of minor children, and employment assistance program. Consequently, community members risk giving advice to new arrivals that is not reflective of the particularities of their situation. Aware of how such information can get distorted and feed feelings of mistrust, caseworkers warn clients not to discuss the details of their financial assistance with other refugees. During Bonheur and Esperance's twenty-four-hour home visit, their caseworker told them twice during the meeting not to discuss their cash aid with other refugees, since not everyone was enrolled in the same programs or had the same family composition. He explained, "For benefits, you can't compare yourself with your neighbors," and later in the conversation, he reiterated, "Make sure you never talk about your benefits with other people." Nearly a month later, Bonheur and Esperance had befriended another recently arrived Congolese family in their neighborhood who was supported by the same caseworker. One day, the two fathers walked into their caseworker's office asking him to explain their financial assistance again. Understandably, the families had exchanged information about their respective benefits and wanted to know why they were not receiving comparable amounts. In addition to differences in family size and initial housing circumstances, one family was enrolled in the TANF CALWorks program while the other was enrolled in Matching Grant. They were both receiving the assistance that their caseworker believed was best suited to their family, but the complexities of resettlement services and public assistance made both families doubt that they had been offered all available benefits.

Resettlement Agency staff were aware of the prevalence of mistrust, which persisted despite efforts to address it. When I shared preliminary findings about this issue during a meeting with some Resettlement Agency staff in Boise, a member of the casework team dramatically dropped her head into her arms in an exaggerated display of frustration, responding that the Resettlement Agency had put a great effort into dispelling misinformation about R&P spending. Another staff member blamed PRM for increasingly rigid rules about not giving cash to clients, putting Resettlement Agency staff in situations in which they had to implement and enforce top-down regulations that contribute to clients' disappointment, confusion, and ultimately mistrust. Resettlement Agencies are being held accountable by PRM and other funders, and it would be risky to defy directives, especially regarding the allocation of funds. Regardless of their preferences, Resettlement Agencies cannot act independently of the government agencies that give their work legitimacy.[10]

A couple of months later during an interview, this same staff member in Boise elaborated on the challenges of sustaining clients' trust. Their office had sought the support of a program designer who concluded that mistrust was inevitable. She recounted that the program designer had explained, "Every time you introduce the distribution of money into a service program, it switches the relationship into a transactional mode, and within that transactional mode, it is deeply difficult to create that sense of human trust." Importantly, the fact that these transactions involve money that clients cannot "see, choose, or touch" makes maintaining trust all the more challenging. Refugees are given no ownership over the R&P money that they arrive believing belongs to them; money that rarely touches their hands. Despite this staff member's belief that "families should have cash" based on "a lot of evidence showing that people make choices that are most aligned with their needs when they have total control over it," programmatic directives from the federal government left no room for flexible implementation. Giving out large sums of R&P funds to clients as cash could jeopardize their standing as a Resettlement Agency. Given the resource-scarce environment within which they operate, their priority was to ensure that their clients remained housed, even if trust suffered in the process.

Certain administrative choices made by Resettlement Agencies contribute to the mistrust that develops around welcome money. Resettlement Agencies have some discretion over the allocation of each client's $1,125 R&P funds, with the option to reserve up to $200 per person to create an emergency reserve of flex funds for particularly needy cases in the future. Since initial setup costs were so expensive in San Diego, it was not feasible to withhold any of the R&P funds, and so all $1,125 was systematically spent on each arriving client. Additionally, public assistance programs in San Diego provided some level of ongoing support for more vulnerable cases, such as single parent families. As refugees in Idaho do not benefit from a public safety net, the Boise Resettlement Agency made the decision to uniformly reserve $200 of R&P funds per client to build up a flex fund, which they maintained for emergency rental assistance, a strategy for filling the void left by a weak welfare state.

In this sense, clients of the Boise Resettlement Agency were not incorrect in asserting that they had not received the welcome funds that they had been promised. Moreover, other Resettlement Agencies in Boise opted not to reserve flex funds, meaning that refugees resettled by other Resettlement Agencies in the same city did benefit from all $1,125 of the welcome money. An IRC Boise administrator was aware that this decision had the potential to create misunderstandings, but she also had to safeguard the agency's ability to help their clients, particularly in instances of housing insecurity. She told me, "It was our decision, because we have some families with extreme need, and we do pool the flex and push it towards them, single moms that we want to pay more months of rent towards . . . and there's probably mistrust of, you know, 'It was supposed to be $1,125, and what I'm getting is $925.'" In the absence of reliable state-based public assistance in Idaho,

Resettlement Agency leadership made the decision to conserve funds knowing that it risked further damaging their clients' trust.

When refugees lose trust in their caseworker and the Resettlement Agency, the already difficult task of resettlement and the provision of services is further strained. This mistrust also jeopardizes the ongoing relationship between Resettlement Agencies and their clients, affecting the likelihood that they will return for future services. One of the Boise Resettlement Agency's immigration staff members explained that they wanted clients to make use of their office's services to apply for a Green Card one year after arrival, rather than seek assistance elsewhere. The Resettlement Agency's national office expects that former clients will return for this service, and it reflects poorly on the Resettlement Agency when they do not. This staff member knew that the Resettlement Agency risked losing clients' future business if they felt like they had been cheated during the resettlement process.

WHEN CASEWORKERS LOSE TRUST

As refugees are judging the trustworthiness of their caseworkers, so too are caseworkers appraising their clients. The punitive nature of resettlement services and the US approach to welfare coupled with the high-stakes monitoring of Resettlement Agency compliance makes caseworkers and employment specialists hyperaware of clients who may be misrepresenting themselves in their claims for assistance or may be falling short of programmatic requirements. When clients elicit suspicion about the information they are providing to the Resettlement Agency, it damages their credibility in future interactions and makes caseworkers less willing to make exceptions. When clients use up their pocket money quickly, it can raise caseworkers' concerns about reckless spending or dishonesty about where the money has gone. When a single Burmese man in San Diego asked his caseworker for more money, explaining that he had spent his $100 in pocket money as well as

$200 from his US tie in less than a week, his caseworker began to question his client's explanation of what had happened to the money and why he needed more.

Ahead of each monthly check day in Boise, Resettlement Agency staff equipped themselves with compliance notes that contain detailed attendance records for English and job readiness classes as well as any other concerns. Financial assistance programs, whether resettlement specific or welfare based, all come with terms that require recipients to participate in job readiness activities before employment. Resettlement Agency staff used these notes to confront clients about noncompliance, like spotty attendance, relying on this written record as proof should a client try to deny not having participated. This approach sets up adversarial exchanges which assume that clients are being dishonest and taking advantage of the resettlement program. Resettlement Agency staff use the threat of sanctions, which would cut necessary benefits, to coerce compliance.

A Congolese couple in Boise met with a Resettlement Agency staff member on check day to receive their rental check and disbursement of pocket money through the Matching Grant program. The staff member began the meeting by addressing concerns about their attendance at English class: "I know you're here for your check, but first I need to cover a few things. You were only at three classes last month. Same with your wife. Is there a reason you're not going?" The client responded through an interpreter that he had never missed a class. The staff member continued, "[You're] only marked for three days. Everyone else is marked." The client explained that he had signed his name in the class's attendance book. The staff member cautioned him, "I'll give you a warning. If your attendance isn't marked better next month, you'll be sanctioned in Matching Grant. If you go to class, make sure the teacher marks you present." Despite the client's claims to the contrary, he received a warning. Rather than giving him the benefit of the doubt, the staff member presumed that he had missed English class. Though a warning is only a verbal reprimand, any future missteps put this client at risk of being sanctioned, which carried more severe consequences.

In addition to attendance records, clients may also be confronted about rumors that they began working without informing the Resettlement Agency. Because most refugee-specific and general assistance programs are means-tested, benefitting from both resettlement assistance and unreported income puts clients at risk of committing fraud. On several occasions, the Boise Resettlement Agency heard that two brothers had begun working while continuing to receive their Matching Grant benefits. Though these young men denied that they were employed, the Resettlement Agency nonetheless sanctioning them and withheld their benefits based on several other reports that they were indeed working. The Resettlement Agency had even planned to send a staff interpreter to their home to speak with the clients' sibling in the hopes of getting to the truth.

When clients are deemed to have misrepresented their situation or needs, their reputations may be tarnished, and doubts may be sown regarding future requests. Etienne, a young Congolese man, relocated to Boise after originally being resettled in the Midwest eight months earlier. He was ill when he first arrived in the US and struggled with expectations for early employment given his poor health. He told me that his original Resettlement Agency pressured him to take a job at a car factory despite being sick. After three weeks, he suffered a terrifying medical scare on the job. Then winter set in. He was still unwell, and the extreme cold caused him pain in his muscles and bones. He recounted that he did not leave his apartment for three months. He lost weight and thought he was going to die. Etienne decided that he had to move somewhere else. He just wanted a calm place to live. Through social media he reconnected with a friend from the eleven years he spent in a refugee camp. She had been resettled to Boise with her family and invited him to come and stay with her family while he got settled. Etienne hitched a ride with a long-haul truck driver from his church whose route was going through Idaho.

After three days on the road, Etienne arrived in Boise and settled into his friend's apartment. He reached out to the Boise Resettlement Agency for support. He asked for help with financial assistance, finding permanent housing, and getting ongoing medical care, but the Resettlement Agency had no resources to support him. A refugee's case can only be officially transferred to another Resettlement Agency if it is done within the refugee's first thirty days in the US, and Etienne had long surpassed the ninety-day R&P period. He was considered a secondary migrant and thus not part of the Resettlement Agency's official caseload. Nonetheless, Etienne pled his case to the Resettlement Agency. He was concerned about overstaying his welcome with his friend. He wanted the Resettlement Agency to help him find roommates. He also asserted that his health was still too fragile to begin working, so he wanted financial support to pay for rent. Though Etienne had had aspirations as a young student in the DRC, his plans had been derailed by forced migration. In the refugee camp, he had spent all of his time simply trying to survive, and he lamented that life in the US felt the same. Given that Etienne was a single adult of working age without minor children, food stamps were the only benefit that he qualified for in Idaho, which still required participation in job readiness activities.

After internal deliberations, the Resettlement Agency staff made the administrative decision not to use any of their emergency reserve on Etienne, which they felt they needed to conserve for their own clients, particularly single mothers. The staff rationalized that there was bound to be someone in need of emergency support who had children. Like other humanitarian settings where service providers must at times rank what they determine to be their clients' need, Resettlement Agency staff have the power to determine who gets access to limited resources.[11] Etienne could make his case but had no control over the outcome.[12] According to their hierarchy of deservingness, young single men were at the bottom, even those with health issues. The Resettlement Agency assigned a caseworker to Etienne who helped him enroll in the food stamps program. Since Etienne had already been in the US for eight months, he was ineligible for Refugee Medical Assistance, and he did not qualify for Medicaid in Idaho because he was over eighteen years old and unemployed. Over the next several weeks, Etienne continued to make requests of the Resettlement Agency. He needed a place to live and resisted the idea of working until he felt stronger.

After a month of Etienne's continued efforts at claims making, which were premised on no longer being able to stay at his friend's home, he accidentally sent a text message to one of the Resettlement Agency's interpreters that had been intended for his friend. The text message discussed strategizing about how he could convince the Resettlement Agency to give him money for an apartment. This slipup did not go over well with the staff. The interpreter who received the text message later noted that he had sensed that Etienne was being manipulative and that he had been suspicious of him from the beginning. This error only reinforced the impression. The casework staff felt deceived after having spent weeks working to come up with creative temporary housing solutions out of fear that Etienne would become homeless. As other incongruencies emerged, such as the fact that he already had a bank account, Etienne lost credibility and made the Resettlement Agency staff question his claims. Eventually the Resettlement Agency helped Etienne gain employment and find housing. But other misunderstandings from Etienne helped to fill in a broader and more complicated picture. For example, when Etienne received his first paycheck from his hotel housekeeping job, he thought that the portion of his income being withheld was a biweekly fee to the Resettlement Agency, rather than taxes to the state and federal government. Regardless of Etienne's circumstances, his actions made the Resettlement Agency doubt the extent of his deservingness and his trustworthiness. Etienne was nonetheless a recently arrived refugee with ongoing medical concerns who arrived in Boise without any formal systems of support.

While living in refugee camps and urban areas in countries of asylum, refugees develop survival strategies in order to get by and keep their families alive under dire circumstances. Within contexts of protracted displacement where corruption may be commonplace, refugees learn that they are expected to play a certain role as the recipients of humanitarian aid.[13] Yet what may have been necessary prior to resettlement risks clashing with normative expectations for fair assistance in the US. A caseworker in San Diego told me, "I've been betrayed so many times" by clients who, according to him, had overstated their needs. In response to desperate pleas for assistance, this caseworker had given one family $200 of his own money and created a fundraiser for another that netted $1,200, only to find out later that both families had misled him. Though he felt wronged, he nonetheless rationalized such instances, concluding that these refugees were just trying to figure out how to get by and were bringing tactics with them that may have been necessary in corrupt and resource-scarce environments. Refugees must walk a delicate balance between appealing for support without asking for too much or appearing unsatisfied with how little they are receiving.[14]

Even if refugees are not deceiving their Resettlement Agency, they may inadvertently elicit doubts about their deservingness by not playing the part of the archetypal grateful refugee. A couple of months after Bonheur and Esperance's family of four was resettled in San Diego and housed in a one-bedroom apartment, Esperance began pressing her caseworker about moving to a two-bedroom apartment. She was pregnant, and before long, their family of five would be sharing one bedroom. This and other requests along with certain signals like the clothes the family wore drove their caseworker to assume that the family must be from a "rich" background; he surmised that only people who came from money would ask such questions. They had been resettled from a city rather than a refugee camp, which the caseworker took as another indication that they were probably better off than other clients. He complained that clients were always trying to find ways to get more. These requests for more comfortable accommodations were considered incongruent with how a refugee *should* act, as if wanting a two-bedroom apartment for a family of five was unreasonable. By making appeals for better conditions, this family did not fit their caseworker's expectations of an acquiescent client. Though class background and past experiences of wealth are irrelevant to claims of refugee status, they nonetheless shaped how service providers formed opinions of their clients' deservingness.

As the resettlement process unfolds, the accumulation of small infractions and decisions being made on behalf of refugees begins to alter their relationship with the Resettlement Agency. Newly arrived refugees also begin to learn the terms of their membership in US society and grow more comfortable asserting themselves and advocating for their needs. Resettlement Agencies are aware that this erosion of trust can occur and risks damaging their credibility with clients. The Boise Resettlement Agency knew how important it was to build rapport with clients early on and that there was room for improvement. A Resettlement Agency administrator developed plans for new clients and caseworkers to meet informally over tea at the Resettlement Agency office before clients had to jump onto the "conveyor belt" of R&P services. The intention was to create an informal space where clients' preferences, ambitions, and expectations could be acknowledged and heard by staff, an approach that notably contrasted with the implementation of standardized services. The administrator described how the goal of this meeting was to foster an opportunity "to get to know you as a human being before all the crap" of required services begins. Though the intentions behind this initiative were good, it put an additional strain on an already overburdened staff. She explained, "I proposed it first to a former caseworker, supervisor, you know, that every new arrival, before they hit the food stamp interview, before we start going through check, check, check, check, test, test, test, test, [we] should have tea with the family, and we brought a special tea set for it. . . .

Like we did some design work to kind of make it feel like a space that isn't clinical, that doesn't force you into a really sterile, unhuman [environment]." Despite the administrator's good intentions, adding this social function to each new case drove the casework supervisor to quit. Aware of the significant structural challenges inherent in the resettlement process, this administrator was realistic in acknowledging that any adjustments they could make would only modestly improve client experiences. She said, "If we can peg down a couple things and fix those, we're not going to raise the bar to deeply satisfied, but at least not as pissed off."

Resettlement Agency casework staff are chronically overworked as they try to keep up with required services, paperwork, and client needs.[15] When service providers are dealing with the daily stressors of managing refugees' initial resettlement, efforts to change the status quo feel insurmountable, leaving intractable issues unresolved. The combination of resource scarcity and strict federal regulations fosters a dynamic of mistrust between new arrivals and Resettlement Agency staff. New arrivals must continue to function in survival mode, while service providers work in a perpetual state of crisis management.

GAINING TRUST, LOSING TRUST

The accumulation of disappointments and unmet expectations prompts refugees to question their trust in the people and system that welcomed them. This chapter has explored the evolution of trust throughout the resettlement process, as refugees assess their service providers and Resettlement Agency staff gauge the trustworthiness of their clients. Issues of mistrust hinge on the control of and appeal for the distribution of limited resources. When refugees' experiences with financial assistance stray from expectations and rumors that circulate in countries of asylum, their attempts to rationalize this ungenerous reception may leave them to conclude that the resettlement system is corrupt. At the same time, the extent of refugees' financial precarity puts Resettlement Agency staff in situations where they feel like they must take control of the decisions that shape their clients' lives so as not to leave them destitute. Staff become self-consciously trapped by structural features of the USRAP, and they rely on problematic strategies that are infantilizing and coercive.[16] They threaten the termination of essential assistance, they discourage the sharing information with others, and they use financial vulnerability to pressure clients into accepting the housing decisions they have made. Resettlement Agency staff's efforts to care for their clients' immediate needs are intimately tied to practices of control.[17] Such disempowering dynamics are particularly harmful for refugees who have experienced significant past traumas.

With the loss of trust comes a reluctant dependence. Refugees feel like they must continue to sign documents and meet requirements in order to continue accessing the meagre assistance they receive. Any deviation from compliance or attempt at claims making may backfire if it runs counter to expectations about how a "grateful" refugee and acquiescent client should act. Clients who damage their credibility risk getting deprioritized on the hierarchy of deservingness that Resettlement Agency staff feel they must rely on to distribute limited funds.

CONCLUSION

RESETTLEMENT IS A CRITICAL and even life-saving means of humanitarian protection, yet it is nonetheless a displacing process—one that comes with hope, excitement, disappointment, and grief. This book highlights the difficult nature of this undertaking given all the ways that refugees must cope with the past while getting their bearings in a new country.[1] Resettlement brings long-awaited relief as well as new struggles. Traditional benchmarks for studying incorporation such as employment and educational outcomes obscure less measurable yet deeply meaningful aspects of refugees' lives, including familial dynamics, dignity, and emotional well-being.

This book examines both how and why resettlement feels so displacing. While some of the loss and destabilization of early resettlement are consequences of forced migration and protracted displacement, other dimensions are rooted in policy decisions that create coercive conditions for the delivery of essential services. The bureaucratic program that governs resettlement is a humanitarian practice that is both supportive and disciplining.[2] Throughout the resettlement process, refugees are repeatedly put in a position in which they face "immoral proposals"[3] that limit their ownership over decisions critical to their own well-being. Consequently, the gains offered by resettlement become intertwined with hardships that disrupt life in new and unexpected ways. When the rare chance at resettlement necessitates permanent family separations or when ongoing access to essential financial support is contingent upon low-wage manual labor employment, resettlement becomes displacing to an extent that refugees never imagined. Feelings of disillusionment, frustration, mistrust, isolation, disempowerment, and uncertainty are all expressions of the displacing effects of resettlement.

Just because resettlement is difficult for refugees and service providers, however, does not mean that it is not worth doing. In a world without resettlement, refugees in protracted displacement would have little to no alternative to raising future generations in conditions shaped by the restricted mobility, limited rights, food insecurity, and poor healthcare that characterize the imposed temporariness of many contexts of asylum. Moreover, in the absence of resettlement, cities across the US would be without the many small business owners, community leaders, and families who simply want to make a home where their children can enjoy safety and security.

A Resettlement Agency staff member in Boise explained that, despite being the best path forward, resettlement would always be a daunting process for new arrivals. She said, "Most of our families—I felt like they were pretty communicative when they first arrived: . . . 'I know that this is the best thing for my family because I can't go back home.' So many of our families, at least verbally and on the surface, had reconciled with that, of we aren't going back. But how you do that? That's a much easier thing to say than when you are actually going through that process." Models of service delivery that foreground agency and choice while also acknowledging the inherent disruptions of resettlement can make the process less distressing, helping new arrivals to "reorganise the world around them into a world that is not crazy or fragmented, but stable and meaningful."[4] This book shows that familial and economic stability as well as the security of home not only are central to refugees' well-being, but they also facilitate the long process of incorporation.

Despite being free from the persecution and the violence that precipitated their forced migration, many refugees arrive in their resettlement destination only to confront housing instability, economic insecurity, and a loss of agency. Amara summed up how the USRAP's approach to resettlement was at times antithetical to the ethos of the American dream. She said, "We thought everything was made out of gold. . . . So it's a big fall to go from there to, 'Oh, you have to work. Oh, by the way, you know, your credentials? They mean nothing here.' And just understanding that that in and of itself is trauma." She continued, "It's one thing to tell someone to be a proud American, but when you're struggling, what do you have to be proud about? You know, all you think about is how am I going to make it?" When refugees encounter the displacement and disillusionment of initial resettlement, they are doing so already exhausted by the traumas of war and forced migration. As refugees face the uphill climb of acclimating to and settling in a new country, the services and forms of assistance provided to them do not offer the security, peace of mind, and hopefulness that would attenuate the many struggles that inevitably accompany resettlement.

Prior scholarship on the USRAP has typically taken two approaches to studying resettlement. The first compares resettled refugees with other immigrants in the US to show how refugees stand out as the sole group to benefit from a federal program of integration, an exception in a country that takes a hands-off approach to immigrant integration. The second approach focuses on how the USRAP falls short of its stated objectives, failing the refugees who arrive to communities across the country. By extending the literature on the "social condition of displacement" to the resettlement context, this book offers displacement as an alternative framework for understanding the initial resettlement stage.[5] In doing so, I show why resettlement does not live up to the expectations of both refugees and receiving communities. As refugees contend with the many competing challenges of settling in a new country, Resettlement Agency service providers are given inadequate time and resources with which to facilitate their clients' resettlement. The realities of the USRAP are particularly incongruent with frameworks of integration that foreground security and stability across numerous domains of a refugee's life, including employment, housing, health, and social ties,[6] the difference between "a mere life" and "a good life."[7] By understanding the ways that resettlement is displacing, I show that integration is an inappropriate bar with which to measure initial resettlement, and expectations of achieving integration set Resettlement Agencies and newly arrived refugees up for failure despite their tremendous efforts.

This book identifies why resettlement is so challenging, both for arriving refugees and their service providers, as refugees' relief of having won the resettlement "lottery"[8] is quickly tainted by their disillusionment and lack of ownership in shaping the trajectory of their lives. Labeling resettlement as a solution to displacement gives a false sense of closure that does not reflect refugees' lived experiences.

I also show how deficits in the federal resettlement program create tensions between arriving refugees and service providers. Resettlement Agency caseworkers assume responsibilities that far exceed their job description, and the USRAP takes advantage of their hard work and ingenuity.[9] Yet despite caseworkers' tirelessness and dedication, programmatic shortcomings erode their clients' trust, leaving newly arrived refugees feeling deceived and their caseworkers frustrated. Programmatic objectives and the disciplinary nature of service provision clash with the immediate and ongoing needs of refugees, resulting in tensions that weaken the relationship between refugee communities and local Resettlement Agencies. Because the USRAP is made up of many complicated and interconnected programs that differ across states, misunderstanding and confusion can easily arise. As the face of direct service provision, caseworkers become the easiest target of blame from resettled refugees and broader receiving communities.

This book holds a magnifying glass to refugees' early months in the US, drawing attention to initial resettlement as a distinct phase of the forced migration trajectory worthy of analytic inquiry; it becomes the starting point from which refugees begin the process of longer-term incorporation. By offering a comprehensive portrait of the system responsible for welcoming refugees, I account for the tensions and conflicting priorities that arise as refugees and service providers navigate limited resources and programmatic constraints. By examining the USRAP in two contrasting cities and drawing on the experiences of refugees from multiple countries of origin, this book offers a deep understanding of how refugees manage the displacing effects of resettlement as well as how local dynamics do and do not mitigate the challenges of this federally standardized program.

Resettlement is intended to be a meaningful way to restore the political and social rights of particularly vulnerable refugees, but as this book demonstrates, the USRAP can offer humanitarian protection while also being displacing. I bridge the scholarship on immigrant incorporation, refugee resettlement, and the "social condition of displacement"[10] to show how this "solution" to forced migration creates complicating changes and coercive conditions that further disrupt refugees' lives.

By examining how lived experiences of forced migration interact with this standardized program of resettlement, this book makes three main contributions. Firstly, I advance the international migration literature by offering displacement as an alternative framework for understanding refugees' initial experiences of resettlement. Secondly, I contribute to sociological understandings of displacement. While studies have shown how displacement can occur before and in the absence of forced migration, this book reveals how displacement can continue even after a refugee's forced migration has been "resolved." Lastly, by incorporating the perspectives of both arriving refugees and service providers, I not only show how resettlement is displacing but also why it unfolds in this way. The social policies intended to assist refugees also constrain their choices, create economic insecurity, and expose them to new vulnerabilities.

Alongside resettlement's many challenges are stories of success. Refugees start businesses, pursue higher education, and become leaders in their communities. Yet their achievements are often in spite of, not because of, the policies and programs that welcomed them. Refugees succeed, as they did so many times before, because of their resilience, dedication, and ambition. Without a home country to return to, refugees are given no choice but to make their resettlement work. But the USRAP should not take this resilience for granted. Refugees' and Resettlement Agency service providers' tenacity should not be used as an excuse for accepting the programmatic failings of the USRAP, because for some families the obstacles may always be too great. As Didier noted, "You can either succeed or it can go really bad; it's just two things. That's what I keep telling people, you know. Yeah, it's either become very successful or it can horribly go wrong for you." After six years in Boise, Didier was a success story. A leader in the Congolese community, at the time of our interview, he was nearing the end of his bachelor's degree, having held professional internships that put him on the career path he had always dreamed of. But in order to get to this place six years after his arrival, he had to find a way out of his first job as a janitor. Alongside those who do achieve upward mobility and housing security are many others for whom the challenges of early resettlement remain insurmountable.

It is difficult to predict who will succeed in the face of such challenges and who will continue to struggle. A community partner who ran a program that matched Boise residents with refugee families noted, "It's so hard when you see families struggling. We have one family—we just love them. They were one of those families that came in, and we were like, they are going to do great, and they haven't. It's been a struggle, and he's been sick and can't work and you know it's just been one thing. And the girls are just dolls doing really well in school, but financially they're just not making it." When policies fall short of providing a comprehensive welcome, those with the very vulnerabilities that prioritized them for resettlement are at risk of significant precarity, contradicting the humanitarian motivations that supposedly undergird the USRAP. Given that resettlement support is embedded within the US welfare state,[11] such refugees will encounter struggles that are beyond the scope of what their Resettlement Agency can remedy.

ATTENUATING DISPLACEMENT: RECOMMENDATIONS FOR POLICY

It is misguided to assume that any one policy change can definitively resolve the losses that come with forced migration. Though resettlement will always be difficult, it is incumbent upon policymakers to mitigate the stresses put on refugees, and there are ways that policies can make it easier. The following recommendations often arose during interviews with residents of San Diego and Boise who had gone through the resettlement process themselves. From their more secure and stable vantage point several years after arriving in the US, they reflected on what could have eased the displacing effects of resettlement for themselves and their families. Any of the following recommendations must come with commensurate funding and resources to support Resettlement Agencies, who already make do with so little.

Reflecting on the USRAP, a community partner in Boise who worked with refugee youth said, "It's crazy to see, as you start to dig into it, how many pieces of the puzzle are broken, and how that really takes a lot of energy and time and a lot of people to start to fit the pieces together." Many of the challenges faced by Resettlement Agencies, and by extension their clients, come down to issues of implementation. Well-intended policies do not always match the realities faced by the diversity of refugees who arrive to a diversity of communities across the U.S. A former employment specialist in San Diego noted, "Seeing the gap between actual policies and the programs that are being implemented. . . . It's just . . . it's so easy to see something from a policy, or just from on paper, but then when you're actually dealing with people, it does not apply the way you think it will." An employee of the Boise public schools was well aware that "if people are still coming back with the same problems, then something's not working. . . . Because if they are still coming back, if it's the same problem over and over again, then it's something wrong with our system."

Predeparture Cultural Orientation

The USRAP must evaluate how the predeparture Cultural Orientation curriculum is taught in Resettlement Support Centers around the world. The rumors and misinformation that circulate about the USRAP are powerful and uphold falsehoods about the support that awaits refugees in the U.S. To prevent the erosion of trust between refugees and Resettlement Agencies, efforts must be put into place to ensure that refugees receive a thorough orientation about the realities of US resettlement taught by instructors who have a deep knowledge of the terms, conditions, and systems of support that await refugees upon arrival. This predeparture moment is an opportune time to preemptively counteract narratives related to financial assistance and prepare refugees for the fact that their initial economic support may vary based on their resettlement destination. Formerly resettled refugees could act as "resettlement ambassadors," traveling to Resettlement Support Centers to deliver first-hand accounts of the initial resettlement stage.

Formerly resettled refugees are truly the experts of what resettlement is like, and consultations, either in person or virtually, would allow for candid conversations about what lies ahead. If predeparture Cultural Orientation can mitigate refugees' mistrust of their Resettlement Agencies, it will result in a smoother resettlement process.

Postarrival Cultural Orientation

The Cultural Orientation curriculum is delivered over a few days during the ninety-day R&P period. While it serves as an important touchstone for refugees to learn more about their communities and the adjustments to come, it should not be the only opportunity to review important information related to topics as critical as public assistance, laws, and education. Newly arrived refugees are dealing with a significant amount of information related to their resettlement, and frontloading so much within these early months comes at the expense of depth and retention. Once refugees have gained some real-world context for the topics being covered, Cultural Orientation has the potential to be more impactful. An iterative approach would allow refugees to review information pertinent to their financial, social, and emotional lives as they adjust to their new community, offering a structured and predictable timeline in which to ask questions and talk through points of confusion. While it becomes difficult to schedule Cultural Orientation once refugees are employed or enrolled in school, a flexible and ongoing rotation of classes with an open-door policy would allow current and extended clients to drop in as needed. Alternatively, rather than Resettlement Agencies hosting ongoing Cultural Orientation themselves, funding could instead be given to ethnic- and community-based organizations to deliver open sessions, given their ability to better translate misunderstandings and issues of cultural adjustment as well as their intimate knowledge of the needs within their communities.

Twenty-Four-Hour Resettlement Hotline

In an effort to better support the immediate needs of arriving refugees and to alleviate some of the burdens placed on R&P caseworkers, Resettlement Agencies can establish an emergency "on call" number for refugees to use outside of business hours to address questions, concerns, and points of confusion. As in medical professions or with crisis hotlines, Resettlement Agency staff members would rotate who is "on call" during evenings and weekends. When not on call, caseworkers would be better able to protect their nonworking time, while new arrivals would not feel abandoned outside of standard business hours.

Resettlement Agency Staffing

The staff employed at Resettlement Agencies should reflect the refugee populations they work with and those that live in the community. Not only do staff from refugee backgrounds possess a deeper understanding of the forced migration and resettlement experience, but they can also foster greater trust as new arrivals move through the resettlement process. It is important that people from refugee backgrounds are hired in roles beyond interpreters and are sufficiently compensated for the additional labor they take on through this role.[12]

R&P Itinerary

Newly arrived refugees should have access to a simple yet complete mapping of the locally situated services they will receive, the timeline of those services, and the various agencies and caseworkers who will provide these forms of support. Over time, refugees are enrolled in numerous programs within and beyond the Resettlement Agency. This fragmented structure of service provision is not intuitive, which makes it difficult for refugees to know whom to call for what. From the perspective of arriving refugees, all their issues and needs are interconnected, but services are siloed according to discrete parts of their lives. Not only would a map or flowchart of services make the USRAP more legible to new arrivals, but it would also provide refugees with a better understanding of their progress, of the important milestones to come, and of the key points of contact along the way.

Accounting for Flexibility, Agency, and Choice

Time and choice are meaningful aspects of a refugee's resettlement,[13] and the USRAP prioritizes neither. As a former employment specialist in Boise noted, "A family of two should not necessarily have the same boxes to check as family with a single parent with eight kids or six kids." This one-size-fits-all approach to resettlement services is often misaligned with refugees' needs and puts Resettlement Agency staff in a position in which they must counterbalance ill-suited services with supplemental support beyond their required duties. Staff are seldom provided with more than an arriving case's basic biographical information, and there can be many surprises that caseworkers must figure out how to manage within the first twenty-four to forty-eight hours after arrival. Incorporating greater flexibility also comes with recognizing that the standard per capita R&P grant used to support refugees' initial resettlement expenses must be calibrated to the local cost of living. Caseworkers in high cost of living areas are given the impossible task of finding sustainable housing for their clients, and refugees face immediate economic insecurity when their R&P funds do not stretch further than covering initial set-up costs. R&P funds should be adjusted to cover a stipulated number of months of rent; it should not be up to local housing market to determine when refugees reach a financial precipice.

THE CHANGING POLITICS OF RESETTLEMENT

Since I conducted my fieldwork in San Diego and Boise from 2018 to 2019, the political pendulum has twice swung in opposing directions; resettlement expanded during the Biden administration and contracted to new lows under the second Trump administration. Though President Biden's initial promises to revive the USRAP were complicated by the COVID-19 pandemic and the large-scale efforts to quickly resettle thousands of Afghans and Ukrainians, US resettlement gained renewed traction. Between 2022 to 2024, the annual ceiling was set at 125,000 refugees, the highest level in more than two decades. Though arrivals fell short of this ambitious ceiling, the US resettled 100,034 refugees in 2024, a significant improvement from only a few years earlier when fewer than 12,000 refugees were resettled in both 2020 and 2021. As a result, families were reunited and more refugees were given this important alternative to protracted displacement. On January 27, 2025, this progress came to a screeching halt when President Trump's pause on all future resettlement took effect, including for those who were awaiting scheduled flights.

Resettlement Agencies managed to bounce back from the devastating infrastructural damage incurred during the first Trump administration, yet it remains unclear whether the agencies and staff who do the daily work of the USRAP can outlast another assault on the system. Only weeks after President Trump's second inauguration, Resettlement Agencies began shuttering their offices. The challenges experienced from 2017 to 2021 made clear how important it is to ensure that Resettlement Agencies are financially stable so that they can serve as the critical support system they are for both newly arrived refugees as well as extended clients. At the time of this book's writing, the future of the modern USRAP hangs in the balance.

Attacks on the USRAP in conjunction with increased xenophobia risk destabilizing refugees' sense of security. New resettlement pathways through private sponsorship, co-sponsorship, and educational institutions offer promise for expanding the number of refugees afforded this opportunity. Regardless of how a refugee is resettled, it is imperative not to lose sight of the displacing effects of this process and to think critically about how alternative pathways may attenuate or exacerbate certain dimension of resettlement.

WHEN DOES DISPLACEMENT END?

When I asked a Resettlement Agency staff member if she thought resettlement in Boise was successful, she responded that it worked "by the skin of its teeth." Nonetheless, she noted how shorter-term struggles during the early years of resettlement often gave way to longer-term stability, especially for the second generation. She said, "People make it, they make it short-term by the skin of their teeth, and many, many, many people thrive, become rooted." Moise, a young Congolese man, shared during a Cultural Orientation class that initially life in Boise felt hard because "it's very different. Many things are different than home. Some might be good, like good schools, but still there can be sadness and loneliness." When the instructor asked him what advice he would give to other refugees, he replied with the assistance of an interpreter, "Tell people that Boise is hard upon arrival but as days pass by you get adjusted." Just because initial resettlement is displacing does not mean that disorientation and disruption last forever. Acclimating to a new country and community is hard, particularly when so many aspects of the initial process are out of a refugee's control. Nonetheless, over time people settle into the rhythms of life in a new place. Raphael, a single father from the DRC, had been in San Diego for three years at the time of our interview. He explained that "three, four, five months [in the] United States for a new immigrant, it is hard. But after . . . things will start becoming normal, a normalized situation. At the end, within one year to two years, the situation will be in a good situation." A caseworker in San Diego noted a similar pattern. He observed how over time his clients get settled, and "slowly, slowly, they just disappear," no longer needing the depth of support that had once been essential at the beginning.

When refugees find stability in the various domains of their lives through employment, financial security, family reunification, educational attainment, and housing, displacement gives way to incorporation. Yet as this book demonstrates, attaining stability is not inevitable, and some refugees may continue to feel unmoored long after their arrival. Many continue to experience lingering feelings of displacement as crises arise and as they interact with other local and federal institutions, such as law enforcement, schools, and health care.

Despite these enduring challenges, many people I met in San Diego and Boise repeatedly noted that the benefits of resettlement were not for those who had arrived in the US as adults. Rather, it was for their children. Just as the migration literature has long shown, the 1.5 and second generation adapt and integrate in ways that feel impossible to their parents. The gains and losses of resettlement are unequally distributed across generations and within families. Resettlement cannot repair many of the sorrows that come with forced migration, protracted displacement, and resettlement, but a brighter and more secure future for their children can make the daily struggles all seem worth it, a light to believe in during moments of darkness.

For many of the people I met throughout my fieldwork, the pursuit of resettlement was fueled by aspirations for the next generation. Given the obstacles and disappointments of their own experiences, success became defined by the opportunities available to their children. Aadam, an Afghan father of two explained, "Me and my wife, it will be difficult to [live] our life in here. . . . I'm grateful for being here for my kids, that they are having a better life in here. . . . To give a better life for my kids, I have to be away from my home country, from my friends and my family." Raphael expressed a similar sentiment about his two children, "The main objective is my children to get a good education, that's it. Other things, no. Me, I didn't come here for making money or getting good life, because I'm almost old. But I want at least my children to achieve their future." This finding echoes what sociologist Laila Omar calls "foreclosed futures," which describes how resettlement can be a conscious calculation for parents, resettling to secure their children's future in place of their own.[14]

A Resettlement Agency staff member in Boise explained, "I think just it doesn't matter who you are; starting over later in life, or at an older age just is harder. So yeah, it depends on the measurement of success, but children's, the next generation's fight is incredible." Myint, a young man from the Karen ethnic group in Myanmar who arrived in San Diego as a young child, was fully aware of how much his parents had lost and that he and his sibling had motivated their decision to leave the refugee camp in Thailand where they had become community leaders. He said, "I mean, they left everything. They left the church. They left the students, everything that they created over there. They left everything for us so we can have a better future." The opportunities created by resettlement are calculated differently across generational lines, challenging assumptions that everyone benefits equally.

Hafiz told me that one of his friends who had also been resettled was working at Starbucks for $10 per hour despite having been an engineer with the US military in Afghanistan. When Hafiz asked his friend, "What happened?" his friend replied, "Okay, I lost my career, but I won for my children." During our interviews, both Hafiz and Raphael each showed me their children's school report cards. Neither father could conceal his deep pride for what his children had accomplished in a few short years. Raphael said, "That is what makes me just feel comfortable. . . . When they perform like this, I hope they will get a good future."

"WE ARE PEOPLE LIKE THEM, TOO"

While resettlement may ultimately be a "good" displacement, it is nonetheless disruptive. This book reveals that resettlement does not easily resolve displacement, as refugees continue to experience new and ongoing instabilities that affect their families, economic security, and psychosocial well-being.

When I asked Rosine what she wished people better understood about what it was like to come to the US as a refugee, she said, "I wish they understood that we are people like them, too." Farah made a similar point, "Refugees are just normal people." She explained, "maybe they never thought of leaving their countries" until they were forced to do so. Ashina wished that people understood that "even if they are refugees, they used to have a home, they used to have a life. They used to have things." Thierry explained that "being a refugee is not a choice, but a circumstance. No one chooses to be a refugee. Everyone can be a refugee anytime, anywhere." Once re-settled, he continued, refugees want to "mostly just live peacefully" without worrying about the threats and violence that drove them to leave their homes.

As this book has shown, resettlement is never going to be an easy task, but policies and methods of service delivery that acknowledge and accommodate the displacing effects of resettlement can help to ease the disruption and disorientation of starting over in a new country, especially when refugees have so little say over the process. When resettlement services are delivered through underfunded and over-stretched Resettlement Agencies that function as an extension of the US welfare state, newly arrived refugees encounter a system that feels unwelcoming and punitive. As Grace observed, "There's so many stresses that are under the surface that people don't see, and I think that is what makes it most difficult." It is imperative to improve upon traditional models of resettlement, because, as Karam explained, "when you go through that process, you feel how valuable your life is and how important it is for you and your family to be in a safer place and start a new life. So, you do your best to survive and to prove to yourself and your family and everyone that you can make it again."

Methodological Appendix

THE PATH THAT LED ME to San Diego and Boise from 2018 to 2019 started twelve years earlier when I spent the summer before my junior year of college as an intern at a Resettlement Agency in Boston. Knowing very little about resettlement at the time, I had no idea that those eight weeks would leave me with questions that I would spend the next decade trying to answer. During that summer, my time was focused on tasks that the Resettlement Agency caseworkers did not have the capacity to do given all of the cases they were managing. I escorted clients to doctor's appointments, collected furniture donations throughout the city, provided in-home literacy tutoring for Somali Bantu women, and organized a recreational outing for mothers and children. It quickly became apparent that resettlement was so much more complicated than government policies let on. When I sat at one woman's kitchen table as she practiced writing her name and address, cockroaches fell from the ceiling. Within days of arriving in Boston, one family of four was adamant that they wanted to go back to their country of asylum, distraught by their living conditions and the realities of how their resettlement would continue to unfold. At the same time, I saw the Resettlement Agency's seasoned and knowledgeable caseworkers working around the clock to support their clients. Despite everyone's efforts, the realities of resettlement were falling far short of its promise. Why were these refugees not finding the security and stability they desired? Why did it seem like caseworkers were always fighting an uphill battle?

In the years that followed, I read everything I could get my hands on about US resettlement. I pursued the topic as a master's student at the American University of Paris, and then several years later it motivated me to apply to PhD programs in Sociology. While at UCLA, I immersed myself in the international migration literature, always trying to draw connections with refugee resettlement. Prior to commencing my fieldwork in San Diego and Boise, I carried out two smaller projects that helped to build the foundations of what became my dissertation research. I spent more than a year conducting ethnographic fieldwork at a Resettlement Agency in California where I worked as a volunteer, helping around the office and teaching Cultural Orientation classes. Through this fieldwork, I gained a deep appreciation for the work that Resettlement Agency staff carry out as they move back and forth between strict policy directives and the varying needs of their clients. Subsequently, I spent a summer conducting interviews with refugees who were undergoing the final stages of their resettlement processing in Vienna, Austria, and were anxiously awaiting approval to come to the US. As the people I met in Vienna shared their excitement, fears, and apprehensions, it became clear to me that resettlement has profound effects on refugees' lives long before they have even landed in the US.

As I developed my dissertation project, I wanted to understand the resettlement process from the perspectives of both arriving refugees and service providers, two key groups that were often kept separate in research. By that point, my only frames of reference for the USRAP had been in large immigrant gateway cities that had the established infrastructure to incorporate immigrants and where refugees joined a diversity of foreign-born residents. I knew I also wanted to study how resettlement unfolds in the new immigrant destinations that were such an important part of the USRAP but with which I had little firsthand experience.

ETHNOGRAPHIC FIELDWORK, 2018–2019

Using city-level data from the US Refugee Processing Center, I set out to better understand where refugees were being resettled across the US, in what numbers, and in which groups. I complied an aggregate list of the top fifty cities of resettlement from 2002 to 2017 in order to select my two field sites. I was looking for two cities with sizeable and established resettlement programs that welcomed similar refugee groups but differed in type. Ideally, both cities would also have an affiliate office of the same national Resettlement Agency in order to minimize the organizational variability that exists across the ten national agencies. These criteria led me to San Diego, California, and Boise, Idaho, two cases that ticked all of the boxes.

Eager to study these two contexts of resettlement, I began the long process of gaining research access. Given my interest in the initial formal resettlement period as well as my prior experience within Resettlement Agencies, I chose to anchor my ethnography within a Resettlement Agency in each city from which I could extend my fieldwork to other locations and organizations. I also knew how chronically understaffed Resettlement Agencies were, and I wanted my time in the field to contribute to the everyday work of resettlement. As an ethnographer, it was important to me to be in a role where I could carry out "observant participation."[1] The International Rescue Committee (IRC) had Resettlement Agency offices in both San Diego and Boise, and given the breadth of the IRC's work in forced migration, it seemed like a strong fit.

After carrying out desk-based research on resettlement in these two cities, I visited Boise for the first time to attend the Idaho Conference on Refugees. During three intense days, I learned about the issues and dynamics of resettlement in this city. I also proposed my project idea to the director of the IRC Boise office, who seemed similarly excited about the research. Upon my return to Los Angeles, I began the process of gaining formal research access through IRC's research office based at their headquarters in New York, engaging in consultations and writing a research proposal. Subsequently, I made several trips to San Diego where I met with the IRC San Diego's director and other staff before they also approved my fieldwork plan. After four months of negotiating access and gaining IRB approval from UCLA, my home institution, I moved to San Diego on June 2, 2018.

I spent the following six months in San Diego dividing my time between the IRC's resettlement office for several days per week, where R&P caseworkers were based, and one day per week with the economic empowerment office that housed several of the Resettlement Agency's vocational training programs. From my very first day at the El Cajon office, the R&P caseworkers took it upon themselves to train me in nearly every aspect of their jobs. In addition to shadowing the caseworkers as they set off for hours at a time making home visits, taking clients to appointments, and preparing for new arrivals, I also became a casework assistant in a volunteer capacity, supporting the two staff caseworkers as they assisted their clients. I set up apartments, attended airport pickups, and witnessed interactions between refugees and public services agencies, including the Department of Social Services, the Department of Public Health, the Social Security Administration, and educational institutions. Given the geographic spread of San Diego County, I spent a significant amount of time driving clients around and accompanying them to appointments.

I also became an ad hoc French interpreter for the caseworkers, neither of whom spoke French. Given that my fieldwork took place following the Trump administration's travel bans, Congolese refugees became the predominant group of new arrivals, many of whom had been educated in French. Refugees from the DRC were a relatively new group to arrive in San Diego at the time, and the Resettlement Agency was still catching up to accommodate their language needs. With advanced proficiency in French, I became an asset to the caseworkers who could rely on me in a pinch during airport pickups, walk-ins at the office, or impromptu home visits. This shared language with many Congolese arrivals became a significant asset during my fieldwork. Not only did I get first-hand experience with many of the complicated and difficult conversations between caseworkers and clients, but I was also able to communicate freely with many new arrivals without the mediation of an interpreter and without putting refugees in a position where they had to express themselves in English. Speaking French provided the opportunity for many more informal conversations in the car, in waiting rooms, or at the Resettlement Agency.

During my time in San Diego, I also made a concerted effort to engage in participant observation beyond R&P casework and the Resettlement Agency. I volunteered with three local tutoring programs, one during weekends for community college and university students from refugee backgrounds, one after-school program at a local elementary school for refugee-background students, and one after-school community-based program for Congolese youth. I also attended a monthly meeting for refugee-serving organizations, church services, meetings with a group of local "mentors," and local community festivals that fundraised for resettlement. Through these activities, I learned about many of the issues important to refugee families beyond what emerged in their interactions with their Resettlement Agency. I also made contacts that facilitated the interview component of this project.

After I wrapped up fieldwork in San Diego at the end of November 2018, I moved to Boise on December 1, 2018. I deliberately timed my fieldwork so that I would be in Boise during the winter months, as climate is a meaningful and often underrecognized dimension of initial resettlement experiences. I spent the next six months based at the IRC Boise office in a similar capacity. I supported the R&P casework staff several days per week and spent one day per week assisting the development and community outreach staff. Because of the six months I had spent at the Resettlement Agency in San Diego, the R&P casework staff in Boise considered me to be "trained" already, and I immediately jumped in as a casework assistant at a time when they were short staffed. Along with shadowing the casework staff, I took on similar duties as I had in San Diego, transporting clients, making home visits, assisting clients at appointments, and providing ad hoc French interpretation for Congolese arrivals. As I grew more familiar with the organizational landscape in Boise and as various issues arose, the Resettlement Agency staff became eager to hear points of comparison about how housing and financial matters played out differently in San Diego. Given that Boise did not yet have the same proliferation of refugee-serving organizations beyond Resettlement Agencies, most of my ethnographic fieldwork focused on Resettlement Agency activities, though I attended community meetings and events when possible. Additionally, the time I spent with the development and community outreach staff offered a window into the supplemental work that Resettlement Agencies must do in states that are politically hostile to resettlement. In this role, I conducted research on newly elected state senators and attended legislative meetings and events at the Idaho State Capital. After six months in Boise, at the end of May 2019, I wrapped up fieldwork.

Given my role as a casework assistant in two Resettlement Agencies, I gained a significant understanding of both the professional and embodied dimensions of Resettlement Agency casework. The responsibilities that a caseworker takes on with each new arrival are tremendous, juggling both required services and accompanying paperwork along with their clients' individualized needs and circumstances. It is a job that takes significant stamina; workdays can reach twelve to fourteen hours, particularly when evening airport pickups come after a full day of work. R&P casework also requires significant resolve, as caseworkers often become the targets of blame when resettlement falls short of refugees' and community members' expectations. Resettlement Agency casework is physically and emotionally taxing in ways that I could only fully understand by doing it for a year, as caseworkers try to make their clients' lives tenable despite limited resources and time. I came to deeply appreciate the invisible labor carried out by R&P caseworkers, as they missed lunch breaks, assembled furniture, and cleaned up vomit from the back of their cars.

My positionality as a white American researcher embedded within a Resettlement Agency shaped my interactions and access. I was cognizant that I was associated with Resettlement Agency staff who are in a position of authority and control. In this capacity, I functioned as an insider and outsider and maintained self-awareness of how my presence affected interactions.[2] Given the extensive time I spent within the Resettlement Agency as a volunteer supporting staff and refugee clients, I became a "trusted outsider,"[3] which often resulted in Resettlement Agency staff and many clients sharing candid and critical perspectives on the resettlement process. Within both Resettlement Agencies, I was presented to staff as an external researcher, and on many occasions I had conversations with staff about my project and comparative cases.

Because I spent so much time with Resettlement Agency staff, there were many moments for extended conversations about their responsibilities, particularly challenging cases, and the accumulating frustrations about the nature of their work. These deeper discussions during car rides, shopping trips, apartment setups, and airport pickups gave casework staff the time and space to explain or justify earlier actions. As a casework assistant, I also saw and felt many of the obstacles that Resettlement Agency staff navigate daily, and over the course of a year, I was socialized to understand the USRAP from the vantage point of Resettlement Agency staff. Though I also had many open conversations with clients during trips to the office, home visits, and car rides, my affiliation with the Resettlement Agency likely did not allow for the same level of unencumbered discussion. Nonetheless, as I discuss below, the sixty interviews I conducted with people who had come through the USRAP helped to balance out the potentially skewed perspective of my participant observation, as these interlocutors were no longer reliant on a Resettlement Agency and had little to lose by offering unfettered critiques and evaluations that were enriched by their longer-term reflections on resettlement. These interviews were critical for filling in the perceptions and insights that new arrivals may not have been comfortable sharing with me.

Moreover, I was particularly aware of my dual roles within the Resettlement Agency as an ethnographer and volunteer casework assistant. In order to protect refugees' and service providers' identities, I relied on oral consent to avoid a written record of names, and my access was revisited in informal ways as I conducted fieldwork within the Resettlement Agency and through community events and interactions in each city. The IRC maintains its own general research consent form that new clients are asked to voluntarily sign, as many of their standard activities also include research and data collection internal to the IRC. In addition to this generic consent, it was also important to me to be forthcoming about my role as a student and researcher as I supported clients through the Resettlement Agency. These conversations came up during car rides, in waiting rooms, or before I sat in on meetings between Resettlement Agency staff and their clients. Additionally, my role as a volunteer casework assistant was under the supervision of and in support of the Resettlement Agency staff caseworkers. The caseworkers were in charge of their cases, and they would delegate particular tasks to me, such as providing transportation, running errands, assisting at appointments, and dropping off paperwork. In this capacity, I deferred to the caseworkers on matters relating to their clients' resettlement, and it was made clear to their clients that I deferred to the caseworkers and other Resettlement Agency staff. As I connected with people and organizations beyond the Resettlement Agency, my intimate knowledge of resettlement casework combined with my outsider status enabled a number of very frank conversations about resettlement in both cities.

Throughout my fieldwork it was important to me to take a contributory approach considering the resource-scarce context of resettlement. At the same time, my position within the Resettlement Agency meant that I could not go beyond the scope of what staff can ethically provide. Consequently, time and transportation became two resources that I could give to newly arrived refugees without overstepping professional boundaries—which monetary support would have. I provided transportation that extended beyond the scope of what caseworkers could feasibly offer, and I assisted with client enrollments at agencies that exceeded those required of R&P casework. For example, I spent one afternoon waiting outside of the emergency room so that I could give a client a ride home from the hospital to avoid what would have been a $50 taxi ride. In these small ways, I tried to do what I could to make the lives of new arrivals that much easier while still staying within the bounds of Resettlement Agency regulations.

I regularly wrote detailed fieldnotes based on jottings taken in the field. Throughout this book, I only use direct quotations when I was able to write down what someone said verbatim at the time or when it came from interviews. In instances where it was socially acceptable to take notes, such as during meeting, I wrote detailed notes by hand. Otherwise, I made jottings in my phone that I expanded upon in more comprehensive fieldnotes each evening. Ultimately, I ended up with more than 450 single-spaced pages of fieldnotes, approximately evenly divided between my two field sites.

INTERVIEWS

Along with participant observation, I conducted 102 semi-structured interviews with resettled refugees, service providers, and community partners. My ethnographic fieldwork helped me to build a network in each city, and through these contacts I began recruiting for interviews. I recruited through local Resettlement Agencies, community events, and snowball sampling, which helped to expand the scope of my research beyond the setting of the Resettlement Agency. I focused on two groups in each city (see table 8): people who had been resettled for at least one year (to gain perspectives on longer-term incorporation) and service providers and community partners. Some interviews were conducted with people I had come to know well through my fieldwork, whereas others took place during our first meeting. I carried out interviews at coffee shops, offices, and homes. I offered suggested locations when I reached out but left it up to the interlocutor to decide a place that was both comfortable

TABLE 8
Demographics of interviewees

Refugees	City	San Diego	30
		Boise	30
	Country of origin	Afghanistan	8
		Burundi	3
		Democratic Republic of the Congo	20
		Eritrea	2
		Ethiopia	1
		Iran	1
		Iraq	8
		Kenya	1
		Liberia	1
		Myanmar	5
		Somalia	6
		Sudan	1
		Syria	2
		Uganda	1
Service providers	City	San Diego	19
		Boise	23
	Role	Resettlement Agency staff (including caseworkers, employment specialists, administrators, etc.)	13
		External service providers (including social service agencies, schools, law enforcement, local government, etc.)	15
		Community partners (including ethnic- and community-based organizations, faith-based organizations, etc.)	14

NOTE: I have categorized interviewees according to their role at the time of the interview. Many interviewees have held many professional roles in resettlement over their careers, including several of the refugee interlocutors, which resulted in an even more robust sample of service providers in each city.

and convenient. Though I did not financially compensate interlocutors, I did buy many cups of coffee and tea.

For interviews with people who had arrived through the USRAP, the key criterion was that they had been resettled for at least one year so that they could offer a sense of how refugees' lives unfold once they have moved beyond formal resettlement services. I conducted thirty interviews per city. Though these interviews offer a range of forced migration and resettlement experiences, they are not representative of all refugees who were resettled to these two cities. One third of my interlocutors were Congolese, which reflected the growing focus on Congolese resettlement across the US. Interviews lasted an average of one hour and included a range of questions about their lives prior to resettlement, early resettlement experiences, interactions with service providers, and longer-term incorporation. I was deliberately vague in asking interlocutors about their lives prior to arriving in the US, allowing them to choose what they felt comfortable sharing about their experiences of forced migration and protracted displacement. Many interlocutors did offer great detail about their lives in refugee camps and urban areas as well as the period leading up to their departure for the US, which I draw on throughout chapter 1.

All but two interviews were audio recorded. For the two that were not audio recorded, I instead took detailed notes by hand as was requested by the interlocutor. Two interviews were conducted in French, as requested by the interlocutor, and the rest were conducted in English. Though the interlocutors represented a diversity of countries of origin, experiences of displacement, age, and socioeconomic status, the majority had intermediate to advanced levels of English proficiency at the time of the interview, which leaves questions about how much their language proficiency shaped my findings. Nonetheless, many interlocutors talked extensively about family members during interviews, including immediate family members in the US who still had limited English proficiency years later. There were both gendered and generational reasons why members of the same family had not all gained similar ease with English. In many cases, interlocutors acted as spokespeople for their families by raising issues that affected other members, shedding light not only on their own personal resettlement experiences but the challenges that their loved ones continued to face.

I also carried out interviews with service providers at local Resettlement Agencies and social service agencies, local government officials, law enforcement, educators, and community partners. Many of these contacts were facilitated by my fieldwork, as I began to map out the key organizations and individuals in each city. I received oral consent ahead of each interview, and all interviews were conducted in English, audio recorded, and subsequently transcribed. Interview questions focused on the interlocutors' particular role, perceptions of key issues related to resettlement in that city, and overall perceptions of resettlement. Several interviews were with former Resettlement Agency staff, allowing for candid and illuminating conversations now that they had moved on to other roles and professions.

I have used pseudonyms throughout this book to protect the anonymity of the people who participated in this research. In instances in which it would make them more easily identifiable, I am also vague about certain details of refugees' lives. I have chosen not to use pseudonyms for service providers and instead refer to them by their professional role as "a caseworker," "an employment specialist," and so on. Resettlement Agencies are small organizations, and providing any more detail about the service providers would make it difficult to protect their identities. For this reason, I refer to some people simply as "casework staff" because any additional specification of their role as a youth caseworker or housing specialist would make them more easily identifiable.

ANALYSIS

In addition to memos written during my fieldwork, I carried out several iterative phases of coding and analyzing fieldnotes and interview transcripts, and I relied on abductive analysis during and after my time in the field.[4] My findings about the displacing effects of resettlement emerged inductively as I reached the end of my fieldwork. Given all of the challenges that refugees faced upon arrival, I asked myself what differed between refugees' earlier migrations and their resettlement, and I began to see all of the ways that resettlement also had displacing effects as it disrupted families, curtailed agency, engendered instability, and created trauma.

Once I returned to UCLA in 2019 and began systematically coding and analyzing the data, I also benefitted from the perspective gained by separation and space from my field sites. As I read through fieldnotes and interview transcripts, I came to see how desensitized I had become to many of the injustices and harms that the USRAP imposes on refugees' lives. In the thick of fieldwork and given the pragmatic approach that caseworkers must take in order to fulfill the requirements of their jobs, many of the harms done in the name of resettlement had become normalized over time, particularly as they related to refugees' economic lives. When agencies are simply trying to keep themselves and their clients afloat, seeing the same patterns unfold with each new arrival can give the false impression that this is the only way resettlement can be done. Distance from this seeming inevitability provided me with a deeper analytic lens as I worked through my data.

I recoded all of my data in 2022 and 2023 as I began the revisions for this book, which helped me to further home in on what makes resettlement so displacing, bringing some clarity to the questions that had plagued me since I was a resettlement intern in Boston in 2006. I also consulted nearly five hundred pages of programmatic and policy documents that I collected through participant observation and interviews to triangulate my findings. Heeding the call of migration scholars to develop analytic categories that are more responsive to empirical data[5] and to learn from the wisdom that comes with lived experience,[6] I sought to center refugees' perspectives of resettlement rather than policy priorities and frameworks. My hope is that this book will join the growing body of research that reveals all of the ways that policies and organizational structures meaningfully shape refugees' lives, for better and for worse.

Notes

PREFACE

1. The White House (2025).

INTRODUCTION

1. Balakian (2023), Maghbouleh and Omar (2025), Fee (2025c).

2. President of the United States (2024); Garnier et al. (2018).

3. UNHCR (2023).

4. Espiritu et al. (2022).

5. The UN Refugee Agency considers voluntary return to the home country, local integration in the country of asylum, and resettlement to a third country to be the three durable solutions for refugees in situations of protracted displacement (Stein 1983).

6. FitzGerald (2019, 3), Arar et al. (2025).

7. Fredricksson (2000).

8. Massey and Bartley (2005), Menjívar (2000), Menjívar and Abrego (2012), Galli (2023).

9. Waters and Pineau (2015), FitzGerald and Arar (2018), Fitz-Gerald (2022).

10. Waters and Pineau (2015, 131).

11. Gowayed (2022), Grace et al. (2018), Kreisberg et al. (2022), and Tran and Lara-García (2020) emphasize labor; Abramitzky et al. (2023) and Portes and Rumbaut (2006)

emphasize language; and Khuu and Bean (2021) emphasize education.

12. Espiritu (2014, 5).

13. Fee (2025b).

14. Fee (2025b), Cicek-Okay et al. (2023), Rodgers et al. (2023).

15. On resettlement as an exceptional pathway, see Androff (2022), FitzGerald (2019). On those who remain in difficult situations, see Arar and FitzGerald (2023). On those who take dangerous routes, see Bermudez Tapia (2023); Mandić Simpson (2017).

16. Menjívar (2023), Menjívar and Gómez Cervantes (2020).

17. Menjívar (2023).

18. Ali (2023), Lubkemann (2008a, 2008b), Vaz-Jones (2018).

19. Adey et al. (2020), Ali (2023), Lubkemann (2008a, 2008b), Vaz-Jones (2018).

20. Ali (2023), Cullen Dunn (2017).

21. Ali (2023).

22. Lubkemann (2008b, 454).

23. Ali (2023, 1987).

24. Cullen Dunn (2017).

25. Lubkemann (2008a, 188).

26. Lubkemann (2008b, 468).

27. Lubkemann (2008a, 188).

28. Vaz-Jones (2018).

29. Adey et al. (2020, 7).

30. Adey et al. (2020, 32).

31. Brown (2011), Bloemraad (2006).

32. Ong (2003), Sriram (2020).

33. Abdi (2015), Gowayed (2022), Grace et al. (2018), Ong (2003), Sackett and Lareau (2023), Tang (2015), Nawyn (2011), Darrow (2015, 2018), Tran and Lara-García (2020), Kreisberg et al.(2022), Tesfai (2023).

34. Bloemraad (2006), Marrow (2011), Fox (2012), Menjívar and Abrego (2012).

35. Zuberi (2006), Menjívar and Abrego (2012), Katz (2013), Gowayed (2022), Menjívar (2023), Galli (2023), Canizales (2024).

36. Galtung (1969), Farmer (2004), Canning (2017).

37. Mayblin (2020), Farmer (1996, 2004), Jackman (2002), Menjívar and Abrego (2012), Zhao et al. (2021).

38. Jackman (2002).

39. Galtung (1969).

40. Anglin (1998).

41. Galtung (1969, 171).

42. Esping-Andersen (1990).

43. Nasiali (2016).

44. Centeno and Cohen (2012).

45. Weigt (2006).

46. Zuberi (2006), Wacquant (2009), Katz (2013), Weigt (2006), Schram et al. (2009).

47. Weir et al. (1988), Somers (2008), Katz (2013). On immigrants and welfare, see Fox (2012).

48. Fox (2012).

49. Pedraza-Bailey (1985), Portes and Rumbaut (2006), Brown (2011).

50. Gowayed (2022).

51. Pedraza-Bailey (1985), Haines (2010), Fee (2019).

52. On reduction in assistance see Haines (2010), on minimal increases in funding see Lugar (2010).

53. Menjívar (2006), Canning (2017), Mayblin (2020), Galli (2023).

54. Fredriksson (2015), Abdi (2015).

55. Gowayed (2022).

56. Office of Refugee Resettlement (2022). Gowayed (2019), Frazier and van Riemsdiik (2021).

57. Ong (2003), Nawyn (2011), Tang (2015), Grace et al. (2018).

58. On career ambitions, see Gowayed (2022); on the sense of home, see Tang (2015); on belonging, see Ong (2003).

59. Lubkemann (2008a, 188).

60. Ferris and Kerwin (2023).

61. Ferris and Kerwin (2023), Lubkemann (2008b), Espiritu (2014).

62. UNHCR (2020, emphasis added).

63. President of the United States (2021, emphasis added).

64. On the inherently political nature of these programs, see Scott-Smith (2016); on the lack of impartiality, see Harrell-Bond (2002) and Garnier et al. (2018).

65. Garnier et al. (2018).

66. Office of Refugee Resettlement (2022).

67. Fee (2019).

68. Gowayed (2022), Garnier et al. (2018).

69. Hamlin (2021).

70. Phillimore (2024, 388).

71. Lugar (2010).

72. Barnett (2005).

73. Lanphier (1983), Gowayed (2022).

74. Brown et al. (2007).

75. Brick et al. (2010), Watson (2022), Fee (2025a).

76. Hein (2006), Gowayed (2020), Sackett and Lareau (2023), Besteman (2016), Abdi (2015), Tang (2015), Watson (2022), Bose (2020), Chambers (2017).

77. WRAPS (2020), Marrow (2011), Singer and Wilson (2006).

78. Portes and Böröcz (1989).

79. Fee (2025a).

80. Watson (2022); Fee (2025a); Haines (2010).

81. Fee (2025a).

82. Kastner (n.d.).

83. WRAPS (2020).

84. Fee (2025a).

85. A Welcoming City is a formal designation that recognizes local policies that promote immigrant inclusion.

86. Fee and Arar (2019), Darrow and Howsam Scholl (2020).

87. Galli and Fee (2023).

88. Fee et al. (2025).

89. Dromgold-Sermen (2022).

90. Abdi (2015), Brown (2011), Gowayed (2022), Omar (2023), Pearlman (2019), Espiritu et al. (2022).

CHAPTER 1. DEPARTURE

1. Arar et al. (2025).

2. Watson (2025), Dinçer (2025), Fee (2022).

3. Arar and FitzGerald (2022).

4. Fee (2022).

5. Fee (2022).

6. Balakian (2025); Nandi et al. (2025).

7. Pearlman (2024).

8. Crawley and Jones (2021).

9. Omar (2023, 3).

10. Loescher and Scanlan (1986), García (2017).

11. Crawley and Jones (2021, 3232).

12. Crawley and Jones (2021).

13. Balakian (2025), Nandi et al. (2025).

14. van Selm (2014, 518).

15. Crawley and Jones (2020).

16. Pearlman (2024).

17. Fee and Arar (2019).

18. Fee (2022).

19. Arar and FitzGerald (2022).

20. Castles (2003), Gowayed (2022).

21. Omar (2022).

22. Omar (2022), Dromgold-Sermen (2020).

23. Um (2015).

24. Fee (2022).

CHAPTER 2. ARRIVAL

1. Gowayed (2022), Abdi (2015), and Sackett and Lareau (2023).

2. See MacLeod (1987) for a discussion of aspirations and expectations.

3. Fee (2019).

4. Fee (2025b).

5. Gowayed (2022).

6. Fee (2025b).

7. Fee (2025b).

8. Arar and FitzGerald (2022).

9. UNHCR (2020).

10. Lindley (2009); Abdi (2015).

11. Levitt (1998).

12. Jansen (2008).

13. Jansen (2008).

14. Ali (2023).

15. Um (2015).

16. Massey et al. (1987); Hagan (1998); Hernández-León (2008).

17. Kunz (1973, 128).

18. Rumbaut (1989); Portes and Rumbaut (2006).

CHAPTER 3. FAMILY

1. Fullerton Rico (2025).

2. Enchautegui and Menjívar (2015), Wilmsen (2011).

3. Gubernskaya and Dreby (2017), McCleary (2017).

4. Abrego (2014), Dreby (2010), Warren (2022).

5. Lindley (2009).

6. Lim (2009).

7. Menjívar et al. (2016), Enchautegui and Menjívar (2015), Abrego (2014), Dreby (2010).

8. On inadvertent family separation, see Wilmsen (2011); on strategic, see Arar and FitzGerald (2023).

9. Arar and FitzGerald (2023).

10. Fee (2022).

11. Fee and Arar (2019).

12. UNCHR (2023).

13. On family unity as the basis for US immigration policy, see Balakian (2023), Enchautegui (2013), Enchautegui and Menjívar (2015), Menjívar et al. (2016), and Gubernskaya and Dreby (2017). For conceptions of legitimate families, see Smith (1993).

14. Crawley and Jones (2021).

15. Balakian (2023, 216).

16. Fee (2022).

17. Balakian (2023), Warren (2023).

18. Abrego (2014), Dreby (2010), Gubernskaya and Dreby (2017).

19. Warren (2022), Balakian (2023).

20. Martin (2005). On the importance of extended family units, see Maghbouleh and Omar (2025), Balakian (2023), Omar (2022).

21. Gowayed (2022).

22. McCleary (2017).

23. Balakian (2023).

24. Fee (2019).

25. Omar (2022).

26. Portes and Rumbaut (2006).

27. Dery (1998).

28. Hasenfeld (1987, 470).

CHAPTER 4. WORK

1. Office of Refugee Resettlement (2022).

2. Jacobsen (2014).

3. Gowayed (2022), Abdi (2015), Tang (2015), Sackett and Lareau (2023), Kriesberg et al. (2022).

4. Esping-Andersen (1990), Orloff (1993), Somers (2008).

5. Orloff (1993).

6. Gowayed (2022).

7. Gowayed (2019), Frazier and van Riemsdijk (2021).

8. FRED (2024).

9. Tran and Lara-García (2020).

10. Shaw (2014), Fee (2019), Fee and Arar (2019), Fee (2025b).

11. Fee (2025b).

12. Brown (2011).

13. Harrell-Bond (2002).

14. Code of Federal Regulations (351).

15. Living wage data sourced from the Living Wage Institute via https://livingwage.mit.edu/counties/06073.

16. Living wage data sourced from the Living Wage Institute via

https://livingwage.mit.edu/counties
/06073.

17. Gowayed (2022).

18. Canizales (2024).

19. Fee (2022).

20. Gowayed (2022).

21. Barnett (2005).

22. Johnson and Thompson (2008).

23. Rohde et al. (2016), Kopasker et al. (2018).

24. Gowayed (2022, 47).

25. Fee (2019).

26. Schmidt et al. (2024).

27. Zuberi (2006), Wacquant (2009), Katz (2013), Gowayed (2022).

28. Fee (2019).

CHAPTER 5. TRUST

1. Harrell-Bond (2002, 53).

2. Harrell-Bond (2002).

3. Hasenfeld (1987, 471).

4. Watson (2025); Fee (2022).

5. Jansen (2008).

6. Jansen (2008).

7. Voutira and Harrell-Bond (1996).

8. Cullen Dunn (2017).

9. Schilke et al. (2021).

10. Belloni (2007).

11. Ticktin (2014).

12. Harrell-Bond (2002).

13. Harrell-Bond (2002).

14. Harrell-Bond (2002).

15. Fee (2025b).

16. Ticktin (2014).

17. Garnier et al. (2018).

CONCLUSION

1. Omar (2023).

2. Ticktin (2014).

3. Ali (2023).

4. Cullen Dunn (2017, 63).

5. Lubkemann (2008a, 187), Vaz-Jones (2018), Adey et al. (2020), Ali (2023), Kraly et al. (2023).

6. Ager and Strang (2008).

7. Phillimore (2024).

8. FitzGerald (2019).

9. Fee (2025b).

10. Lubkemann (2008a, 187).

11. Gowayed (2022).

12. Fee (2025b).

13. Gowayed (2022).

14. Omar (2022).

METHODOLOGICAL APPENDIX

1. Seim (2024).

2. Small and Calarco (2022).

3. Bucerius (2013).

4. On abductive analysis, see Tavory and Timmermans (2014).

5. Zetter (2018), Kraly et al. (2023).

6. Pearlman (2024).

Bibliography

Abdi, Cawo. 2015. *Elusive Jannah*. University of Minnesota Press.

Abramitzky, Ran, Leah Boustan, Peter Catron, Dylan Connor, and Rob Voigt. 2023. "The Refugee Advantage: English-Language Attainment in the Early Twentieth Century." *Sociological Science* 10(27):769–805.

Abrego, Leisy. 2014. *Sacrificing Families*. Stanford University Press.

Adey, Peter, Janet C. Bowstead, Katherine Brickell, Vandana Desai, Mike Dolton, Alasdair Pinkerton, and Ayesha Siddiqi. 2020. "Introduction to Displacement Studies: Knowledges, Concepts, Practices." In *The Handbook of Displacement*, edited by Adey, Bowstead, Brickell, Desai, Dolton, Pinkerton, and Siddiqi. Palgrave Macmillan.

Ager, Alastair, and Alison Strang. 2008. "Understanding Integration: A Conceptual Framework." *Journal of Refugee Studies* 21(2):166–91.

Ali, Ali. 2023. "Conceptualizing Displacement: The Importance of Coercion." *Journal of Ethnic and Migration Studies* 49(5):1083–102.

Androff, David K. 2022. *Refugee Solutions in the Age of Global Crisis*. Oxford University Press.

Anglin, Mary K. 1998. "Feminist Perspectives on Structural Violence." *Identities* 5(2):145–51.

Arar, Rawan, and David Scott FitzGerald. 2022. *The Refugee System*. Polity Press.

Arar, Rawan, Molly Fee, Heba Gowayed, and Blair Sackett. 2025. "Refugee Resettlement as an Institution." *Ethnic and Racial Studies* 48(12):2259–72.

Balakian, Sophia. 2023. "Of Aunts and Mothers: Refugee Resettlement, the Nuclear Family, and Caring for 'Other' Children in Kenya." *Ethnic and Racial Studies* 46(2):213–32.

Balakian, Sophia. 2025. "Working on Resettlement: Refugees in Kenya and Everyday Practices in Pursuit of Migration Futures." *Ethnic and Racial Studies* 48(12):2420–37.

Barnett, Michael. 2005. "Humanitarianism Transformed." *Perspectives on Politics* 3(4):723–40.

Belloni, Roberto. 2007. "The Trouble with Humanitarianism." *Review of International Studies* 33(3):451–74.

Bermudez Tapia, Bertha A. 2023. "From Matamoros to Reynosa: Migrant Camps on the U.S.-Mexico Border." *Contexts* 22(1):30–7.

Besteman, Catherine. 2016. *Making Refuge*. Duke University Press.

Bloemraad, Irene. 2006. *Becoming a Citizen*. University of California Press.

Bose, Pablo. 2020. *Refugees in New Destinations and Small Cities*. Springer.

Brown, Hana E. 2011. "Refugees, Rights, and Race: How Legal Status Shapes Liberian Immigrants' Relationship with the State." *Social Problems* 58(1):144–63.

Brown, Lawrence A, Tamar E. Mott, and Edward J. Malecki. 2007. "Immigrant Profiles of U.S. Urban Areas and Agents of Resettlement." *The Professional Geographer* 59(1):56–73.

Brick, Kate, Amy Cushing-Savvi, Samia Elshafie, Alan Krill, Megan McGlynn Scanlon, and Marianne Stone. 2010. *Refugee Resettlement in the United States: An Examination of Challenges and Proposed Solutions*. Columbia University School of International and Public Affairs.

Bucerius, Sandra M. 2013. "Becoming a 'Trusted Outsider': Gender, Ethnicity, and Inequality in Ethnographic Research." *Journal of Contemporary Ethnography* 42(6):690–721.

Canizales, Stephanie L. 2023. "Work Primacy and the Social Incorporation of Unaccompanied, Undocumented Latinx Youth in the United States." *Social Forces* 101(3):1372–95.

Canizales, Stephanie L. 2024. *Sin Padres, Ni Papeles*. University of California Press.

Canning, Victoria. 2017. *Gendered Harm and Structural Violence in the British Asylum System*. Routledge.

Castles, Stephen. 2003. "The International Politics of Forced Migration." *Development* 46:11–20.

Centeno, Miguel A., and Joseph N. Cohen. 2012. "The Arc of Neoliberalism." *Annual Review of Sociology* 38(1):317–40.

Chambers, Stefanie. 2017. *Somalis in the Twin Cities and Columbus*. Temple University Press.

Cicek-Okay, Sevsem, Sarah Jernigan, Ahmed Sam Beydoun, and Riham Mazen Alwan. 2023. "The Perceived Challenges of Resettlement Among Syrian Refugees in the United States." *Journal of Social Service Research* 50(6):921–37.

Code of Federal Regulations. n.d. "45 CFR § 400.2 - Definitions." Cornell Law School, Legal Information Institute. https://www.law.cornell.edu/cfr/text/45/400.2

Crawley, Heaven and Katherine Jones. 2021. "Beyond Here and There: (Re)conceptualising Migrant Journeys and the 'In-Between.'" *Journal of Ethnic and Migration Studies* 47(14):3226–42.

Cullen Dunn, Elizabeth. 2018. *No Path Home*. Cornell University Press.

Darrow, Jessica. 2015. "Getting Refugees to Work: A Street-Level Perspective of Refugee Resettlement Policy." *Refugee Survey Quarterly* 34(2):78–106.

Darrow, Jessica. 2018. "Administrative Indentureship and Administrative Inclusion: Structured Limits and Potential Opportunities for Refugee Client Inclusion in Resettlement Policy Implementation." *Social Service Review* 92(1):36-68.

Darrow, Jessica H., and Jess Howsam Scholl. 2020. "Chaos and Confusion: Impacts of the Trump Administration Executive Orders on the US Refugee Resettlement System." *Human Service Organizations: Management, Leadership & Governance* 44(4):362–80.

Dery, David. 1998. "'Papereality' and Learning in Bureaucratic Organizations." *Administration and Society* 29(6):677–89.

Dinçer, Cemile Gizem. 2025. "Waiting for Resettlement: Experiences of Iranian Refugee Women in Turkey." *Ethnic and Racial Studies* 48(12):2309–25.

Dreby, Joanna. 2010. *Divided by Borders*. University of California Press.

Dromgold-Sermen, Michelle S. 2022. "Forced Migrants and Secure Belonging: A Case Study of Syrian Refugees Resettled in the United States." *Journal of Ethnic and Migration Studies* 48(3):635–54.

Enchautegui, Maria E. 2013. "Broken Immigration Policy: Broken Families." The Urban Institute, Washington, DC.

Enchautegui, María E., and Cecilia Menjívar. 2015. "Paradoxes of Family Immigration Policy: Separation, Reorganization, and Reunification of Families Under Current Immigration Laws." *Law & Policy* 37(1–2):32–60.

Esping-Andersen, Gosta. 1990. *The Three Worlds of Welfare Capitalism*. Princeton University Press.

Espiritu, Yến Lê. 2014. *Body Counts*. University of California Press.

Espiritu, Yến Lê, Lan Duong, Ma Vang, Victor Bascara, Khatharya Um, Lila Sharif, and Nigel Hatton. 2022. *Departures*. University of California Press.

Farmer, Paul. 1996. "On Suffering and Structural Violence: A View from Below." *Daedalus* 125(1):261–83.

Farmer, Paul. 2004. "An Anthropology of Structural Violence." *Current Anthropology* 45(3):305–25.

Fee, Molly. 2019. "Paper Integration: The Structural Constraints and Consequences of the U.S. Refugee Resettlement Program." *Migration Studies* 7(4):477–95.

Fee, Molly. 2022. "Lives Stalled: The Costs of Waiting for Refugee Resettlement." *Journal of Ethnic and Migration Studies* 48(11): 2659–77.

Fee, Molly. 2025a. "Once a Refugee, Always a Refugee? The Social Construction of Refugee Status After Resettlement." *Ethnic and Racial Studies* 48(3):498–519.

Fee, Molly. 2025b. "Resettlement Knowledge: The Expertise of Service Providers." *Refugee Survey Quarterly* 44(1):126–42.

Fee, Molly. 2025c. "Displacing Refugees: Resettlement and the Reconstitution of Families." *Social Problems*. Online first.

Fee, Molly and Rawan Arar. 2019. "What Happens When the United States Stops Taking in Refugees?" *Contexts* 18(2):18–23.

Fee, Molly, Jessica Darrow, Jess Howsam Scholl, Ashley Cureton, and Odessa Gonzalez Benson. 2025. "Refugee Resettlement: A Durable Solution at a Crossroads." *Refugee Survey Quarterly* 44(1):1–11.

Ferris, Elizabeth, and Donald Kerwin. 2023. "Durable Displacement and the Protracted Search for Solutions: Promising Programs and Strategies." *Journal on Migration and Human Security* 11(1):3–22.

FitzGerald, David Scott. 2019. *Refuge Beyond Reach*. Oxford University Press.

FitzGerald, David Scott. 2022. "The Sociology of International Migration." In *Migration Theory: Talking across Disciplines*, edited by Brettell and Hollifield. Routledge.

FitzGerald, David Scott, and Rawan Arar. 2018. "The Sociology of Refugee Migration." *Annual Review of Sociology* 44:387–406.

Fox, Cybelle. 2012. *Three Worlds of Welfare Relief*. Princeton University Press.

Frazier, Emily, and Micheline van Riemsdijk. 2021. "When 'Self-Sufficiency' Is Not Sufficient: Refugee Integration Discourses of US Resettlement Actors and the Offer of Refuge." *Journal of Refugee Studies* 34(3):3113–30.

FRED (Federal Reserve Economic Data). 2024. "Unemployment Rate in Ada County, ID." Federal Reserve Bank of St. Louis Economic Data. https://fred .stlouisfed.org/series/IDADAC1URN

Fredriksson, John. 2000. "Bridging the Gap Between Rights and Responsibilities: Policy Changes Affecting Refugees and Immigrants in the United States since 1996." *Georgetown Immigration Law Journal* 14:757–78.

Fullerton Rico, Kristina. 2025. "Grieving in the 'Golden Cage': How Unauthorized Immigrants Contend with Death and Mourn from Afar." *Social Problems* 72(3):912–27.

Galli, Chiara. 2023. *Precarious Protections*. University of California Press.

Galli, Chiara and Molly Fee. 2023. "Refugees Welcome? Historicizing U.S. Resettlement and Asylum Policy." In *Global Atlas of Refugees and Asylum Seekers*, edited by Vila Freyer and Sirkeci. Transnational Press London.

Galtung, Johan. 1969. "Violence, Peace, and Peace Research." *Journal of Peace Research* 6(3):167–91.

García, María Cristina. 2017. *The Refugee Challenge in Post-Cold War America*. Oxford University Press.

Garnier, Adèle, Liliana Lyra Jubilut, and Kristin Bergtora Sandvik. 2018. *Refugee Resettlement*. Berghahn Books.

Gowayed, Heba. 2019. "Diverging by Gender: Syrian Refugees' Divisions of Labor and Formation of Human Capital in the United States." *Gender and Society* 33(2):251–72.

Gowayed, Heba. 2020. "Resettled and Unsettled: Syrian Refugees and the Intersection of Race and Legal Status in the United States." *Ethnic and Racial Studies* 43(2):275–93

Gowayed, Heba. 2022. *Refuge*. Princeton University Press.

Grace, Breanne L., Stephanie J. Nawyn, and Betty Okwako. 2018. "The Right to Belong (If You Can Afford It): Market-Based Restrictions on Social Citizenship in Refugee Resettlement." *Journal of Refugee Studies* 31(1): 42–62.

Gubernskaya, Zoya, and Joanna Dreby. 2017. "US Immigration Policy and the Case for Family Unity." *Journal on Migration and Human Security* 5(2):417–30.

Hagan, Jacqueline Maria. 1998. "Social Networks, Gender and Immigrant Settlement: Resource and Constraint." *American Sociological Review* 63(1):55–67

Haines, David W. 2010. *Safe Haven?* Kumarian Press.

Hamlin, Rebecca. 2021. *Crossing*. Stanford University Press.

Harrell-Bond, Barbara. 2002. "Can Humanitarian Work with Refugees Be Humane?" *Human Rights Quarterly* 24(1):51–85.

Hasenfeld, Yeheskel. 1987. "Power in Social Work Practice." *Social Service Review* 61(3):469–83.

Hein, Jeremy. 2006. *Ethnic Origins*. Russell Sage Foundation.

Hernández-León, Rubén. 2008. *Metropolitan Migrants: The Migration of Urban Mexicans to the United States*. University of California Press.

Jackman, Mary R. 2002. "Violence in Social Life." *Annual Review of Sociology* 28(1):387–415.

Jacobsen, Karen. 2014. "Livelihoods and Forced Migration." In *The Oxford Handbook of Refugee and Forced Migration Studies*, edited by Fiddian-Qasmiyeh, Loescher, Long, and Sigona. Oxford University Press.

Jansen, Bram J. 2008. "Between Vulnerability and Assertiveness." *African Affairs* 107(429):569–87.

Johnson, Howard, and Andrew Thompson. 2008. "The Development and Maintenance of Post-Traumatic Stress Disorder (PTSD) in Civilian Adult Survivors of War Trauma and Torture: A Review." *Clinical Psychology Review* (28)1:36–47.

Kastner, Alton. n.d. "A Brief History of the International Rescue Committee." International Rescue Committee, New York. https://www.rescue.org/sites/default/files/document/999/abriefhistoryoftheirco.pdf

Katz, Michael B. 2013. *The Undeserving Poor.* Oxford University Press.

Kopasker, Daniel, Catia Montagna, and Keith A. Bender. 2018. "Economic Insecurity: A Socioeconomic Determinant of Mental Health." *SSM - Population Health* (6):184–94.

Khuu, Thoa V., and Frank D. Bean. 2021. "Refugee Status, Settlement Assistance, and the Educational Integration of Migrants' Children in the United States." *International Migration Review* 56(3):780–809.

Kraly, Ellen Percy, Mohammad Jalal Abbasi-Shavazi, Lorraine Lizbeth Torres Colón, and Holly E. Reed. 2023. "Social Consequences of Forced and Refugee Migration." *Annual Review of Sociology* 49(1):129–53.

Kreisberg, A. Nicole, Els De Graauw, and Shannon Gleeson. 2022. "Explaining Refugee Employment Declines: Structural Shortcomings in Federal Resettlement Support." *Social Problems* 71(1):271–90.

Kunz, Egon F. 1973. "The Refugee in Flight: Kinetic Models and Forms of Displacement." *International Migration Review* 7(2):125–46.

Lanphier, Michael C. 1983. "Refugee Resettlement: Models in Action." *The International Migration Review* 17(1):4–33.

Levitt, Peggy. 1998. "Social Remittances: Migration Driven Local-Level Forms of Cultural Diffusion." *International Migration Review* 32(4):926–48.

Lim, Soh-Leong. 2009. "'Loss of Connections Is Death': Transnational Family Ties Among Sudanese Refugee Families Resettling in the United States." *Journal of Cross-Cultural Psychology* 40(6):1028–40.

Lindley, Anna. 2009. "The Early Morning Phonecall: Remittances from a Refugee Diaspora Perspective." *Journal of Ethnic and Migration Studies* 35(8):1315–34.

Loescher, Gil, and John Scanlan. 1986. *Calculated Kindness.* Macmillan.

Lubkemann, Stephen C. 2008a. *Culture in Chaos.* University of Chicago Press.

Lubkemann, Stephen C. 2008b. "Involuntary Immobility: On a Theoretical Invisibility in Forced Migration Studies." *Journal of Refugee Studies* 21(4):454–75.

Lugar, Richard G. 2010. "Abandoned upon Arrival: Implications for Refugees and Local Communities Burdened by a U.S. Resettlement System That Is Not Working." U.S. Senate Committee on Foreign Relations, Washington, DC.

MacLeod, Jay. 1987. *Ain't No Makin' It.* Westview Press.

Maghbouleh, Neda and Laila Omar. 2025. "'Heaven Without People Is Not Worth Going to': Refugee Resettlement, Time, and the Institutionalization of Family Separation." *Ethnic and Racial Studies* 48(12):2438–56.

Mandić, Danilo, and Charles M. Simpson. 2017. "Refugees and Shifted Risk: An International Study of Syrian Forced Migration and Smuggling." *International Migration* 55: 73–89.

Marrow, Helen B. 2011. *New Destinations Dreaming*. Stanford University Press.

Martin, David A. 2005. *The United States Refugee Admissions Program*. Migration Policy Institute.

Massey, Douglas, and Katherine Bartley. 2005. "The Changing Legal Status Distribution of Immigrants: A Caution." *International Migration Review* 39(2):469–84.

Massey, Douglas, Rafael Alarcon, Jorge Durand, and Humberto González. 1987. *Return to Aztlan*. University of California Press

Mayblin, Lucy. 2020. *Impoverishment and Asylum: Social Policy as Slow Violence*. Routledge.

McCleary, Jennifer Simmelink. 2017. "The Impact of Resettlement on Karen Refugee Family Relationships: A Qualitative Exploration." *Child and Family Social Work* 2:1464–71.

Menjívar, Cecilia. 2000. *Fragmented Ties*. University of California Press.

Menjívar, Cecilia. 2023. "State Categories, Bureaucracies of Displacement, and Possibilities from the Margins." *American Sociological Review* 88(1):11–23.

Menjívar, Cecilia, and Leisy J. Abrego. 2012. "Legal Violence: Immigration Law and the Lives of Central American Immigrants." *American Journal of Sociology* 117(5):1380–421.

Menjívar, Cecilia, Leisy Abrego, and Leah Schmalzbauer. 2016. *Immigrant Families*. Wiley.

Menjívar, Cecilia and Andrea Gómez Cervantes. 2020. "Bureaucracies of Displacement: From Immigrants' Social and Physical Exclusion to Their Judicial Removal." In *The Handbook of Displacement*, edited by Adey et al. Palgrave Macmillan.

Nandi, Sarah, Oroub El Abed, Megan Bradley, and Hamzah Qardan. 2025. "Being 'Resettlement-Minded': Intersectional Dimensions of Refugee Resettlement Strategies and Refusals in Jordan." *Ethnic and Racial Studies* 48(12):2383–400.

Nasiali, Minayo. 2016. *Native to the Republic*. Cornell University Press.

Nawyn, Stephanie J. 2011. "'I Have So Many Successful Stories': Framing Social Citizenship for Refugees." *Citizenship Studies* 15(6–7):679–93.

Office of Refugee Resettlement. 2022. The Refugee Act of 1980. https://www
.acf.hhs.gov/orr/policy-guidance/refugee-act

Omar, Laila. 2023. "Foreclosed Futures and Entangled Timelines: Conceptualization of the 'Future' Among Syrian Newcomer Mothers in Canada." *Journal of Ethnic and Migration Studies* 49(5):1210–28

Ong, Aihwa. 2003. *Buddha Is Hiding*. University of California Press.

Orloff, Ann Shola. 1993. "Gender and the Social Rights of Citizenship: The
Comparative Analysis of Gender Relations and Welfare States." *American
Sociological Review* 58: 303–28.

Pearlman, Wendy. 2019. "Becoming a Refugee: Reflections on Self-Under-
standing of Displacement from the Syrian Case." *Review of Middle East Studies* 52(2):299–309.

Pearlman, Wendy. 2024. *The Home I Worked to Make*. W. W. Norton.

Pedraza-Bailey. 1985. *Political and Economic Migrants in America*. University of
Texas Press.

Phillimore, Jenny. 2024. "From Mere Life to a Good Life: Shifting Refugee Integration Policy from Outcomes to Capabilities." *Refugee Survey Quarterly*
43(4):387–409.

Portes, Alejandro, and Józsf Böröcz. 1989. "Contemporary Immigration: Theoretical Perspectives on its Determinants and Modes of Incorporation." *International Migration Review* 23(3):606–30.

Portes, Alejandro, and Ruben G. Rumbaut. 2006. *Immigrant America*. University
of California Press.

President of the United States. 2021. "Proposed Refugee Admissions for Fiscal
Year 2022."

President of the United States. 2022. "Proposed Refugee Admissions for Fiscal
Year 2023."

President of the United States. 2024. "Proposed Refugee Admissions for Fiscal
Year 2025."

Rodgers, Graeme, Stacey Shaw, Karin Wachter, and Jodie Boisvert. 2023. "Com-
passion Satisfaction, Burnout and Secondary Traumatic Stress Among Refugee Resettlement Workers in the United States," Switchboard, International
Rescue Committee. https://www.switchboardta.org/wp-content/uploads
/2024/01/Research-Manuscript_Compassion-Satisfaction-Burnout-and

-Secondary-Traumatic-Stress-among-Refugee-Resettlement-Workers-in-the
-United-States.pdf

Rohde, Nicholas, K. K. Tang, Lars Osberg, and Prasada Rao. 2016. "The Effect of Economic Insecurity on Mental Health: Recent Evidence from Australian Panel Data." *Social Science and Medicine* 151:250–8.

Rumbaut, Rubén G. 1989. "The Structure of Refuge: Southeast Asian Refugees in the United States, 1975–1985." *International Review of Comparative Public Policy*: 97–129.

Sackett, Blair, and Annette Lareau. 2023. *We Thought It Would Be Heaven*. University of California Press.

Schilke, Oliver, Martin Reimann, and Karen S. Cook. 2021. "Trust in Social Relations." *Annual Review of Sociology* 47:239–59.

Schmidt, Lucie, Lara Shore-Sheppard, and Tara Watson. 2024. State Safety Net Database, version 2.1 [dataset]. Brookings Institution.

Schram, Sanford F., Joe Soss, Richard C. Fording, and Linda Houser. 2009. "Deciding to Discipline: Race, Choice, and Punishment at the Frontlines of Welfare Reform." *American Sociological Review* 74(3):398–422.

Scott-Smith, Tom. 2016. "Humanitarian Dilemmas in a Mobile World." *Refugee Survey Quarterly* 35:1–21.

Seim, Josh. 2024. "Participant Observation, Observant Participation, and Hybrid Ethnography." *Sociological Methods & Research* 53(1):121–52.

Shaw, Stacy A. 2014. "Bridge Builders: A Qualitative Study Exploring the Experiences of Former Refugees Working as Caseworkers in the United States." *Journal of Social Service Research* 40(3):284–96.

Singer, Audrey, and Jill H. Wilson. 2006. From "There" to "Here": Refugee Resettlement in Metropolitan America. The Brookings Institute.

Small, Mario Luis, and Jessica McCrory Calarco. 2022. *Qualitative Literacy: A Guide to Evaluating Ethnographic and Interview Research*. University of California Press.

Smith, Dorothy E. 1993. "The Standard North American Family: SNAF as an Ideological Code." *Journal of Family Issues* 14(1):50–65.

Somers, Margaret. 2008. *Genealogies of Citizenship*. Cambridge University Press.

Sriram, Shyam K. 2020. "Of Acculturative Stress and Integration Distress: The Resettlement Challenges of Bhutanese Refugees in Metro Atlanta." *South Asian Diaspora* 12(1):93–108.

Stein, Barry N. 1983. "The Commitment to Refugee Resettlement." *Annals of the American Academy of Political and Social Sciences* 467:187–201.

Tang, Eric. 2015. *Unsettled*. Temple University Press.

Tavory, Iddo, and Stefan Timmermans. 2014. *Abductive Analysis: Theorizing Qualitative Research*. University of Chicago Press.

Tesfai, Rebbeca. 2023. "Success or Self-Sufficiency? The Role of Race in Refugees' Long-Term Economic Outcomes." *Journal of Refugee Studies* 36(1): 156–89.

Ticktin, Miriam. 2014. "Transnational Humanitarianism." *Annual Review of Anthropology* 43:273–89.

Tran, Van C., and Francisco Lara-García. 2020. "A New Beginning: Early Refugee Integration in the United States." *The Russell Sage Foundation Journal of the Social Sciences* 6(3):117–49.

Um, Khatharya. 2015. *From the Land of Shadows*. New York University Press.

UNHCR (UN Refugee Agency). 2020. "What is Refugee Resettlement?" https://www.unhcr.org/5feo6e8b4

UNHCR. 2023. *Resettlement Handbook*. https://www.unhcr.org/resettlement -handbook/

van Selm, Joanne. 2014. "Refugee Resettlement." In *The Oxford Handbook of Refugee and Forced Migration Studies*, edited by Fiddian-Qasmiyeh, Loescher, Long, and Sigona. Oxford University Press.

Vaz-Jones, Laura. 2018. "Struggles over Land, Livelihood, and Future Possibilities: Reframing Displacement Through Feminist Political Ecology." *Signs: Journal of Women in Culture and Society* 43(3):711–35.

Voutira, Eftihia, and Barbara Harrell-Bond. 1996. "In Search of the Locus of Trust: The Social World of the Refugee Camp." In *Mistrusting Refugees*, edited by Daniel and Knudsen, 207–24. University of California Press.

Wacquant, Loïc. 2009. *Punishing the Poor*. Duke University Press.

Warren, Kamryn. 2023. "Resettlement Divorce: The Hidden Costs of Family Separation During Refugee Resettlement." *Social Currents* 10(3):271–85.

Waters, Mary C. and Pineau, Marisa G., eds. 2015. *The Integration of Immigrants into American Society*. National Academies Press.

Watson, Jake. 2022. "Rescaling Resettlement: Local Welcoming Policies and the Shaping of Refugee Belonging." *Social Problems* 71(3):858–74.

Watson, Jake. 2025. "Between Hope and Harm: The Fragmentary Effects of Resettlement for Congolese Refugees in Uganda." *Ethnic and Racial Studies*, 48(12):2344–61.

Weigt, Jill. 2006. "Compromises to Carework: The Social Organization of Mothers' Experiences in the Low-Wage Labor Market After Welfare Reform." *Social Problems* 53(3):332–51.

Weir, Margaret, Ann Shola Orloff, and Theda Skocpol. 1988. "Introduction: Understanding American Social Politics." In *The Politics of Social Policy in the United States*, edited by Weir, Orloff, and Skocpol. Princeton University Press.

The White House. 2025. "Realigning the United States Refugee Admissions Program." Presidential Actions. https://www.whitehouse.gov/presidential -actions/2025/01/realigning-the-united-states-refugee-admissions-program/

Wilmsen, Brooke. 2011. "Family Separation: The Policies, Procedures, and Consequences for Refugee Background Families." *Refugee Survey Quarterly* 30(1):44–64.

WRAPS. 2020. Refugee Processing Center. https://www.wrapsnet.org/

Zetter, Roger. 2018. "Conceptualising Forced Migration." In *Forced Migration*, edited by Bloch and Donà. Routledge.

Zhao, Linda, Philipp Hessel, Juli Simon Thomas, and Jason Beckfield. 2021. "Inequality in Place: Effects of Exposure to Neighborhood-Level Economic Inequality on Mortality." *Demography* 58(6):2041–63.

Zuberi, Dan. 2006. *Differences That Matter*. Cornell University Press.

Index

barriers: to communication, 204; cultural, 141; English proficiency, 167; to job placement, 161–62; linguistic, 141, 143, 256

Biden administration, 247

bipartisanism, Refugee Act of 1980 and, x

Boise, 31–33; rental market in, 151; as resettlement area, 63–64, 65, 66, 69, 72, 124, 125; securing housing in, 145–47, 148–49; service providers from, 261*tab.*

Boise Resettlement Agency, 24–29; flex funds and, 226–27; hotel costs, 150

Bracero Program, 32

bureaucracy of resettlement: expectation of confidence in, 205; separations and, 119–20; as supportive and disciplining, 237

Bureau of Population, Refugees, and Migration (PRM), 199, 214, 225

Burmese refugees, in San Diego, 227

Burundi, refugee camps in, 43

Burundian refugees: in Boise, 163; interviewees, 261*tab.*

CALWorks Programs, 156, 224

caregiving: imposed by resettlement programs, 138; plural marriage breakups and, 123

caseworkers: appraisal of clients, 203–4; asymmetrical relations of, 201–2; author's experience with, 257–60; client accusations of misappropriating funds, 220–21; dependency of clients on, 201–2, 203; empathy from, 127; as face of direct service provision, 240; frustration of, 239; housing decisions, 209–10; as inattentive and absent, 206;

R&P funds management, 213–14, 215–20; responsibilities exceeding job description, 239; securing housing, 145–49, 209; significance of, 89–93

cash aid: CALWorks Programs and, 156; pocket money, 211; requirements to receive, 138; TANF program, 176*tab*, 188. *See also* R&P funds

Central African Republic refugees, 163

childcare, workfare requirements and, 137–38

child protective services, threat of, 143

children: acculturation of, 141; benefits of resettlement for, 249; childcare for, 137–38; preschool aged, 140; school aged, 140; social media and, 143–44

choice, limitations on, 203

citizenship, pathway to, 14

City Heights, 30

climate, initial resettlement experience and, 69–70, 207, 257

coercion: asserting agency under, 20; role in displacement, 13

community leaders: Congolese, 142, 153, 206, 213, 219, 220; Karen refugees as, 250; refugees as, 237; in San Diego, 112–13

community support, 111–13

Congolese refugees: in Boise, 142, 145, 148, 164, 213, 214, 220, 222–23, 228; ethnic divisions and, 152–53; interviewees, 261*tab.*; in San Diego, 206, 221–22, 256

conveyor belt of services, 80–89, 207, 233

co-sponsorships, 248

countries of asylum: central problems in, 79; conditions in, 212; corruption in, 205; housing in, 144; lack of stability in, 64; local integration in, 265n5;

resettlement process in, 43; single
mothers in, 123; waiting in, 125
countries of resettlement, variety of, 44
COVID-19 pandemic, 247
Crawley, Heaven, 53
Cultural Orientation classes, 31, 248; in
Boise, 32; postarrival, 244; predeparture, 45, 107, 212, 213, 243–44; on R&P
funds, 215–16; self-sufficiency pathway
and, 180

Democratic Republic of Congo (DRC):
ethnic divisions and, 152–53; strategic
separation and, 120
Department of State (DOS): Bureau of
Population, Refugees, and Migration
(PRM), 199, 214, 225; screenings by, x
departure, scheduling of, 45
deskilling, 168–69
disillusionment of resettlement, 238;
misinformation leading to, 213; over
housing, 209–11
displacement of resettlement: acknowl-
edgment and accommodation of, 236,
251; circumstances of, 14; confronting
expectations, 114; effects of, 7, 237;
ending of, 248–50; expectations and,
93–103; forced migration and, 12; need
for acclimation and adjustment, 41;
plural marriage breakups and, 123;
prearrival resettlement process and,
42; social condition of, 239, 240; as
trauma, 107
disruption of resettlement: experience of,
7, 41, 237; plural marriage breakups
and, 123–24
divided families, separation of, 123–24

EBT cards, 188
economic issues: affecting organization
and local businesses, xii; economic
demands of resettlement, 144;
economic insecurity, 185–90; economic self-sufficiency, 175–85; financial
constraints of resettlement program,
209; of plural marriage breakups, 123;
public assistance, xi; Reception &
Placement (R&P) funds, 155; self-
sufficiency pathway, xi, 197; stability as
central, 238; taxes, xi. See also financial
assistance; R&P funds; self-sufficiency
pathway; work
education: high school credits, 5, 6,
182–83; reviewing information about,
244; school aged children, 182
El Cajon, 30; arrival at, 76; as resettlement
location, 191
employment: career loss, 158, 167, 168, 197,
238, 250; deskilling, 168–69, 172;
displaced livelihoods, 158; early
employment, 159–75; economic
self-sufficiency and, 175–85; injuries and,
179–80; job placement decisions, 209,
229–31; living wage, 176tab; Matching
Grant employment programs, 214;
necessity for, 156–57, 197, 211, 239;
parenthood and, 138–39; poverty wage,
176tab; professional recertification,
171–72; rates of, xi; Refugee Act of 1980
and, 158; survival jobs, 169–71
employment specialists, 79, 187–88, 189
Eritrean refugees: interviewees, 261tab.;
in San Diego, 63
estranged spouses, outdated information
and, 127

hotels: overspending on, 218–19; prearrival resettlement process and, 67; as
temporary accommodations, 147
housing: affordable, 26, 30, 146, 150–51,
165, 191, 193, 210; cost of, 145, 147, 149,
151, 167, 191, 193, 209, 216, 218, 219, 223;
decisions on, 208–11; discrimination
against refugees, 145; as foundational,
144, 238, 239; guidelines and regulations, 145–46, 147, 209–10; high costs
of, 137; hotel costs, 198; household
item purchases, 198–200; housing
supply checklist, 200*tab.*; quality of,
147–48; R&P funds and, 155; rental
payments, 197; risk of unhousing, 151;
in San Diego, 215; separations and,
144–54; substandard, 206. *See also*
homelessness
Housing Choice Voucher (HCV)
program (Section 8 housing), 151
housing specialists, 198–99, 201
humanitarian programs, asymmetrical
relations of, 201–2
humanitarian protections, USRAP offer
of, 240

Idaho Office for Refugees, 197
information, withholding of, 125
initial expenses, R&P funds for, 197–200
initial resettlement experience: disillusionment of, 238; as distinct phase of
forced migration, 240
insecurity, distress of economic insecurity, 185–90
internal relocations, instability of, 40–41
International Organization for Migration
(IOM), 24*fig.*, 67

International Rescue Committee (IRC).
See IRC (International Rescue
Committee)
Iran, fleeing, 119
Iranian refugees, interviewees, 261*tab.*
Iraqi refugees: in Boise, 143, 145, 205;
displacement before being refugees,
12; employment, 174; interviewees,
261*tab.*; SIV holders, 129–30, 168
IRC (International Rescue Committee),
11, 27, 29, 30, 32, 215–16, 226, 255–56,
257, 259

Jansen, Bram, 205–6
jobs, Resettlement Agencies layoffs, xii
Jones, Katherine, 53
Jordan: departing, 204; family left in, 116;
fleeing to, 40–41, 115; layovers in, 122

Kakuma refugee camp (Kenya), 206
Kampala, Uganda, asylum in, 120
Kenya: health care in, 137; refugee camps
in, 66, 206, 211; Resettlement Support
Center in, 63
Kenyan refugees: in Boise, 206; interviewees, 261*tab.*; in New England,
206–7
kinship structures: extended family
separations, 129–32; US law and, 123.
See also plural marriages

landlords, 88, 145–46, 149, 152, 178, 188,
191, 215
language: English classes, 81*tab.*, 84, 86,
111, 132, 138, 161, 172, 174, 194, 228;
English language, 5, 10, 23, 68, 78, 167,
170, 171; learning a new language, 41;

postarrival Cultural Orientation, 215–16, 244

poverty, 169, 176*tab*, 195–96

prearrival resettlement process: approval, 42–47; flights, 63, 66, 67–70; journeys and destinations, 62–73; with refugees' lives, 41–42; refugees' trajectory, 50–62

precarity: context of, 125; economic insecurity, 185–90; Medicaid and, 179; ongoing, 41

predeparture Cultural Orientation, 107, 212, 213, 243–44

predeparture medical screenings, 44

pregnancy: housing and, 148; resettlement and, 139

private sponsorships, 248

PRM (Bureau of Population, Refugees, and Migration), 199, 214, 225

professional recertification, 171–72

protracted displacement: consequences of, 236; refugees in, 237; resettlement process and, 42; USRAP and, 42

PTSD: parenting and, 135; resettlement stressors as triggering, 188, 190. *See also* trauma

public assistance programs: absence of in Idaho, 226; in California, 191; for daycare, 138; enrollment in, 156, 211; food stamps, 156; qualification for, 156; resettled refugees reception of, xi; reviewing information about, 244; single mother families and, 124; support for vulnerable cases, 226; workfare requirements, 137–38

public safety net, as absent in Idaho, 204

R&P funds: administrative choices and, 226; amounts and usage of, 155–57, 190, 211; decisions on spending of, 208; doubts over, 198–99, 201, 202; flex funds, 226–27; hotel costs beyond, 150; for initial expenses, 157, 197–201, 211, 214–15; initial resettlement experience and, 137, 217; leftover, 191, 215, 216; limitations of, 145; misinformation over, 213–14, 215, 220–21, 221; pocket money, 211, 227–28; postarrival Cultural Orientation and, 215; PRM and, 199, 225; as welcome money, 199, 214, 218

Reception & Placement (R&P) funds. *See* R&P funds

Reception and Placement (R&P): assistance, 18*tab*.; itinerary, 245–56; as short period, 157. *See also* R&P funds

Refugee Act of 1980, x, 20, 158

Refugee Cash Assistance Program, 18*tab*., 24*fig*., 197

Refugee Medical Assistance (RMA), 18*tab*., 179, 231

remittances: sent by refugees, 123; sent to family in refugee camps, 126

resettlement: difficult nature of, 236; as humanitarian protection, 236; meaningful aspects of, 236. *See also* displacement of resettlement

resettlement (U.S.): acceptance for, 44; disorienting nature of, 45; as percentage of global resettlement, x–xi; as humanitarian protection, 42; importance of, 47–50; as migratory pathway, 42; politics of, 20–22, 247–48; as refugee pathway, x; as risk to national security,

resettlement (U.S.) (*continued*)
x; standardized program of, 240;
Trump administration's rationale for
halting, x; as unanticipated migration,
50–62; US model of, x
Resettlement Agencies, 91, 92–93;
caseworker assignment, 76; employment assistance programs enrollment, 77–78; home tour, 76; housing
preparation, 76; implementation
issues, 243; layoffs, xii; 24-hour home
visit, 77; notification of arriving
refugees, 75–76; preparations for
arrivals, 76; time limitations, 79;
under Trump administration, x;
during Trump administrations, 247;
as underfunded and overstretched,
251. *See also* caseworkers; staffing
resettlement process, corruption
during, 205
Resettlement Support Centers, interim
stays at, 67
resources: as minimal, 209; scarcity of,
201, 207
reunification: after approval, 126; after
long separation, 120; families awaiting
have longer separations, xi
reunions: of plural marriage families,
124–25; unexpected reunions, 133–35
rights, limited, 237
rights of refugees, as lacking, x
Rohingya refugees, Boise community
of, 138
Rwanda, 6

safety: concerns over housing, 208–9;
fears over school aged children's safety,
140–41; importance of, 252; from
persecution, 119; physical, 107–8; from
resettlement, 41; in San Diego, 119
San Diego, 29–31; housing in, 137; life in,
122; as resettlement area, 124;
resettlement in, 119; securing housing
in, 145–47, 148–49; service providers
from, 261*tab.*
San Diego Resettlement Agency, 24–29;
on abusive relationships, 129;
administrator at, 121; diaper supplies,
136–37; housing practices of, 149–50
scholarship on USRAP, 238–39
secondary migration, costs of, 25
Section 8 housing (Housing Choice
Voucher program), 151
security: frameworks of integration
foregrounding, 239; not provided by
services or assistance, 238; from
resettlement, 41; in San Diego, 119;
threats to sense of, 107; xenophobia
risk to sense of, 247
self-sufficiency pathway: economic
self-sufficiency and, 175–85; immediate placement on, xi; rental payments
and, 197; single mother families
and, 124
Selm, Joanne van, 55
separations: creation of new separations,
121–27; extended families and, 129–32;
familial integrity and, 132–33, 154;
housing disruptions, 144–54; nuclear
families, 117–29; parenthood disruptions, 135–44; precarity and, 119;
unexpected reunions, 133–35; from
unmarried children, 122–23; US law
and, 154

violence: in countries of asylum, 43; structural harms, 13–14, 15–20

voluntary return to home country, as durable solution for refugees, 265n5

vouchers, 151

vulnerability, plural marriage breakups and, 123–24

war, impacts of, 107

Welcome Housing solution, 150–51

welcome money, 199. *See also* R&P funds

Welcoming Cities, formal designations of, 267n85

welfare: state-based welfare, 14, 180, 190–95; structural harms and, 15–20

workfare requirements: as depleting parental time and energy, 144; parents complying with, 137–38

xenophobia, increase in, 247

Yemen, fleeing to, 118–19

Zimbabwe, refugee camps in, 43

Founded in 1893,
UNIVERSITY OF CALIFORNIA PRESS
publishes bold, progressive books and journals
on topics in the arts, humanities, social sciences,
and natural sciences—with a focus on social
justice issues—that inspire thought and action
among readers worldwide.

The UC PRESS FOUNDATION
raises funds to uphold the press's vital role
as an independent, nonprofit publisher, and
receives philanthropic support from a wide
range of individuals and institutions—and from
committed readers like you. To learn more, visit
ucpress.edu/supportus.